How Scholars Write

....

How Scholars Write

AARON RITZENBERG

SUE MENDELSOHN

New York   Oxford

OXFORD UNIVERSITY PRESS

Oxford University Press is a department of the University of Oxford.
It furthers the University's objective of excellence in research, scholarship,
and education by publishing worldwide. Oxford is a registered trade mark of
Oxford University Press in the UK and certain other countries.

Published in the United States of America by Oxford University Press
198 Madison Avenue, New York, NY 10016, United States of America.

© 2021 by Oxford University Press

Library of Congress Cataloging-in-Publication Data
Names: Ritzenberg, Aaron, author. | Mendelsohn, Sue, author.
Title: How scholars write / Aaron Ritzenberg, Sue Mendelsohn.
Description: New York : Oxford University Press, 2021. | Includes
  bibliographical references and index. | Summary: "How Scholars Write is
  an affordable, pocket-sized research and composition guide that offers a
  descriptive approach to research. It can be used in conjunction with
  readings of the instructors' choosing, Instead of providing specific
  rules or formulas, this book describes how actual researchers work. How
  Scholars Write demystifies the writing process by explaining tools and
  techniques that all writers can use"—Provided by publisher.
Identifiers: LCCN 2019033371 (print) | LCCN 2019033372 (ebook) | ISBN
  9780190296735 (paperback) | ISBN 9780190095840 (ebk) | ISBN
  9780190095833 (ebk)
Subjects: LCSH: Academic writing—Handbooks, manuals, etc. |
  Research—Methodology—Handbooks, manuals, etc.
Classification: LCC LB2369 .R556 2021 (print) | LCC LB2369 (ebook) | DDC
  808.06/6378—dc23
LC record available at https://lccn.loc.gov/2019033371
LC ebook record available at https://lccn.loc.gov/2019033372

Printing number: 9 8 7 6 5 4 3 2 1
Printed by LSC Communications, Inc., United States of America
on acid-free paper

TABLE OF CONTENTS
....

PREFACE

....

We begin this book with a problem: we set out to write a straightforward, linear guide to something that is neither straightforward nor linear—academic writing. Some years ago, this problem came alive for us when we began talking about the gaps between how we taught our students to write and how we approached our own writing. While we taught our students rather formulaic strategies that would approximate academic writing—find a controversy you're passionate about; take a strong stand; place a thesis statement in your introduction; begin paragraphs with topic sentences—we seldom use those strategies in our own projects. We instead start our research with questions sparked by reading others' research; we think about crafting responses to those questions that move the larger scholarly conversation forward; we look for gaps and complications. We wondered if our students experienced academic writing as we do: creative, exploratory, and often exciting. Since those early conversations, we have worked on teaching writing and research in ways that are less mystified and more real.

So we set out to write a guide that introduces academic writers— undergraduates, graduate students, and other researchers—to the often surprising realities of how seasoned scholars research and write. Though the book contains a fair amount of practical advice, this is not an advice book. Merely describing what works for *us* would capture only our personal preferences or idiosyncrasies. Instead, our project here is to present a transparent, principled, research-based description of how scholars actually get things written. We offer here not unbreakable rules but a mindset, not formulas but tools and techniques.

To fulfill this project, we looked to research in writing studies, cognitive psychology, educational psychology, and applied linguistics to answer questions such as "How do scholars come up with ideas?" and "How do researchers read their sources?" We also invited a host of published researchers to describe how they approach their writing. You'll find narratives from scholars in neurobiology, writing studies, law, literary studies, media studies, library science, music, engineering, and creative nonfiction. Together, these voices suggest the ways that people can read and write themselves into belonging in a scholarly community. We've divided each chapter into two sections:

Mindset: The first section of each chapter explains how researchers think through various challenges. We offer here the principles, attitudes, and approaches that scholars bring to their research.

Tools & Techniques: The second part of each chapter presents practical strategies that researchers use at various stages of academic writing. We describe scholars' reading methods, research techniques, and writing practices that you can apply to your own projects.

Each chapter also includes the following features that take you inside scholars' writing practices:

Scholar's Story: These short narratives highlight expert researchers' own experiences when tackling common challenges in the research process. You'll see that research can be humbling, maddening, and revelatory even for the experts. These stories illustrate the ways that professional scholars use the same strategies we describe.

Key Terms: We define the words that describe the sometimes difficult to identify but crucial concepts and components that drive academic writing.

Practice: Throughout the book, we offer quick exercises for readers to practice honing the skills we describe.

Research on Writing: We highlight research in the fields of writing studies, rhetoric, psychology, and linguistics to explain the ideas that inform scholars' approaches to writing, research, and thinking. Each includes a takeaway, showing how you might apply the research to your own writing.

Myth vs. Reality: This feature dispels common misperceptions about writing—misperceptions that can inhibit your ability to move forward, such as "A thesis statement must be one sentence long," "It's always inappropriate to use 'I,'" and "Researchers start with a claim."

Common Pitfalls: We describe typical ways that research can go wrong, and we share strategies that scholars use to avoid these pitfalls.

Time Savers: This feature offer tricks and tools scholars use to avoid wasting time with unfocused or inefficient work.

Turn to Your Research: Chapters end with a feature that prompts you to apply concepts and strategies to your own research project.

Writers who are newer to academic research may find the gap between their own writing and published writing daunting. Published writing often appears to present brilliant thinking with ease. However, during the writing process, the scholars who publish are themselves learning, experimenting, writing and rewriting (and rewriting some more), asking for help, and sometimes running into road blocks. This book is our effort to take you behind the scenes of scholars' writing in order to dispel the notion that only people born brilliant can be academic writers. Rather, successful scholars practice principled strategies that anyone can adopt in order to craft academic writing that matters.

ACKNOWLEDGMENTS

Don't let the cover of this book fool you. While it lists just two authors, many people contributed their wisdom and effort. These acknowledgments reflect the advice we give in the book, which is to seek out many perspectives that challenge us to complicate thinking and clarify writing. We're fortunate to have a generous community in which to do that.

Our closest collaborator was Shyanne Figueroa Bennett. As our research assistant, Shyanne read every word of this manuscript multiple times and helped us not only catch mistakes but sharpen our explanations. We relied on her keen-eyed notes in the margins to better envision how readers would experience each chapter. In future years, we look forward to reading books with her name on the cover.

Our thinking about writing and teaching has been shaped in profound ways by our colleagues in the Columbia University Undergraduate Writing Program—Nicole Wallack, Glenn Michael Gordon, and Jason Ueda—whose thoughts have helped shape this book, likely in more ways than they realize. We hope that the pages that follow capture some of the wisdom and compassion they bring to their work every day.

Throughout this process, we have also relied on Undergraduate Writing Program colleagues to read chapter drafts and talk through the challenges of putting slippery concepts into accessible language. Thank you to Allen Durgin, Vanessa Guida, Valerie Seiling Jacobs, Xander Landfair, Simon Porzak, Abby Rabinowitz, Hal Sundt, Avia Tadmor,

Rebecca Wisor, and Tana Wojczuk for many illuminating conversations and much encouragement. Writing a book takes the luxury of time. Alan Stewart, Nicole Wallack, John Stobo, and the Columbia University Department of English and Comparative Literature championed this project and made it possible for us to carve out that time. We do not take for granted our good fortune to have found ourselves in such a supportive department. We are avid users of the Columbia University Writing Center. The consultants there gave us many hours of their time. Kirkwood Adams, Maria Baker, Mira Baum, Samantha Caveny, Sam Chanse, Tara Gallagher, Rachel Greenspan, Priyanka Mariwala, Alyssa Pelish, Bridget Potter, Steve Preskill, Noah Shannon, and Shelby Wardlaw all moved this book forward with their thoughtful feedback.

We relied on a tremendous amount of support from colleagues, friends, and family while we wrote this book. Advice and inspiration came from John Brereton, Ellen Crowell, Rosa Eberly, Chris Eichler, Lester Faigley, Karin Gosselink, Alfie Guy, Briallen Hopper, Celerstine Johnson, Alyssa Mendelsohn, Bill Mendelsohn, Joan Mullin, Ken Ritzenberg, Barbara Rockenbach, Eliana Schonberg, Fred Strebeigh, and Ryan Wepler. Thanks go particularly to Mookie Kideckel, Susi Ritzenberg, and Matt Wildman, who read chapter drafts to help us see how people inside and outside academe would respond to our ideas.

In the early stages of writing the book we made a list of scholars we admire: those who not only produce compelling scholarship but have rich language for thinking about writing. This dream team—Renee Brown, Nicholas Chong, Ellen Crowell, Brian Fallon, Stuart Firestein, Richard Thompson Ford, Elisabeth Heard Greer, Briallen Hopper, Kelly Kessler, Jessica Lott, Sharon Marcus, Elizabeth Matthews, Elizabeth Mintie, Anice Mills, Elsa Olivetti, and Simon Porzak—took time from their own research and teaching to contribute Scholar's Story pieces for this project. Their contributions represent the commonality of scholars' experiences whether they be senior researchers, graduate students, or undergraduates and whether they come from community colleges or research-focused universities.

Working with Oxford University Press has been a pleasure. We thank Carrie Brandon, who was the book's first supporter. Garon Scott carefully shepherded the project through its long middle stages. And we feel supremely lucky that Steve Helba, an enthusiastic and knowledgeable advocate, arrived to carry it through to the end.

We appreciate the work of many people at the press who helped with the final stages of the book, including Patricia Berube, Jill Crosson, Kora Fillet, Alexander Foley, Louise Karam, Jodi Lewchuk, Tracey MacDonald, Tony Mathias, and Anne Sanow.

We are grateful to the reviewers of this text, who drew on their years of expertise to offer excellent advice: Anne Buison, College of Saint Elizabeth, Eric Cimino, Molloy College, Jane Collins, Pace University, Heidi Diehl, Brooklyn College, CUNY, Iris Jamahl Dunkle, Napa Valley College, Kristine Gussow, George Mason University, Sara Hillin, Lamar University, Glenn D. Jackson, Eastern Kentucky University, Rebecca Kern-Stone, Manhattan College, Michael Krull, Georgetown University, Kristopher Michael Lotier, Hofstra University, Steven E. Nash, East Tennessee State University, Diana Hope Polley, Southern New Hampshire University, Psyche Ready, George Mason University, Crystal S. Rudds, Malcolm X College, and other anonymous readers. Their feedback—productive, smart, and attentive—guided our many revisions. The work of reviewing texts-in-progress often far outweighs its rewards, so we especially honor and appreciate their professional generosity.

Finally, we thank our students for their enduring goodwill. We experimented with the lessons contained in this book with students in Saint Louis University's educational opportunity programs, Elite Scholars of China in Beijing, and Columbia University's colleges for traditional and nontraditional students. We are especially grateful for those students who were brave enough to speak up when a lesson didn't ring true or didn't translate clearly into practice. Your observations stayed with us. They pushed us to search for better explanations for what actually happens when scholars write. Thank you for everything you have taught us.

How Scholars Write

CHAPTER 1

The Pursuit of Ignorance

SCHOLAR'S STORY

Neurobiologist Stuart Firestein on Discovering Better Ignorance

One evening in graduate school more than thirty years ago, I was alone in the laboratory, finishing up some experiments that hadn't been going so well. I was trying to record the electrical responses of a single cell in the olfactory system exposed to a tiny amount of an odor. Suddenly, or so it seemed after fourteen straight hours of recording unsuccessfully from one cell after another, I pushed the button that delivered a little puff of odor, and the single brain cell produced this simple and beautiful response. A long, slow, curved line appeared on the oscilloscope, representing the electrical response of this living cell to the odor. At that moment I was the only person on the planet who knew this response existed. It was curiously sobering—like I should be careful tonight because I won't be able to show this to anyone until tomorrow, and what a pity if I should get run down by a bus. So I walked home, carefully, with this silly thought in my head and began going over what had just happened.

I realized that the crucial thing was not what I had seen in the lab but what this simple discovery would allow me to do for the next few

continued

months—the new questions I could formulate and test, the mysteries I could now explore. How does this response vary with odor concentration? How does this cell recognize this particular odor from the thousands, millions of other odors? How does this single cell's response turn into a perception deeper in our brains? What I really discovered that night was that, contrary to what I had thought, the great joy in science is not those rare eureka moments of discovery but the vistas of questions that open up because of that discovery. The next few months? My discovery kept me happily busy asking and answering questions I could never have imagined for some three decades.

Read the research: Stuart Firestein is a professor of biological sciences at Columbia University. His most recent books are *Ignorance: How It Drives Science* and *Failure: Why Science Is So Successful*.

Mindset: "Knowledgeable Ignorance" Propels Research

This academic writing guide begins in a place that might feel counterintuitive: ignorance. While published academic writing features what a writer knows, Stuart Firestein's neurobiology research emerged from a keen understanding of what he *didn't* know. His discovery in the laboratory was momentous because it opened up questions that he could not have asked before conducting this research. Firestein shows us why ignorance is crucial in science: researchers make advances only when they respond to gaps in scientific knowledge. Researchers in all disciplines depend upon a similar approach: they seek out ignorance.

We might imagine that established scholars effortlessly write down ideas they have already fixed in their minds. However, this is a false notion of academic writing. For even the most accomplished researchers, writing is a process not of transcribing preformed thoughts, but of delving deeply into what they don't yet understand. Scholars are learners.

The appearance of effortless mastery that often comes across in high-level scholarship is the result of a tremendous amount of deliberate practice. Think of a professional basketball player whose three-point shot looks automatic, a world-class dancer whose leaps across the stage seem effortless, or a famous musician whose intricate guitar riffs appear to be second nature (see Photo 1.1). What appears to be spontaneous, unthinking performance is the result of years of training and practice.

PHOTO **1.1**
Ballerina Misty Copeland performs difficult moves seemingly effortlessly. Copeland writes in her 2014 memoir that she still takes class every day: "It never becomes boring, even though I've done all these movements in this very studio a million times over thirteen years. It's my safe place, where I can experiment . . . It's the time to push myself beyond my limits so that my performances can feel effortless, fresh" (3).

Many thinkers have noted the ways that a display of easy mastery is in fact a crafted performance. During the Renaissance, Baldesar Castiglione coined a word for this kind of practiced ease: *sprezzatura*. Castiglione portrayed the ideal courtier as someone who possessed *sprezzatura* in all things and appeared to perform duties "naturally and without any effort" (34). With this book, we hope to help you practice *sprezzatura* in your own research and writing. We treat writing not as an innate talent but rather a learned skill that offers the appearance of ease only through informed practice.

"Knowledgeable Ignorance"

In *Ignorance*, a book about the real work that scientists do, Stuart Firestein offers examples of scholars who contributed to the world's knowledge precisely because they were able to recognize their own ignorance. Firestein makes the distinction between "willful stupidity" and "knowledgeable ignorance" (6, 7). People display willful stupidity when they cling to beliefs and practices even in the face of opposing evidence (11). Individuals display knowledgeable ignorance, on the other hand, when they seek out what they don't know (11). Knowledgeable ignorance is researched and informed—mindful not only of what the researcher doesn't yet know but also of what the larger community of scholars doesn't yet know. Firestein's description of ignorance asks us to redefine our notion of expertise: being an expert is not to have all the answers but to articulate compelling questions.

Indeed, many academic articles conclude not with definitive answers but with the promise of new avenues of inquiry. For instance, in their article "Modeling the Past: Digital Technologies and Excavations in Polis, Cyprus," archaeologist Joanna S. Smith and computer scientist Szymon M. Rusinkiewicz detail the methods behind their three-dimensional drawings of ancient buildings and artifacts. Their final paragraph raises new questions that their research prompts:

> The project led us to ask new questions in archaeology and computer graphics that point to new directions for the study and exhibition of cultural heritage through digital technologies. Importantly, it has begun to suggest approaches for representing uncertainty and change. In computer graphics, the fragmentary nature of archaeological remains continues to inspire new ideas about how best to represent and reconstruct them. Archaeologically, the modeling has led to new ideas about these buildings, their urban contexts, and contemporary structures. (421)

Smith and Rusinkiewicz use the word "new" four times in their concluding paragraph. Instead of emphasizing definitive findings, they focus on the questions that became possible to ask only as a result of their findings. Their ignorance has become more knowledgeable, and they can now ask new questions that are important for the fields of computer graphics and archaeology.

Many writers recognize how difficult it is to push toward ignorance. Nobel Prize-winning psychologist Daniel Kahneman writes, "sustaining doubt is harder work than sliding into certainty" (114). It is no easy task to remain unsettled and open-minded, especially when your eventual goal may be to make a confident, convincing claim. Nineteenth-century poet John Keats referred to the hard work of sustaining doubt as "negative capability," which he described as "when man is capable of

MYTH VS. REALITY

Myth: Researchers start with a claim.
Reality: Researchers start with a problem that needs resolving.

When we read published research, we often imagine that the scholars started out already knowing the answers. This myth persists because we typically witness only the final, published product. From this perspective, we don't see any uncertainty the researcher encountered or any evidence that they (very likely) revised their thinking many times. What we don't see, then, is the process. As you'll observe throughout this book, the search for problems and their implications evolves throughout the research process.

being in uncertainties, Mysteries, doubts" (109). For Keats, writers who practice negative capability are able to dwell in uncertainty and thus do not settle on comfortable, received ideas. When we draw inspiration from Keats, we value the capacity to change our minds.

As a mindset, the quest for knowledgeable ignorance asks us to resist settling for our first ideas. It allows us to stay in a place where we can use our curiosity to discover layers of complexity. After all, if a writer merely offers their first thoughts about an issue, it is quite likely that those same first thoughts have already occurred to the reader as well. Readers are invigorated not by having their preconceptions echoed back to them but by encountering new thinking.

You may be tempted to hide your uncertainty as you write. But researchers sometimes display their negative capability as a strategy. When writers perform the uncertainty that motivated their research, they suggest a capacity for open-mindedness that readers find reassuring. Michael Pollan, for instance, begins his essay "An Animal's Place" with a moment that reflects on his own knowledgeable ignorance. He indulges in a steak at the very moment that he reads Peter Singer's influential book on animal rights:

> The first time I opened Peter Singer's *Animal Liberation*, I was dining alone at the Palm, trying to enjoy a rib-eye steak cooked medium-rare. If this sounds like a good recipe for cognitive dissonance (if not indigestion), that was sort of the idea. Preposterous as it might seem,

to supporters of animal rights, what I was doing was tantamount to reading *Uncle Tom's Cabin* on a plantation in the Deep South in 1852. (58)

Instead of leading with a claim about the ethics of eating meat, Pollan demonstrates the intellectual conflict that drives his essay and emphasizes the fact that he has not reached a conclusion. What are the effects of demonstrating this kind of knowledgeable ignorance so openly? Pollan shows us that his ethos—the character qualities that his writing exudes—is open-minded and self-aware. Readers will likely trust a writer who considers multiple viewpoints, who is open to new evidence, who is subject to the frailties of being human. The writer invokes sympathy with readers who may feel similarly conflicted.

Notice, too, that the strategy of demonstrating knowledgeable ignorance hooks readers, who wonder how the author will resolve this cognitive dissonance. Scholars stay on the lookout for cognitive dissonances—those places of uncertainty and conceptual difficulty that may invite intellectual indigestion. These dissonances may be uncomfortable, as Pollan points out, but they also make for excellent launching points for writing. We'll call these launching points "problems."

Problems

Throughout this book, we'll use the word "problem" in a specialized way. By "problem," we don't mean mistake or fault. We mean an intellectual tension that merits resolving. When scholars analyze a text—a novel, a building, a journal article, a film, a performance, an event—they're mining for problems. They search for tensions or dissonances: things that don't quite fit together in expected ways. Scholars then work to make sense of the tensions or dissonances. If the scholar can show how making sense of the problem matters to others, it can become the foundation of a research project. Stuart Firestein, for instance, used a problem that he noticed in the laboratory—why does a brain cell respond in this particular way to this particular smell?—to launch an array of research projects that help other researchers understand how the brain processes odors. As we move through this book, we'll return to the idea of a problem. In Chapter 2, we'll look at some examples of scholarly problems. We'll ask, "How can we come up with problems? How can we best articulate these problems? How can we show why readers should care about these problems?"

RESEARCH ON WRITING

Nancy Sommers and Laura Saltz's "The Novice as Expert: Writing the Freshman Year"

Sure, pushing oneself toward knowledgeable ignorance may work for cutting-edge physicists or professional art historians, but what about nonexperts? For instance, wouldn't student writers be better off displaying mastery of a subject to their teachers rather than raising more questions? Researchers in the field of composition studies have asked similar questions. These scholars have found, in fact, that college writers develop more quickly and more fully when they adopt open-minded, questioning attitudes.

In their article "The Novice as Expert: Writing the Freshman Year," Nancy Sommers and Laura Saltz look at why some college students thrive as writers while others seem stuck. They examine the writing experiences of over 400 undergraduates throughout the course of their college careers. Sommers and Saltz conclude that the key factor that determines writerly success is student disposition. They argue that the "students who make the greatest gains as writers throughout college (1) initially accept their status as novices and (2) see in writing a larger purpose than fulfilling an assignment" (124). Through writing, students in their freshman year begin to see themselves not as visitors to a foreign land but as active participants in an intellectual community (131). What does being a novice mean? For Sommers and Saltz, being a novice means opening yourself to "instruction and feedback," experimenting with fresh ideas and new methods, and allowing yourself to be changed by intellectual discoveries (134). This disposition allows writers to view assignments not as hoops to jump through but as invitations to participate in the intellectual life of the university.

Takeaway: Less-seasoned writers develop most when they embrace the role of a novice who wants to try new approaches and when they find internal motivation to write.

Read the research: Sommers, Nancy, and Laura Saltz. "The Novice as Expert: Writing the Freshman Year." *College Composition and Communication*, vol. 56, no. 1, Sept. 2004, pp. 124–149. *Google Scholar*, doi:10.2307/4140684.

Tools & Techniques: Reading and Writing to Discover

This section describes strategies for maintaining a questioning attitude that generates knowledgeable ignorance. We offer here strategies that we see scholars use, particularly in the opening phases of research. These phases present opportunities to explore unfamiliar ideas and to resist finalizing them too early. Eventually, you'll discard many of your ideas. But some will launch you further into your research project. To emphasize the fact that early-stage research seeks knowledgeable ignorance, we've divided the rest of this chapter into two sections: 1) "Read before You Know" and 2) "Write before You Know."

Read before You Know

How you read likely depends on your purpose. Readers of poems often examine the same lines over and over, while readers of websites often skip most of the content as they scan for what they need. Neither one of these strategies is inherently better than the other, but they serve different purposes and offer potential for different findings. Researchers employ reading practices that serve their particular purposes, especially at the opening stages of a research project. No one has enough time to read every word of every article and book that may be useful in a research project. In Chapter 7, we discuss reading strategies at length. But here we want to introduce reading strategies that researchers use when they embark on a project.

- Reading to explore. In the early stages of a project, researchers read broadly, resisting the urge to narrow their focus immediately. They sample many ideas quickly to spur further thinking.
- Reading to map the scholarly conversation—the way that researchers respond to one another through scholarship. They note the names of scholars that appear repeatedly. They ask, "Who are the established voices and who are the emerging voices?"
- Reading to discover key terms. Scholars track the words that appear to be at issue in the scholarly conversation. They note the words that texts take care to define or redefine. They ask themselves, "Which words have contested or evolving definitions?"
- Reading with negative capability. Researchers stay open to things that they can't explain at first. They look for contradictions, gaps, or cognitive dissonance, but they do not rush to judgment about these problems. Instead, they read to better grasp them.

Write before You Know

While less-seasoned writers often approach writing as a single, high-pressure performance, research by Nancy Sommers shows us that expert writers usually think of writing as a series of low-pressure activities, a process rather than a performance (382, 386–87). By "low-pressure," we mean that no one will judge the writing, so the stakes for succeeding or failing are low. You can use low-pressure writing to experiment with new techniques and new forms. Most important, you can use low-pressure writing to write your way into new thoughts.

Here, we offer low-pressure strategies that professional researchers use in the beginning stages of their projects.

Low-Pressure, High-Reward Strategies for Advancing Thinking

- Focused freewriting. Freewriting means writing down one's thoughts without rereading, revising, or editing. When scholars freewrite, they disregard grammar and spelling, instead trying to get their thoughts onto the page quickly. They strive to use writing as a way of thinking. *Focused* freewriting simply means that you focus your freewriting energies on a specific prompt or question. Focused freewriting will not produce polished writing, but it will often yield new avenues for exploration.

- Writing to remember. Researchers use writing to download thoughts onto the page. According to research by cognitive psychologist Ronald Kellogg, less-experienced writers tend to tax their working memories by holding too many ideas in their heads at once (8). Experienced writers, on the other hand, write down ideas to free their minds for new thinking: (Kellogg 16, 21).

- Writing with others. Researchers write in communities, sharing their writing at various stages, from brainstorming to final polishing. Talking through thoughts with peers can be a powerful way to develop early ideas. When they're speaking, researchers often ask colleagues to take notes and to say back what they heard.

- Visiting a writing center. Most schools and many communities have writing centers, whose staffs help writers develop their thinking in low-pressure settings.

- Starting early. Researchers start projects early to give themselves time to try out many ideas and avoid committing to a dull idea under the pressure of a deadline.

- Recording speech. Writers sometimes speak into voice recorders or speech-to-text programs, talking through ideas they would like to explore. They then listen to the recordings or read the transcriptions. Many people speak more fluidly than they write, so speaking can be an effective way to generate new thoughts.
- Emailing or messaging ideas. People often put less pressure on themselves when they write emails or text messages than when they write for a formal purpose. For some people, this kind of uninhibited writing can also take the form of lists, drawings, or diagrams.

Researchers in the early stages of their projects use strategies like these not to prove what they know but to find out what they don't yet know. In the next chapter, we'll examine the kinds of knowledgeable ignorance researchers seek out to form the foundation of meaningful research.

TURN TO YOUR RESEARCH

Generate Ideas Using Low-Pressure Strategies

The following exercises help writers come up not with answers but with informed questions. They will help you approach your work with "negative capability," asking you to dwell in uncertainty at the earliest phases of your research.

1. *Freewrite your way to ignorance*: Write nonstop, beginning with what you know about a subject, then moving to what you'd like to find out. What is most mysterious to you? What are you most eager to understand? Don't worry about grammar or punctuation; rather, practice writing as a way of thinking on the page.

2. *Seek expert ignorance*: Find an expert and ask questions that might reveal a shared ignorance. You might ask the following: What research problems are you working on now? What remains mysterious in your field? What is most surprising to you? What are the classic questions scholars grapple with? What are emerging questions? What terms or concepts in your field are most contested?

Works Cited

Castiglione, Baldesar. *The Book of the Courtier.* Translated by Charles S. Singleton, Norton, 2002.

Copeland, Misty. *Life in Motion: An Unlikely Ballerina.* Simon and Schuster, 2014.

Firestein, Stuart. *Ignorance: How It Drives Science.* Oxford UP, 2012.

Kahneman, Daniel. *Thinking, Fast and Slow.* Farrar, Straus and Giroux, 2011.

Keats, John. *Keats's Poetry and Prose: Authoritative Texts, Criticism.* Norton, 2009.

Kellogg, Ronald T. "Training Writing Skills: A Cognitive Developmental Perspective." *Journal of Writing Research,* vol. 1, no. 1, 2008, pp. 1–26. *EBSCOhost,* doi:10.17239/jowr-2008.01.01.1.

"Misty Copeland." *Misty's Gallery Images,* 2015, mistycopeland.com/images/.

Pollan, Michael. "An Animal's Place." *New York Times Magazine,* 10 Nov. 2002, pp. 58+.

Smith, Joanna S., and Szymon M. Rusinkiewicz. "Modeling the Past: Digital Technologies and Excavations in Polis, Cyprus." *Progress in Cultural Heritage Preservation,* edited by Marinos Ioannides, et al., vol. 7616, Springer Berlin Heidelberg, 2012, pp. 414–22. *SpringerLink,* doi:10.1007/978-3-642-34234-9_42.

Sommers, Nancy. "Revision Strategies of Student Writers and Experienced Adult Writers." *College Composition and Communication,* vol. 31, no. 4, Dec. 1980, pp. 378–88. *JSTOR,* doi:10.2307/356588.

Sommers, Nancy, and Laura Saltz. "The Novice as Expert: Writing the Freshman Year." *College Composition and Communication,* vol. 56, no. 1, Sept. 2004, pp. 124–49. *Google Scholar,* doi:10.2307/4140684.

CHAPTER 2

....

Scholarly Problems

SCHOLARS' STORY

Writing Studies Researchers Renee Brown, Brian Fallon, Jessica Lott, Elizabeth Matthews, and Elizabeth Mintie on Entering a Scholarly Conversation

The five of us—four undergraduates and one graduate student—worked together as tutors at the Indiana University of Pennsylvania writing center. At the time, our campus asked students to use a plagiarism prevention program called *Turnitin.com*. We noticed that students were coming to the writing center confused about how and why *Turnitin* had flagged their texts for plagiarism. Further, students often received little direction from their instructors on how to read the results or correct the flagged content. We agreed that *Turnitin* did not address the true causes of plagiarism, and it did not contribute to students' understanding of proper citation.

These issues elicited questions about how *Turnitin* functions. We moved from anecdotal experiences to research by delving into *Turnitin*, uploading papers, playing around with it, and then being genuinely surprised by how it worked. We spoke about our discoveries with each other and with other writing tutors, who shared our concerns and inspired us to keep working at this problem. We then developed a presentation for

English Department faculty. Their responses to our findings pushed us to continue the project, asking questions of people in authority and eventually presenting at the National Conference on Peer Tutoring in Writing.

After hearing feedback from these professionals, we realized that something we viewed as a local issue was really a national issue, prompting us to consider how our research could inform a broader community and how, as tutors, we were uniquely positioned to advocate for all students affected by *Turnitin*. We wanted to share what we learned with students and tutors at other universities, so we wrote an article about our experiences. After lots of writing and revising, our work appeared as "Taking on *Turnitin*: Tutors Advocating Change" in *Writing Center Journal*. Our experience taught us that research was the language of the institution, and it allowed our voices to resonate.

Read the research: Brown, Fallon, Lott, Matthews, and Mintie are now all graduated and have embarked on their careers. Their article "Taking on *Turnitin*: Tutors Advocating Change" appears in the *Writing Center Journal*.

Mindset: Research Is a Form of Scholarly Conversation

In the last chapter, we emphasized the ways that scholars use writing to seek out "knowledgeable ignorance" (Firestein 11). In this chapter, we focus on the kinds of ignorance that researchers pursue. How, for example, did Renee Brown, Brian Fallon, Jessica Lott, Elizabeth Matthews, and Elizabeth Mintie decide to pursue the research that led to their published article? Notice that their project began with an experience of dissonance: they observed confusion among students who came to the writing center. They explored the source of that confusion, *Turnitin*, and were "genuinely surprised" by some of their findings. Their surprise, like the bewilderment that Stuart Firestein describes at the beginning of Chapter 1, indicates a **scholarly problem**—a moment when the researcher is not sure how to make sense of their observations.

The famous playwright and screenwriter David Mamet gave the following advice to writers of *The Unit*, a television show about Special Forces operatives: "Start, every time, with this inviolable rule: The *scene must be dramatic*. It must start because the hero has a problem, and it must culminate with the hero finding him or herself either thwarted or

KEY TERM

Scholarly Problem

In common usage, the word "problem" calls to mind a regrettable dilemma, something to avoid. Researchers, however, *seek out* scholarly problems: difficulties that arise from a gap in understanding. Scholarly problems take the form of tensions or dissonances that, when made sense of, advance our understanding. When a scholar articulates a problem—something that doesn't yet make sense—they create for the reader an expectation that their research will resolve the problem.

educated that another way exists" (qtd. in Haralovich 302). As Mamet suggests, a dramatic problem keeps viewers glued to a television show; so can a scholarly problem keep readers interested in research. They must ask, "How will the writer make sense of the problem?" Typically, writers present the scholarly problem in the introductions of their books and articles in order to provide a reason why readers should care about their research: research projects aim to make sense of the problem.

After the research team of Brown, Fallon, Lott, Matthews, and Mintie discovered an initial tension between the way students and faculty encountered *Turnitin*, they sought out a more sophisticated understanding of the problem. They moved from a conversation among students in the writing center to a conversation among scholars—faculty and experts. To use Stuart Firestein's language, they made sure not to dwell in "willful stupidity" but to push toward "knowledgeable ignorance" (11). They knew that their ignorance was knowledgeable when they saw that "something we viewed as a local issue was really a national issue." Thus, when the research team made sense of the shared dissonance, they advanced the **scholarly conversation**.

In this section, we'll discuss the ways that researchers use conversation to find scholarly problems that then allow them to carry that conversation further. These two concepts—scholarly conversation and scholarly problem—are so fundamental to understanding how scholars research that they will be the focus of this chapter and the core of the book.

KEY TERM

Scholarly Conversation

When scholars write, they participate in a scholarly conversation—reading other scholars, responding to them, and expecting other scholars to write in response. New research takes on significance when it demonstrates how it advances this ongoing conversation.

Intervening in the Scholarly Conversation

Conversation is both a part of the research process and something that scholars enact in their writing. Psychologist Daniel Kahneman writes about the conversation-based research process that he and his collaborator Amos Tversky used: "Our research was a conversation in which we invented questions and jointly examined our intuitive answers" (Kahneman 6). Kahneman and Tversky used their initial "intuitive answers" as a starting point. The back and forth of their conversation pushed both scholars beyond their first thoughts.

While Kahneman and Tversky engaged in actual conversation, many scholars generate a virtual conversation with participants who are not physically present but whose ideas provide the back-and-forth exchange that makes a conversation illuminating. Mathematics Professor Steven Strogatz explains, "A very central part of any mathematician's life is this sense of connection to other minds, alive today and going back to Pythagoras. . . . We are having this conversation with each other going over the millennia" (qtd. in Cook). Strogatz participates in a conversation that is not bound by time and space but exists instead in the realm of research, where thinkers from any time can come together.

What does a scholarly conversation look like on the page? In academic writing, scholars reference the studies that came before them and allude to studies that they hope will grow out of their research. Let's look at how historian Edward E. Baptist scaffolds his new ideas onto research by historians who came before him. In *The Half Has Never Been Told: Slavery and the Making of American Capitalism*, Baptist sets out to revise some historians' contentions that American slavery would have died out on its own because it diminished the United States' power and wealth. He demonstrates that, in fact, slavery was central to the modernization

RESEARCH ON WRITING

L. S. Vygotsky on Transferring Knowledge to New Contexts

PHOTO **2.1**
Mathematician and avid juggler Ron Graham. Photo by Peter Vidor.

L. S. Vygotsky, a Russian psychologist, did influential work on the cognitive development of young learners in the 1920s and 1930s. His research has been tremendously influential for researchers today who study something called "learning transfer." Learning transfer refers to a person's ability to take a skill they learned in one setting (a class, for example) and apply that skill in another setting (at work, for example). Transferring learning is essential if we actually want to put to use all the things we spend years in school learning; unfortunately, transferring learning to new contexts is not very intuitive for learners (81–82).

However, Vygotsky demonstrates that people are more likely to transfer a skill to a new setting when they are taught the new learning in terms of what they already know—a technique called *scaffolding* (90). To take one example, how might someone use scaffolding to teach juggling (see Photo 2.1)? Handing a learner three balls and asking them to practice keeping them all in the air is likely to end in failure and frustration.

However, most people have experience tossing a single ball. So instructions for new jugglers typically start by asking the learner to do something they are already familiar with: tossing a single ball from hand to hand. Gradually, the instructor scaffolds onto that familiar skill by adding a second ball and finally a third.

Vygotsky's concept of scaffolding has powerful implications for writers. In a sense, writers are teachers, and readers are their students. If writers can explain their scholarly problem in terms of what readers already know—by scaffolding the problem onto what has already been said in the scholarly conversation—readers are more likely to carry those ideas to new settings, and the ideas are more likely to become influential.

Takeaway: Readers are more likely to apply new ideas when writers explain how those ideas respond to and advance the existing scholarly conversation.

Read the research: Vygotsky, L. S. *Mind in Society: The Development of Higher Psychological Processes*. Harvard UP, 1978.

of the United States and a driver of its economic success. Baptist knows that in order for readers to grasp his ideas, he needs to contextualize his research within the studies that came before him. He writes,

> Thus, even after historians of the civil rights, Black Power, and multicultural eras rewrote segregationists' stories about gentlemen and belles and grateful darkies, historians were still telling the half that has ever been told. For some fundamental assumptions about the history of slavery and the history of the United States remain strangely unchanged. (xviii)

Notice that Baptist first shows that historians responded to one another: scholarship changed when historians questioned "segregationists' stories." Baptist then says, though, that even these historians weren't questioning other "fundamental assumptions" about the history of slavery. He goes on to reveal that his research will overturn some of these assumptions. The scholarly problem that Baptist addresses—how historians have not fully grasped the links between slavery and capitalism—doesn't come out of nowhere. It is a response to the scholarly conversation.

What did Edward E. Baptist have to do in order to understand the existing scholarly conversation and formulate a problem in response to it? And how can you adapt the practices of expert researchers like

Baptist in your own writing? The Tools & Techniques section suggests strategies that you can employ.

Tools & Techniques: Locating a Scholarly Problem with Stakes

We can imagine objections you might have to adopting the conversation-based practices of expert researchers. After all, seasoned researchers often work on longer projects over more time. They have years, sometimes, to explore the existing conversation and to respond. Newer researchers, on the other hand, not only have more to learn about the existing conversation, they are also often working on shorter projects with tighter deadlines. Is taking the time to discover problems that rise out of scholarly conversation a luxury only for experts? We want to argue that, in fact, the differences between seasoned and newer researchers come not primarily from the time they have but the practices they employ. Emulating experts' practices can make the research process more effective and efficient for any researcher, no matter their level of experience.

A Problem-Driven Writing Process

Think about the process you typically go through to arrive at an idea to write about. Which of these writers' processes comes closest to describing your first few steps?

Writer A: Topic-driven Approach	Writer B: Problem-driven Approach
1. Find a topic or controversy that interests me.	1. Discover a puzzling tension or dissonance: a scholarly problem.
2. Formulate a forceful claim about the topic or controversy.	2. Map out the conversation about this problem.
3. Search for published writers who echo or oppose my claim.	3. Seek a next step in the conversation that makes better sense of the problem.

Researchers Linda Flower and John R. Hayes studied the ways that two different groups of writers—college students and professional academics—approached these early, exploratory stages of the writing process. They discovered that the less-experienced college writers tended to take approaches similar to Writer A's, while the more-experienced research writers tended to take approaches similar to Writer B's (26–30).

Flower and Hayes concluded that less-experienced writers "are merely trying to express a network of ideas already formed and available in memory," while more-seasoned researchers "are consciously attempting to probe for analogues and contradictions, to form new concepts, and perhaps even to restructure their old knowledge of the subject" (28). Their findings may seem counterintuitive at first: why would more-experienced writers take a problem-driven approach that seems less efficient? After all, by the second step, the topic-driven Writer A has already nailed down a claim, while the problem-driven Writer B hasn't even started to consider a claim. Are experienced writers just less efficient? Not necessarily. Instead, they hold different assumptions about what academic writing should accomplish for themselves and others. Let's examine those assumptions:

Assumptions behind Writer A's Topic-Driven Approach	Assumptions behind Writer B's Problem-Driven Approach
1. Find a topic or controversy that interests me.	1. Discover a puzzling tension or dissonance, a scholarly problem.
Assumption: My personal interest in an issue is sufficient to motivate a project about it.	*Assumption*: Interesting problems are motivated by tensions or dissonances that I *and* my readers don't yet understand. If I can make sense of them, I and my readers will arrive at a new understanding.
2. Formulate a forceful claim about the topic or controversy.	2. Map out the conversation about this problem.
Assumption: I earn credibility with readers by taking a side and staunchly supporting it. My claim will be original if I avoid being influenced by others' ideas at this stage.	*Assumption*: I can better formulate a problem that captures shared ignorance if I research what others have written. Then I can understand the stakes of resolving the problem not only for myself but for others.
3. Search for published writers who echo or oppose my claim.	3. Seek a next step in the conversation that makes better sense of the problem.
Assumption: Academics measure their success by proving that their claims are more persuasive than others' claims. So my goal is to rally a team of scholars who can prove that my claims are right and my opposition is mistaken.	*Assumption*: Academic writing is an ongoing conversation. My goal is not to defeat others in the conversation but to contribute to it, helping my fellow researchers and myself take a step forward in our understanding.

You might notice from these assumptions that the topic-driven Writer A measures success by their ability to prove something about *themselves*: that they are right. The problem-driven Writer B measures success by helping themselves *and others* arrive at a richer understanding of the conversation. Writer B's goal is outward-focused; it is a response to and for others that comes out of careful listening to the ongoing conversation.

Which Scholarly Problems Are Worth Pursuing?

Not every tension or gap in understanding constitutes a problem worth writing about. In Stuart Firestein's *Ignorance*, mathematician Maria Chudnovsky explains that she decides to pursue research problems only 1) when they connect to other problems and 2) when they can take the conversation somewhere new (61). Notice how similar her criteria are to L. S. Vygotsky's concepts of scaffolding (connecting to other problems) and learning transfer (taking the conversation somewhere new). Chudnovsky's criteria are simple but useful for any writer to apply when deciding whether to pursue a scholarly problem:

1. Is the problem connected to an existing scholarly conversation? In other words, does evidence exist that others already care about it?
2. Will my making sense of the problem take us somewhere new? In other words, can I make an original contribution to the conversation?

When answering this second question, researchers consider an additional factor: the **stakes** of the contribution:

3. Will my original contribution to the conversation have meaningful stakes, or consequences, for the conversation? In other words, will my research influence others' interpretations in ways that are meaningful for them?

Notice that the criterion of stakes demands that researchers think about what matters to their readers early in a project. That might feel daunting before you even know what you're going to claim, but you don't necessarily need to raise problems with world-changing stakes. Sometimes making sense of a seemingly small problem in a **text** can carry important implications for how another person understands it.

KEY TERM

Stakes

Stakes answer the question, "So what?" In a research project, writers articulate stakes by offering evidence that the scholarly problem represents a meaningful next step in the conversation. This evidence answers the questions, "Why does this problem matter in this conversation? Why does it matter to my readers? Why does it matter here and now?"

KEY TERM

Text

When we use the word "text," we mean any object that one can analyze. A text might mean a book or a poem, of course, but it can also mean a film, a data set, a musical composition, a work of architecture, a performance, an event, a conversation, and so on.

Strategies for Generating Scholarly Problems

The following examples describe reading strategies that researchers use to make observations that lead to scholarly problems. They employ these strategies to identify problems within single texts and across multiple texts. You will find that some problems could fall under more than one category.

Notice that each problem requires two parts. Like a rubber band that can only be stretched when you pull each end in opposite directions, a scholarly tension requires two elements to be at odds. For instance, merely noticing that something seems strange doesn't constitute a scholarly problem until the researcher places it in tension with a second element: what we think of as typical. As you read the highlighted passages, you'll notice that we have underlined language that indicates the kind of tension the author is calling attention to.

As they research, scholars generate problems to drive their research by looking for tensions or dissonances between . . .

Common Understanding and Complication

Begin by observing a tension between the way others have understood the text and some aspect of the text that appears to diverge from that understanding.

Example: In this excerpt from his essay "The Trouble with Wilderness," William Cronon complicates our common understanding of the idea of "wilderness" as a realm separated from civilization (passage highlighted in light gray). Cronon observes that, in fact, wilderness is a product of civilization (passage highlighted in dark gray):

The common understanding of wilderness	For many Americans wilderness stands as the last remaining place where civilization, that all too human disease, has not fully infected the earth. It is an island in the polluted sea of urban-industrial modernity, the one place we can turn for escape from our own too-muchness. Seen in this way, wilderness presents itself as the best antidote to our human selves, a refuge we must somehow recover if we hope to save the planet. As Henry David Thoreau once famously declared, "In Wildness is the preservation of the World."
A complication: reasons to rethink the common understanding of wilderness	But is it? The more one knows of its peculiar history, the more one realizes that wilderness is not quite what it seems. Far from being the one place on earth that stands apart from humanity, it is quite profoundly a human creation—indeed, the creation of very particular human cultures at very particular moments in human history. (7)

Locate this type of problem by first researching the common understanding. Then look for elements that this understanding can't account for.

Consider the stakes by asking how this new complication might challenge the common understanding of the text.

COMMON PITFALL

The Unproven Common Understanding

Writers who are new to the stakes of a scholarly conversation sometimes revert to a strategy that deflates the tension they seek to create: the unproven common understanding. The unproven common understanding takes the form of an assertion that is detached from existing conversation or evidence: for instance, "For centuries, people have valued education,"

"Society punishes those who are different," or "Everyone loves an under-dog." We could easily find many exceptions to these sweeping generaliza-tions. Even when an unproven common understanding has some truth to it, it can be too broad to make a reader care about complicating it. How does one create a meaningful common understanding? Research. Writers can uncover the common understanding by study-ing the existing scholarly conversation or the popular conversation. The popular conversation may be expressed in newspapers, magazines, social media, and so forth.

Whole and Part

Begin by observing a tension between the whole text and one part of it that appears to be an outlier.

Example: In an essay arguing that the French painter Puvis de Cha-vannes is more innovative and provocative than previously acknowledged, the art historian Jennifer L. Shaw focuses on one of his murals called *Sum-mer*. Shaw finds a scholarly problem in the painting by noting that while the whole painting seems harmonious (passage highlighted in light gray), a part of the painting interrupts this harmony (passage highlighted in dark gray).

The whole mural	In *Summer*, incomplete or inexplicable bodies are set into what seems from a distance to be a pleasing composition aimed at delighting, rather than disturbing, its viewers. However, while the painting, taken as a whole, appears harmonious
A part that complicates our understanding of the whole	because of its decorative patterning, it is less so when the viewer focuses on individual figures. (591)

Locate this type of problem by re-reading (or re-viewing, re-listening, and so on). Study the text(s) first to grasp the big picture. In your notes, describe your overall sense of its claim, structure, and style. Then read again, this time annotating parts that diverge from your sense of the whole.

Consider the stakes by asking how making sense of the tension will offer a new interpretation of the outlier or the text as a whole.

Part and Part

Begin by observing a tension between one part of a text and another part.

Example: Literary critic Barbara Johnson locates a surprising tension between two paragraphs in Zora Neale Hurston's 1928 essay "How It Feels to Be Colored Me." Johnson explains that, while the essay answers the implicit question, "What does it feel like to be colored?", two parts of the text offer different definitions of the word "colored." One part of the text suggests that "colored" is a stable identity (passage highlighted in light gray). Another part of the text suggests that "colored" is an identity one acquires (passage highlighted in dark gray).

One part of the text describes "colored" as something one always *is*.	While the first paragraph thus begins, "I am colored," the second starts, "I remember the very day that I *became* colored." The presuppositions of the question are again undercut. If one can become colored, then one is not born colored, and the definition of "colored" shifts. (174)
Another part describes "colored" as something one *becomes*.	

Locate this type of problem by labeling the parts of the text. In your annotations, name the components or attributes of each section. Then read your labels. Notice any incongruities among the component parts.

Consider the stakes by asking how interpreting the tension can help us understand the functions of both parts, and, further, how making sense of the tension can advance our understanding of the whole text.

Pattern and Break

Begin by observing a tension between a pattern that a text establishes and a break in that pattern.

Example: Ecologists Philippe Perret and Jacques Blondel study the behavior of bird populations in two different habitats: on mainlands and on islands. They find a tension between the pattern of aggressive behavior among birds living on mainlands (passage highlighted in dark gray) and the break in that pattern of behavior among less-aggressive island birds (passage highlighted in light gray):

Island birds don't follow the same pattern as mainland birds. The pattern observed in mainland birds is aggression.	The reduced aggressiveness of birds in crowded insular populations runs counter to the trend usually observed in mainland populations where increased densities often result in increased situation-specific aggression. (97)

Locate this type of problem by reading for repetition. Annotate patterns you see in language, structure, imagery, and so on. Then read again, this time looking for places that don't adhere to the pattern. *Consider the stakes by asking* how making sense of the break in the pattern offers a new understanding of the text.

Form and Function

Begin by observing a tension between the structure or appearance of the text (its form) and what the text actually accomplishes (its function).

Example: In this excerpt from "Enteroviruses," public health scientist Peter Muir articulates a scholarly problem by explaining the tension between the apparent structure of enteroviruses (passage highlighted in light gray) and the ways that enteroviruses operate in the world (passage highlighted in dark gray) (see Photo 2.2):

Locate this type of problem by noting the difference between how the text appears and what the text does. For each section of the text, describe

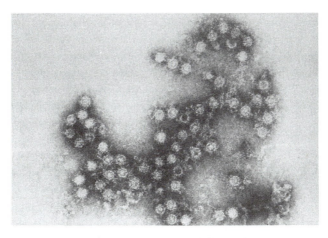

PHOTO **2.2**
An immunoelectron microscopic image of an enterovirus called Coxsackie B4. Image courtesy of the Centers for Disease Control and Prevention.

The form of enteroviruses suggests simplicity.	Enteroviruses continue to fascinate taxonomists, molecular biologists, and physicians. Their
	small size, nondescript appearance and simple
But enteroviruses serve functions that are diverse and complex.	genomic structure belies their biological diversity and the broad clinical spectrum of their associated illnesses. (57)

the structure and form and what you would expect this structure and form to accomplish. Then describe what each section actually accomplishes.

Consider the stakes by asking how making sense of the incongruity between the form of the text and the function it serves can advance our understanding.

Presence and Absence

Begin by observing a tension between something you expect to be present and its actual absence.

Example: In "Denial of Power in Televised Women's Sports," kinesiologists Margaret Carlisle Duncan and Cynthia A. Hasbrook articulate a scholarly problem by noting a stark contrast between the widespread presence of televised male sports (passage highlighted in light gray) and the comparative absence of televised female sports (passage highlighted in dark gray):

Sports featuring men receive a lot of television coverage. Sports featuring women receive minimal television coverage.	More significant yet, though, is the disproportionate amount of television coverage devoted to team sports, particularly men's team sports, and to "male appropriate" individual sports. By comparison, females competing in team contests and certain individual sports receive a negligible amount of air time. Why are team sports and certain individual sports considered to be a male domain? Why is there such a notable lack of female participation in these areas? And why are these imbalances underscored by disproportionate media coverage, especially television coverage? (83)

Locate this type of problem by first naming the aspects of the text that are present or that you expect to be present. Next, describe what is notably absent, given what else is there or what your expectations were.

Consider the stakes by asking how interpreting the conflict between what we expect to be present and its absence helps further our understanding.

Expectation and Observation

Begin by observing a tension between what we expect to encounter and what we actually observe.

Example: In *Our Declaration: A Reading of the Declaration of Independence in Defense of Equality*, historian Danielle Allen articulates a scholarly problem rising out of the tension between how we expect signers of the Declaration of Independence to have acted based on their words (passage highlighted in light gray) and observations of their actual actions (passage highlighted in dark gray):

The signers' words make us expect one thing. But the actions we observe suggest another.	What are we to make of the fact that the signers, who formally declared a commitment to equality, also protected slavery and ruthlessly sought to deracinate, if not exterminate, Native Americans? (240)

Locate this type of problem by first noting your expectations. Before reading a text for the first time, note what you expect (and why) based on what you know about the author, the publication, the genre, the date of publication, the subject, and so on. When you read, annotate any passages that don't meet your expectations.

Consider the stakes by asking how making sense of the mismatch between what we expect and what we actually observe furthers our understanding.

Audience and Text

Begin by observing a tension between the approach that a text takes and the audience it addresses.

Example: In "Materiality and Genre in the Study of Discourse Communities," rhetorical theorists Amy J. Devitt, Anis Bawarshi, and Mary Jo Reiff examine the disjuncture between specialized legal language used in jury instructions (passage highlighted in dark gray) and the nonspecialist jury members who must interpret it (passage highlighted in light gray).

The audience for jury instructions are not legal specialists.	The inclusion of nonspecialists is vital to the U.S. judicial system, with the usually final decisions made not by all-knowing judges but by every-
Yet jury instructions rely on specialized legal language.	day citizens. . . . But jury instructions are written by lawyers, with their details hammered out by lawyers and the judge arguing privately, away from the ears of the jurors who must use them. By the time the judge gives a jury instructions, those instructions contain presumptions, implications, specifications known well by the law community but unknown to the unsuspecting jury members. . . . As a result, juries do not and cannot interpret the genre the way its creators intended. (544)

Locate this type of problem by reading through the intended audience's eyes. As you read, discover whom the text is aimed at. Specialists or generalists? Americans or another nationality? Contemporary readers or past readers? Skeptics or believers? And so on. What clues can the publication, the date, and the text itself offer? What beliefs and interests might those readers bring to the text? Annotate any passages that are in tension with their beliefs or interests.

Consider the stakes by asking how making sense of the conflict between the audience's interests and the text's approach furthers our understanding.

Text and Context

Begin by observing a tension between a text and the context surrounding it, including its historical moment, its creator's body of work, the intellectual tradition it comes out of, and so on.

Example: In "A Shopping Mall at Ground Zero, Uninformed by Its Sacred Land," *New York Times* architecture reviewer David W. Dunlap describes his experience visiting the Westfield World Trade Center shopping mall within the Oculus, the grand transit hub opened on the former site of the destroyed World Trade Centers (see Photo 2.3). He finds a tension between the shopping mall's rather everyday appearance (passage highlighted in light gray) and the grandeur of the Oculus's design (passage highlighted in dark gray):

A "heartening" context	The experience was at once heartening and dispiriting. Heartening, because Santiago Calatrava's soaring Oculus now teems with people. The cantilevered "diving boards" over the great hall have instantly become downtown's version of the crowded balconies at Grand Central Terminal, the ideal spot to take that perfectly symmetrical
A "dispiriting" text	architectural panorama. . . . Dispiriting, because there is little to suggest that Westfield World Trade Center occupies consecrated ground. Apart from the bravura of Mr. Calatrava's design, and the snow-white marble floors, this mall could be just about anywhere. (A19)

Locate this type of problem by researching the context. Before you read, briefly research the text, author, and time period. If you're reading a book, you might look at book reviews, which typically situate the book within the author's body of work and within an intellectual tradition. Then find aspects of the text that don't seem to fit the context.

Consider the stakes by asking how making sense of the gap between the text and the context in which it was produced or situated furthers our understanding of the text and/or the context.

PHOTO **2.3**
The Westfield Mall in One World Trade Center, designed by Spanish architect Santiago Calatrava.

And Others . . .

Many more categories of scholarly problems exist. All that's required is to observe two things in tension that, when made sense of, would further our understanding. Other common tensions that scholars form into problems include tensions between . . .

- Theory and practice
- Method and findings
- Prominence and significance
- Past, present, and future
- Genre conventions (meaning the features typically shared by this type of text) and observations

The next two chapters address the steps that researchers take after they find scholarly problems to motivate their research: defining a project and making a claim (see Figure 2.1).

FIGURE **2.1**
Scholarly problems provide reasons, or motive, for scholars to pursue a project that leads to a claim.

PRACTICE

Generate Scholarly Problems

Task #1: Imagine that you're analyzing the Militärhistorisches Museum der Bundeswehr (Military History Museum) in Dresden, Germany (see Box Photo 2.4). List and describe all the types of scholarly problems that the building presents for you. Choose from the pairs of tensions listed in the section "Strategies for Generating Scholarly Problems."

Task #2: Imagine that you've begun researching the Militärhistorisches Museum der Bundeswehr. You learn that the original neoclassical building was constructed in 1876 to serve as an armory (Studio Daniel Libeskind). In later years it became a military museum, first showcasing Nazi, then Soviet, and later East German military histories (Studio Daniel Libeskind). In 1989, the year the Berlin Wall fell, the German government shut down

PHOTO 2.4
The Militärhistorisches Museum der Bundeswehr in Dresden, Germany. Photo courtesy of Bundeswehr/Andrea Bienert.

the museum to rethink how it wanted to tell the nation's military history (Studio Daniel Libeskind). A newly conceived museum opened in 2011, dedicated to exploring the human experience of war (Heckner 366–67). As part of its reopening, the German government commissioned Polish American architect Daniel Libeskind to design an addition to the original building (Heckner 365). Libeskind, who lost most of his relatives in the Holocaust, created a steel-encased five-story wedge that juts out from the center of the original building (Meisler). Given this research about the museum, list and describe additional types of scholarly problems that you would consider writing about.

ANSWERS:

Task #1: One possible answer is a tension between whole and part. The whole of the Militärhistorisches Museum der Bundeswehr is a white stone façade that features classical Roman architectural elements. However, the new part disrupts that old design by using a different color, material, and shape.

Task #2: One possible answer is a tension between past and present. In the past, the Militärhistorisches Museum der Bundeswehr encouraged visitors to appreciate the various German governments' military triumphs. In its present redesigned form, it encourages visitors to question the governments' military actions.

TURN TO YOUR RESEARCH

Choose Scholarly Problems That Spark Conversation

Not all tensions and dissonances will make for meaningful scholarly problems. To figure out which problems are worth pursuing, let's return for a
moment to the metaphor of research as a form of conversation. What separates people who spark lively conversation from those who tend to shut
down conversation? Earlier in the chapter, we highlighted mathematician
Maria Chudnovsky's two requirements for pursuing scholarly problems:
they must both 1) connect to already-known problems and 2) take the
conversation somewhere new (in Firestein 61).

Chudnovsky's requirements help us realize that people can shut
down scholarly conversation in two ways: either by raising a problem that
doesn't clearly build on what's already known (violating the first requirement) or by repeating what listeners already know (violating the second
requirement). To visualize which scholarly problems will spark conversation, first list all the possible pairs of tensions you might address in your
own writing project. Then sort each problem into one of the three sections
in Figure 2.2.

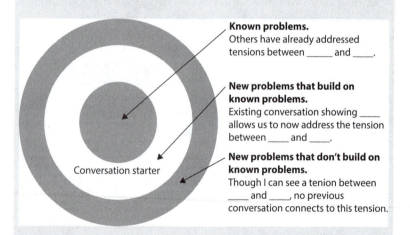

Known problems.
Others have already addressed
tensions between _____ and _____.

**New problems that build on
known problems.**
Existing conversation showing _____
allows us to now address the tension
between _____ and _____.

**New problems that don't build on
known problems.**
Though I can see a tenion between
_____ and _____, no previous
conversation connects to this tension.

Conversation starter

FIGURE 2.2
Scholarly problems scaffold on top of what's already known and move into
the unknown.

Works Cited

Allen, Danielle. *Our Declaration: A Reading of the Declaration of Independence in Defense of Equality.* Norton, 2014.

Baptist, Edward E. *The Half Has Never Been Told: Slavery and the Making of American Capitalism.* Basic Books, 2014.

Bienert, Andrea. *Außenaufnahme Des Militärhistorischen Museums in Dresden,* 12 Sept. 2011. *Wikimedia Commons,* commons.wikimedia.org/wiki/File:Militärhistorisches_Museum_Dresden_(außen).jpg.

Centers for Disease Control and Prevention. *Coxsackie B4 Enterovirus Virions.* 1981. *Centers for Disease Control and Prevention Public Health Image Library,* phil.cdc.gov/Details.aspx?pid=5630.

Cook, Gareth. "The Singular Mind of Terry Tao." *New York Times,* 24 July 2015, www.nytimes.com/2015/07/26/magazine/the-singular-mind-of-terry-tao.html.

Cronon, William. "The Trouble with Wilderness: Or, Getting Back to the Wrong Nature." *Environmental History,* vol. 1, no. 1, 1996, pp. 7–28.

Devitt, Amy J., et al. "Materiality and Genre in the Study of Discourse Communities." *College English,* vol. 65, no. 5, 2003, pp. 541–58. *Google Scholar,* doi:10.2307/3594252.

Duncan, Margaret Carlisle, and Cynthia A. Hasbrook. "Denial of Power in Televised Women's Sports." *Gender and Sport: A Reader,* edited by Sheila Scraton and Anne Flintoff, Psychology Press, 2002, pp. 83–93.

Dunlap, David W. "A Shopping Mall at Ground Zero, Uninformed by Its Sacred Land." *New York Times,* 5 Sept. 2016, p. A19.

Firestein, Stuart. *Ignorance: How It Drives Science.* Oxford UP, 2012.

Flower, Linda, and John R. Hayes. "The Cognition of Discovery: Defining a Rhetorical Problem." *College Composition and Communication,* vol. 31, no. 1, 1980, pp. 21–32. *JSTOR,* doi:10.2307/356630.

Haralovich, Mary Elizabeth. "Those at Home Also Serve: Women's Television and Embedded Military Realism in Army Wives." *A Companion to the War Film,* edited by Douglas A. Cunningham and John C. Nelson, Wiley & Sons, 2016, pp. 289–304. *Crossref,* doi:10.1002/9781118337653.ch17.

Heckner, Elke. "Fascism and Its Afterlife in Architecture." *Museum & Society,* vol. 14, no. 3, Nov. 2016, pp. 363–81.

Johnson, Barbara. *A World of Difference.* Johns Hopkins UP, 1987. *Google Books,* books.google.com/books/about/A_World_of_Difference.html?id=8TPibhJxoyQC.

Kahneman, Daniel. *Thinking, Fast and Slow.* Farrar, Straus and Giroux, 2011.

Meisler, Stanley. "Daniel Libeskind: Architect at Ground Zero." *Smithsonian*, vol. 33, no. 12, Mar. 2003, pp. 77–84.

Muir, Peter. "Enteroviruses." *Medicine*, vol. 42, no. 1, 2014, pp. 57–59. *Google Scholar*, doi:10.1016/j.mpmed.2013.10.009.

Perret, Philippe, and Jacques Blondel. "Experimental Evidence of the Territorial Defense, Hypothesis in Insular Blue Tits." *Experientia*, vol. 49, no. 1, 1993, pp. 94–98. *SpringerLink*, doi:10.1007/BF01928800.

Shaw, Jennifer L. "Imagining the Motherland: Puvis de Chavannes, Modernism, and the Fantasy of France." *Art Bulletin*, vol. 79, no. 4, Dec. 1997, p. 586. *Crossref*, doi:10.2307/3046277.

Studio Daniel Libeskind. "Dresden's Military History Museum / Studio Libeskind." *ArchDaily*, 14 Oct. 2011, www.archdaily.com/172407/dresden%e2%80%99s-military-history-museum-daniel-libeskind/.

Vidor, Peter. *Ron Graham.* 19 Nov. 2007. *Wikimedia Commons*, commons.wikimedia.org/wiki/File:Ronald_graham_juggling.jpg.

Vygotsky, L. S. *Mind in Society: The Development of Higher Psychological Processes.* Harvard UP, 1978.

CHAPTER 3

Projects

Mindset: A Project Provides a Plan to Address a Problem

Consider how you might respond as a researcher to this problem: in 2017, countries spent $3.1 billion to fight malaria; despite this massive effort, 219 million people contracted the mosquito-borne illness, and 435,000 died (World Health Organization 4, 37, 42) (see Photo 3.1). The majority of those who died were children under the age of five (World Health Organization 42).

Researchers around the world address this problem every year. For example, in their article "The Economic and Social Burden of Malaria," economists Jeffrey Sachs and Pia Malaney review close to fifty studies examining the ways the disease impedes nations' economic and social development (680). In another article, a medical research group called the South East Asian Quinine Artesunate Malaria Trial (SEAQUAMAT) compared the effectiveness of two different treatments for 1,382 malaria sufferers (718–20). Both articles address the same scholarly problem—the disease's continuing devastation in spite of the many efforts people have made to fight it—but they approach the problem differently. Put another way, these researchers grapple with the same problem, but they each do so guided by different **projects**. Designing a project is the step researchers take after identifying a problem. The project determines *how* the researchers will address the problem and arrive at a claim (see Box Figure 3.1).

In describing the project as the step between scholarly problem and claim, we're drawing on the work of composition studies scholar Joseph

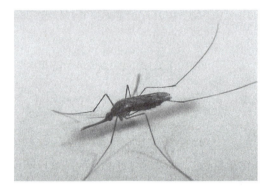

PHOTO **3.1**
Researchers develop many projects in response to the disease spread by this small insect. What project would you design to fight malaria? Photo by Edward McCellan and courtesy of the Centers for Disease Control.

KEY TERM

Project

A project is the approach that a researcher takes to address a scholarly problem. Researchers carry out the project in order to discover a claim.

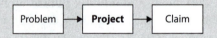

Problem → **Project** → Claim

FIGURE **3.1**
A scholar's project determines how they will move from a problem to a claim.

A project consists of four components:

1. The purpose of the study: What might making sense of the scholarly problem accomplish?
2. The object(s) of analysis: Which text(s) or data will the study analyze?
3. Method of analysis: How will the object(s) be analyzed?
4. Stakes: Why does making sense of the problem in this way matter for readers?

Harris, who describes project as "a plan of work" (17). While a researcher's scholarly problem provides the motive for research, the project determines which pathway they will take to make sense of the problem. Because a single scholarly problem invites many possible projects, scholars must prove that their projects carry meaningful stakes to address the problem.

Projects Respond to Conversation

Fortunately, researchers don't have to invent projects out of thin air. The ongoing scholarly conversation serves as a foundation; researchers look to others' projects to discover fruitful models to draw from or common approaches that could use revision or expansion.

In the two passages that follow, political scientist Peter Mandaville describes the purpose, objects of analysis, methods of analysis, and stakes of the project of his book *Transnational Muslim Politics: Reimagining the Umma*. "Umma" refers to the sense of community that unites Muslims across nations and cultures. As you read these excerpts, notice how Mandaville justifies his project (highlighted in light gray) by describing it as a response to others' scholarly projects on Islamic political life (highlighted in dark gray).

Mandaville begins by addressing two components of his book's project, the purpose and methods:

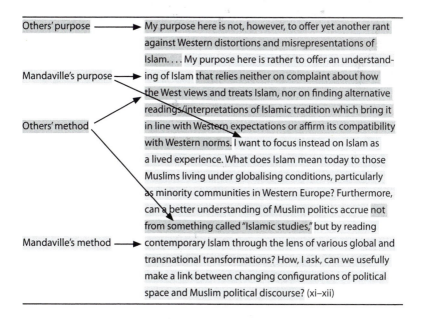

Others' purpose ⟶ My purpose here is not, however, to offer yet another rant against Western distortions and misrepresentations of Islam. ... My purpose here is rather to offer an understand-

Mandaville's purpose ⟶ ing of Islam that relies neither on complaint about how the West views and treats Islam, nor on finding alternative readings/interpretations of Islamic tradition which bring it

Others' method in line with Western expectations or affirm its compatibility with Western norms. I want to focus instead on Islam as a lived experience. What does Islam mean today to those Muslims living under globalising conditions, particularly as minority communities in Western Europe? Furthermore, can a better understanding of Muslim politics accrue not from something called "Islamic studies," but by reading

Mandaville's method ⟶ contemporary Islam through the lens of various global and transnational transformations? How, I ask, can we usefully make a link between changing configurations of political space and Muslim political discourse? (xi–xii)

Mandaville acknowledges that he is taking on a scholarly problem that political scientists before him have also addressed: the tension between the appearances and realities of Muslim political life in the West. Yet he also explains how his project offers something new. As Mandaville describes what his purpose *isn't*, he points to what he sees as the limitations of other scholars' projects: their purpose is to view Islam in terms of its relationship to the West, which produces merely "rant[s]." Mandaville's purpose instead is to study Western Muslims' lives on their own terms.

Mandaville also adopts a different method than previous scholars. Others delve into analysis typical in Islamic studies to show how the Western world accommodates Islam. In contrast, Mandaville will study Muslims' lives by focusing on elements of Islamic culture that are changing in similar ways across the globe.

The book goes on to describe its objects of analysis and stakes. As you read, note the way Mandaville designs his project to address the shortcomings of other scholars' projects:

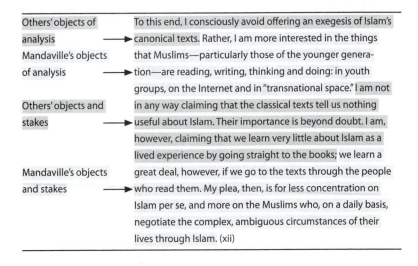

Others' objects of analysis ⟶	To this end, I consciously avoid offering an exegesis of Islam's canonical texts. Rather, I am more interested in the things
Mandaville's objects of analysis ⟶	that Muslims—particularly those of the younger generation—are reading, writing, thinking and doing: in youth groups, on the Internet and in "transnational space." I am not
Others' objects and stakes ⟶	in any way claiming that the classical texts tell us nothing useful about Islam. Their importance is beyond doubt. I am, however, claiming that we learn very little about Islam as a lived experience by going straight to the books; we learn a
Mandaville's objects and stakes ⟶	great deal, however, if we go to the texts through the people who read them. My plea, then, is for less concentration on Islam per se, and more on the Muslims who, on a daily basis, negotiate the complex, ambiguous circumstances of their lives through Islam. (xii)

Here again, Mandaville distinguishes his project from others'. Whereas other scholarship analyzes Islamic scripture (its "canonical texts"), Mandaville analyzes quite different objects. He studies the texts written by contemporary Muslims as they communicate with members of their community throughout the world. Because he draws from as-yet unstudied objects—the web and other everyday texts—he raises new stakes: to arrive at "a better understanding" of Muslims' "lived experience" of political life (xi).

Not all writers explicitly describe their projects as a response to previous scholars' approaches, but the strategy accomplishes something for Mandaville. It suggests that not only his claims but also his approach will make an original contribution to the conversation. Thus, others might respond to Mandaville by adopting similar projects. For instance, one scholar might respond to Mandaville's project by proposing to use a new method to study the same objects, perhaps data mining years of social media posts. Another scholar might suggest examining different objects, like diaries, newspaper articles, or photographs. Each project would contribute a new way of approaching the subject that would, in turn, inform others' approaches.

Tools & Techniques: Designing Do-able Projects

After discovering common approaches to other scholars' projects, Peter Mandaville can design his own project in response to theirs. L. S. Vygotsky's research on cognitive development, presented in the previous chapter, shows why Mandaville's strategy is wise. Vygotsky finds that intellectual development depends upon scaffolding: people are more likely to learn something new when they are taught it in the context of what they already know (Vygotsky 83). In this case, Mandaville's learners are his readers—fellow scholars who are familiar with the scholarly conversation about the political culture of Islam. Mandaville places his new project in the context of what those readers already know about traditional approaches to studying the political life of Islam.

Research Others' Projects

To pursue the kind of work Mandaville is doing, scholars read for and annotate others' projects, just as we did with excerpts of *Transnational Muslim Politics*. They note not only the writer's core ideas but also the way that the writer situates their project within a scholarly conversation. Once you get in the habit of annotating the four components of a study's project—1) purpose, 2) object(s), 3) method, and 4) stakes—you can design projects that scaffold onto others and even advance conversations about the best approaches to a given scholarly problem.

Project descriptions are easy to find: most academic texts begin by defining a scholarly problem, and their logical next step is to describe the ensuing project. In books, project descriptions often appear in the introductions. Humanities and social science journal articles typically place them in the opening sections. And in scientific research reports, project descriptions appear in sections labeled "methods."

Generate Your Own Project

The questions that follow can help you pivot from understanding others' projects to generating and justifying your own project in response.

Purpose: What does the study propose to accomplish? Scientific research often asks, "What information or data would make sense of the problem?" Humanities research often asks, "What interpretation or analysis would make sense of the problem?" Research in engineering, design studies, public policy, and business management often asks, "What action or creation would solve the problem?" Many projects combine purposes: to inform, to interpret, and to propose.

Others' projects:

- For what purposes have other scholars pursued projects to make sense of this scholarly problem?

My own project:

- What new information, interpretation, or proposal will my own study generate?
- Do I have sufficient time and resources to carry out my purpose?

Object(s) of analysis: Which text(s) or data will the study examine? We use the term "object of analysis" instead of "evidence" because evidence suggests that one is merely mining texts or data to support a predetermined claim. "Object of analysis" focuses our attention on the importance of researchers' *interpretations* of texts or data they use to support their claims.

Others' projects:

- Which objects have others analyzed? What do those objects reveal about the scholarly problem? What do they miss?

My own project:

- Which objects are representative of the problem I've identified? Which are intriguing outliers?
- Which emerging objects might invite new interpretations? Which new technologies, different populations of people, new texts, new phenomena, and so on can complicate the conversation?
- How many objects do I have the time and resources to analyze?

Method of analysis: How will I analyze the objects? The answer might entail applying a theoretical lens, designing an experiment, employing a strategy for reading, using a digital tool, and so on. A valid method produces results that others could also arrive at if they employed the method you describe.

Others' projects:

- How have others analyzed the objects? What do those methods reveal about the objects of analysis? What do they miss?

My own project:

- How will analyzing new objects using a common method produce new findings?
- How will analyzing common objects using a new method produce new findings?
- Do I have the time and resources to carry out my method?

Stakes: Why does pursuing the project matter for readers? Which readers or groups of people will be most affected? Stakes can range from matters of life and death to conceptual difficulties that carry subtler implications.

Others' projects:

- Why, according to other scholars, have their projects mattered?

My own project:

- What will change—and for whom—if others adopt the new understanding that my research advances? What will change if they don't?
- What next step does my study make possible?
- Do my findings have implications that go beyond the objects I analyzed?

Narrow Your Project

To convey passion about their research, a scholar might easily fall into the trap of exaggerating the stakes of their project, perhaps asserting that their study carries implications for all of society or a huge span of history. In response, we sometimes see more-experienced researchers advise those who are less experienced to "narrow your focus" or "go deeper." This advice recognizes that significant contributions to a scholarly conversation need not make sweeping claims. Indeed, scholars are often suspicious of sweeping claims, since such claims are less likely to be well proven.

Seasoned scholars maintain their credibility by ensuring that their project's purpose and stakes don't exceed what their objects and methods can actually support. For instance, Peter Mandaville states that his study of communication among young Muslims carries stakes for how we understand Islam as a lived experience in Western Europe. But Mandaville is careful not to claim that his project carries stakes for religions in general or even Muslims in non-Western countries. His objects of analysis can't accurately represent those much larger categories.

Scholars further balance their desire to produce significant projects with the need for feasible projects—research they can realistically carry out. Here we offer four narrowing strategies that scholars use to create feasible projects that are also significant. You'll see that these strategies require the researcher to be realistic about what they can accomplish in a given amount of time: How many objects can they study? What methods can they practically carry out? In each example passage, we have underlined language that signals the narrowing strategy.

Narrowing Strategy 1: Analyze Fewer Objects, and Narrow the Stakes

If you analyze a smaller group of objects, will your project still carry significant stakes?

Literary scholars often analyze a single story or even just a short passage rather than an entire literary period, contending that a deep understanding of a single text more powerfully advances the scholarly conversation than a shallow analysis of many texts. Social scientists, similarly, often analyze a narrowly defined group of people so that they can make more detailed observations. In both instances, scholars must be able to argue that analyzing fewer objects can still carry significant stakes.

Example: Imagine that you study the effects of stress on the health of people who suffer from diabetes. The problem you address rises out of the tension between the presence of many studies of Anglo-European diabetics and the relative absence of studies of indigenous peoples who have diabetes. Your purpose is to discover more information about the effects of stress on indigenous peoples. How might you generate a project that is feasible?

- *The broadest project* would study all subjects. Researchers might contact many groups of indigenous peoples—thousands of groups throughout the world—and study all the diabetes sufferers in those groups. Researchers could then argue that their data carry stakes for understanding the effects of stress on all indigenous peoples with diabetes. However, gathering so much data would require more time than one researcher or even a research team has.
- *A narrower but still unfeasible project* would select a subgroup of subjects. Researchers might study all the diabetic people within a single indigenous identity. Findings from this subgroup would allow researchers to argue that their study carries stakes for every diabetic of that identity. Even this subgroup might require gathering data from thousands of people living far apart from one another, likely overwhelming most researchers.
- *A sufficiently narrow project* would use more limiting criteria to identify an even smaller subgroup.

When faced with this broad question about stress and diabetes, public health researchers Yoshitaka Iwasaki and Judith Bartlett narrowed their subject group in four ways: region, ethnicity, diabetes status, and nationality. They studied stress coping among twenty-six urban, diabetic Aboriginal Canadians (15). Because their study group was quite narrow, they avoided claiming that their findings might apply to other indigenous groups in other regions. They write,

> [O]ur intention here is not to generalize the findings, given the very specific nature of the sample used with a relatively small sample size. . . . [F]urther efforts will be required to better understand the use of human strengths and resilience in coping with stress among Aboriginal populations worldwide. (24)

Notice that Iwasaki and Bartlett present the narrower purpose and stakes of their study not as weaknesses but as an invitation for further research.

Narrowing Strategy 2: Analyze Fewer Objects, but Broaden the Stakes

Can you argue that even though you are analyzing a subgroup of objects, your findings apply to the larger group of objects as well? To effectively narrow your project to study fewer objects but argue for broader stakes, you need to demonstrate that the smaller group of objects accurately represents the larger group.

Example: Imagine that you wanted to learn how the relationships between men and women in Rwanda changed after genocide ravaged the country in the mid-1990s. You decide to address the problem posed by the seeming tension between your *expectation* that Rwandans' efforts to end gender-based violence would be driven mostly by female advocates and the *observation* that these efforts received overwhelming support from men as well. The number of objects you could study are overwhelming: community activism, social support networks, judicial reforms, legal protections, and so on. Rather than analyzing all objects that exemplify a scholarly problem like this one, would analyzing a subset suffice?

In their research, Elizabeth Powley and Elizabeth Pearson study gender relations in postgenocide Rwanda by focusing on a single legislative campaign for a bill designed to combat gender-based violence (15). They make clear, however, that analyzing the gender-based violence bill illuminates the larger issue of Rwandan gender relations:

> While the legacy of the 1994 genocide permeates all aspects of life in Rwanda, including contemporary politics and gender relations, this article does not attempt to comprehensively address the relationship between the genocide or its attendant trauma and current gender relations. Instead, it explores one case of post-conflict policymaking and posits that it is emblematic of the state of gender relations in Rwanda today. (15)

Because they argue that the gender-based violence bill is representative of "the state of gender relations in Rwanda today," Powley and Pearson can make larger claims about "politics and gender relations in Rwanda" without studying all of the possible objects that the broad category of "politics and gender relations" might include (15). This strategy works when you can convince readers that your smaller group of objects accurately represents—or is emblematic of—a larger group of objects.

Narrowing Strategy 3: Analyze Fewer Variables

Can you examine fewer variables about a large group of objects? Perhaps you want to analyze a large number of objects because that large number will offer a more accurate picture of the problem you are addressing. However, when analyzing a large number of objects, you could easily create an overwhelming task in collecting all the data available about each object. One narrowing strategy involves picking only certain aspects of those objects—specific variables—to study. Researchers use this approach when they can show that the variables they have chosen accurately reflect the larger problem they are addressing.

Example: Imagine that you are a researcher who studies changes in people's health at different moments in history. You address a problem rising out of the *absence* of information on Midwesterners health in the nineteenth century, especially compared to the *presence* of such information in the twentieth century. The broadest project might endeavor to gather as much information as possible that might shed light on health: causes of death, access to health care, water quality, mortality rates, and so on. This project could quickly become too demanding to carry out.

Economists Richard H. Steckel and Donald R. Haurin addressed this challenge by narrowing their methods to study a single variable. The title of their study "Health and Nutrition in the American Midwest: Evidence from the Height of Ohio National Guardsmen, 1850–1910" indicates a project that carries an ambitiously broad purpose: to study the health and nutrition of a whole region of Americans. And the set of objects they study is dauntingly large: 13,000 Ohio National Guard enlistees (Steckel and Haurin 117) (see Photo 3.2). However, as their study's subtitle indicates, Steckel and Haurin narrow their focus to a single variable: the height recorded for each soldier on their enlistment record (118). They explain that height is an indicator of nutrition: "adult stature is sensitive to conditions of net nutrition . . . during early childhood" (126). To successfully employ this narrowing strategy, a researcher must convince readers that the variable—height in Steckel and Haurin's study—sufficiently addresses the scholarly problem under examination—the health and nutrition of Midwesterners.

PHOTO **3.2**
Ohio National Guardsman General John C. Speaks was one of the subjects included in Steckel's and Haurin's study (Mercer and Rife 66–67).

Narrowing Strategy 4: Respond to Fewer Scholars

Can you respond to fewer scholars, narrowing your project by addressing only a selection of the existing research?

Perhaps you'd like to enter a long-running scholarly conversation involving hundreds of thinkers. How do you prevent your research from being buried under the sheer number of voices that have taken part? One strategy is to select just a few key voices to respond to.

Example: Imagine that you are studying the extent to which college admissions policies have historically influenced social mobility in the United States. You address a problem emerging from your *observation* that elite colleges did not adhere to the *expectations* they created: their stated mission was to provide a pathway to the middle class for disadvantaged students, yet their admission policies favored the children of well-to-do alumni and elites. Your purpose is to make sense of the gaps between elite schools' claims and their actual admission policies. But you quickly realize that the number of thinkers who have addressed the same problem is overwhelming. How can you narrow your project? In responding to this same scholarly problem, sociologist Jerome Karabel narrows the number of thinkers he will address. In his book *The Chosen: The Hidden History of Admission and Exclusion at Harvard, Yale, and Princeton*, Karabel lays out a study with an ambitious purpose: to study college admissions reforms "throughout the twentieth century" (540). Notice, then, how his last sentence narrows his methods to studying the writings of just three university presidents, each representing a different era:

> There were also periods of profound upheaval when the existing [American social] order seemed precarious—most notably during the Progressive Era, the Great Depression, and the 1960s. It is during just such periods that liberal reformers dedicated to changing the system [of free enterprise] in order to preserve it tend to rise to prominence. At the Big Three [Harvard, Yale, and Princeton], the men who embodied this strand of liberal reformism were Charles W. Eliot, James Bryant Conant, and Kingman Brewster. (540)

Scholars who narrow their projects as Karabel does must justify why the thinkers they address are particularly meaningful to respond to. Karabel, for instance, offers a rationale for why Eliot, Conant, and Brewster are worth focusing on: they were prominent liberal reformers of their respective eras. Thus, studying them carries stakes for understanding liberal reformers more broadly.

Avoid Confirmation Bias

In Greek mythology, the villainous innkeeper Procrustes offers visitors a generous meal and a special bed that he claims fits anyone. Unassuming visitors quickly realize that Procrustes's hospitality comes with a catch: when they lie down on the inn's bed, Procrustes either stretches their bodies or hacks off their legs to make them fit perfectly. Today, a "Procrustean bed" refers to a situation in which we stretch or squeeze whatever evidence we encounter in order to fit our preconceived notions. Researchers who decide on a claim first and *then* hunt for evidence to match the claim risk acting like the mythological Procrustes. They are more likely to overemphasize evidence that fits their claim and downplay evidence that doesn't fit it, a pitfall researchers call "confirmation bias."

Because it prevents researchers from weighing evidence fairly, confirmation bias produces skewed claims. Such bias presents a serious problem in scholarly research. In fact, in a review of studies on the subject, psychologist Raymond S. Nickerson argues that "If one were to attempt to identify a single problematic aspect of human reasoning that deserves attention above all others, the *confirmation bias* would have to be among the candidates for consideration" (175). Nickerson's study finds that the problem is not only damaging to research communities but is also widespread among even seasoned researchers (177–89).

So that they are not tempted to skew their evidence, either by stretching it or downplaying it, seasoned scholars develop projects to guide the gathering and analyzing of evidence *before* forming a claim. Projects therefore capitalize on what Stuart Firestein calls "knowledgeable ignorance," a state in which one consciously pursues better understandings of what they and others, together, don't know (11). This intellectual habit ultimately produces claims that are more likely to be both fair and illuminating.

TURN TO YOUR RESEARCH

Part 1: Design Your Project

Use the following templates to describe the four components of your project that we explain in "Mindset." It can be helpful to return to and revise your project description over the course of your research.

1. *Purpose*: By addressing [the scholarly problem], I will produce [new information, a new interpretation, or a new proposal].
2. *Object(s)*: The objects I will analyze in order to produce this information/interpretation/proposal are [the text(s) or data].
3. *Method*: The method/strategy/tool that will allow me to achieve this purpose is [a method, strategy, or tool].
4. *Stakes*: Addressing the problem in this manner matters to [stakeholders] because [the stakes].

TURN TO YOUR RESEARCH

Part 2: Narrow Your Project

To narrow your project in the early stages of your research, try these writing exercises to apply the four strategies explained earlier:

Strategy 1: Analyze fewer objects, and narrow the stakes.
List all the possible objects you could analyze. For each, write a few sentences describing the stakes that analyzing them might carry. Why do those stakes matter? To whom? Select the smallest group of objects that you find will carry meaningful stakes on their own.

Strategy 2: Analyze fewer objects, but broaden the stakes.
Return to your list of possible objects and their stakes. Reorder the list to group together objects that carry the same stakes. Once you see objects grouped together, ask yourself, "Which of the objects within a group are most representative of the group? Can I use only one or two of these objects to represent the whole group?"

Strategy 3: Analyze fewer variables.
Once you select the objects you'll analyze, list all the possible variables—the specific aspects—you could study about them. For each variable, list the stakes that a study of them might carry. Select the fewest variables that carry the stakes you want to pursue.

Strategy 4: Respond to fewer scholars.
List all the possible scholars you could respond to. Circle the ones who have done the most to shape the conversation. Focus on those scholars, using their ideas as a lens through which to interpret your objects.

Works Cited

Firestein, Stuart. *Ignorance: How It Drives Science*. Oxford UP, 2012.

Harris, Joseph. *Rewriting: How to Do Things with Texts*. Utah State UP, 2006.

Iwasaki, Yoshitaka, and Judith Bartlett. "Stress-Coping Among Aboriginal Individuals with Diabetes in an Urban Canadian City: From Woundedness to Resilence." *Journal of Aboriginal Health*, vol. 3, no. 1, 2006, pp. 15–25.

Karabel, Jerome. *The Chosen: The Hidden History of Admission and Exclusion at Harvard, Yale, and Princeton*. Houghton Mifflin Harcourt, 2006.

Mandaville, Peter G. *Transnational Muslim Politics: Reimagining the Umma*. Routledge, 2003.

McCellan, Edward. *Mosquito.* 2006, Centers for Disease Control and Prevention
Public Health Image Library, phil.cdc.gov/Details.aspx?pid=3169.

Mercer, James K., and Edward K. Rife. *Representative Men of Ohio, 1900–1903.*
Hathi Trust, hdl.handle.net/2027/nnc1.cu54306612.

Nickerson, Raymond S. "Confirmation Bias: A Ubiquitous Phenomenon in Many
Guises." *Review of General Psychology,* vol. 2, no. 2, 1998, pp. 175–220.

Powley, Elizabeth, and Elizabeth Pearson. "Gender Is Society: Inclusive
Lawmaking in Rwanda's Parliament." *Critical Half,* vol. 5, no. 1, Winter
2007, pp. 15–19.

Sachs, Jeffrey, and Pia Malaney. "The Economic and Social Burden of
Malaria." *Nature,* vol. 415, no. 6872, Feb. 2002, pp. 680–85. *Nature,*
doi:10.1038/415680a.

South East Asian Quinine Artesunate Malaria Trial (SEAQUAMAT) group.
"Artesunate Versus Quinine for Treatment of Severe Falciparum Malaria:
A Randomised Trial." *Lancet,* vol. 366, no. 9487, Sept. 2005, pp. 717–25.
ScienceDirect, doi:10.1016/S0140-6736(05)67176-0.

Steckel, Richard H., and Donald Haurin. "Health and Nutrition in the American
Midwest: Evidence from the Height of Ohio National Guardsman,
1850–1910." *Stature, Living Standards and Economic Development,* edited by
John Komlos, U of Chicago P, 1994, pp. 117–28.

Vygotsky, L. S. *Mind in Society: The Development of Higher Psychological
Processes.* Harvard UP, 1978.

World Health Organization. *World Malaria Report 2018.* World
Health Organization, 2018, apps.who.int/iris/bitstream/hand
le/10665/275867/9789241565653-eng.pdf?ua=1.

CHAPTER 4

....

Claims

figure—imagined in the twentieth century as largely benign and action-averse—was in Wilde's day associated with anarchy, terrorism . . . even vendetta. With this insight, I wrote and published an article to help others see this connection. But as a first step, I had to find a way that a personally meaningful connection could also be a starting place for significant scholarship.

Read the research: Ellen Crowell is an English professor at Saint Louis University and the author of the book *The Dandy in Irish and American Southern Fiction: Aristocratic Drag.* You can find her Oscar Wilde article "Scarlet Carsons, Men in Masks: The Wildean Contexts of *V for Vendetta*" in *Neo-Victorian Studies.*

Mindset: Claims Contribute Original and Significant Ideas

Ellen Crowell's research was inspired by a surprising observation that the character "V" and Oscar Wilde wear nearly the same hats and capes (see Photo 4.1 and Figure 4.1). This insight, however original, was not yet a claim. It is instead an observation because it is manifestly true: "V" and Wilde *are* similarly dressed. Crowell's observation became important only when she discovered *why* this unlikely connection between the nineteenth-century writer Oscar Wilde and the twenty-first-century film *V for Vendetta* contributed to a scholarly conversation.

Crowell's contribution takes the form of a claim—an assertion about how we might better understand the objects she analyzes. Her article claims that, in his visual similarity, the firebrand anarchist character "V" challenges other scholars' long-held idea that Oscar Wilde and his writing were disconnected from politics (17). Crowell may have started with a question that would lead her to a new observation: "*What* do I notice that others might not have noticed?" But she pushed herself to ask questions that would lead her to a **claim**: "*How* does my observation help people understand these texts in a new way?" and "*Why* does this new understanding have stakes for others?"

PHOTO **4.1**
Writer Oscar Wilde photographed by Napoleon Sarony in 1882. Image courtesy of the Library of Congress.

Even once we realize that scholars value claims that advance conversation, figuring out what claims matter to readers is challenging. However, academic journals offer some insights. Consider the criteria these academic journals use to select articles:

- *Science* "publishes significant original scientific research" ("Science").

- Geological Society of America journals "encourage submissions that are innovative, provocative (or describe a significant advance in the field), timely, and of interest to a broad audience" ("GSA Bulletin").

- *American Historical Review* looks for "articles that are new in content and interpretation and that make a significant contribution to historical knowledge" ("Article Submission").

FIGURE **4.1**
Poster advertising the 2006 Warner Bros. Pictures film *V for Vendetta*. Literary scholar Ellen Crowell claims that the image's similarity to the portrait of Oscar Wilde is no coincidence.

KEY TERM

Claim

A *claim is* a contention or proposal that resolves, or makes sense of, the scholarly problem. Writers arrive at claims by carrying out their projects (see Figure 4.2). You may use terms like "thesis," "argument," "main idea," or "central point" instead of "claim." We imagine these terms as closely related to "claim."

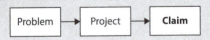

FIGURE **4.2**
Scholars arrive at a claim by carrying out a project to make sense of a problem.

Despite serving different disciplines, all three journals seek articles that are "original" and "significant." To show originality, scholars explain the newness of their ideas relative to the existing conversation. And to display significance, scholars show how their claims advance the conversation.

Originality and significance are potentially daunting standards. But notions of originality and significance are not universal; what counts as original and significant depends on one's audience. The audience for students' writing, for instance, consists of the academic community around them—fellow students and instructors. As writers progress in their educations, ideas of originality and significance will likely shift. Nevertheless, all researchers ask the same questions: "How can I contribute to my own community of scholarship? What new interpretation am I offering my readers that they would not have arrived at on their own?"

Though writers sometimes present their claims to readers early in their texts, writers rarely arrive at their claims in the early stages of their writing process. We discuss claims early in this book not to suggest that you should come up with your claims quickly but rather to emphasize how claims develop out of problems and projects.

PRACTICE

Distinguish Observations and Summary from Claims

Educational psychologist Deborah McCutchen has found that when people are asked to interpret texts that feel unfamiliar to them, they struggle with the task. Feeling overwhelmed, they merely describe or summarize the text rather than take on the more daunting task of interpretation (19–20). McCutchen's findings suggest that when writing about unfamiliar texts, writers need to be sure that their claims are actually claims and not simply observations or summary.

To distinguish between observations/summaries and claims, ask yourself, "Are reasonable alternative interpretations also possible?" If the answer is "no," you have an observation or a summary. If the answer is "yes," you have a claim.

Task: Examine the poster in Figure 4.3, created in the late 1930s or early 1940s by Albert M. Bender. Then read the following six statements

continued

FIGURE **4.3**
Albert Bender's poster "Jobs for Girls & Women" was part of a government program to promote jobs for underemployed groups.

about it. Sort the statements into three claims and three observations/ summaries according to whether reasonable alternative interpretations of them are possible.

- **a.** The poster's bold first word "JOBS" hints at the priorities woman laborers would have had in this era. The availability of jobs mattered before the quality of those jobs.
- **b.** With closed eyes and raised eyebrows, the woman smiles as she dries a dish.
- **c.** The joyful look on the woman's face, her perfect hair, and her neat uniform advance an ideal of domesticity that companies marketed to women in the 1930s.

d. The poster's creator, Albert M. Bender, repeats the word "good" five times.

e. The poster alternates light-colored text on dark backgrounds with dark-colored text on a light background.

f. The poster is a reflection of America's economic crisis in the 1930s, when the country was pulling itself out of the Depression and government agencies took the lead in job creation efforts.

Observations or summaries: Alternative interpretations are not possible.

1. _____ 2. _____ 3. _____

Claims: Alternative interpretations are possible.

1. _____ 2. _____ 3. _____

Tip: One strategy for turning observations into claims is to brainstorm responses to the question, "How does this observation change the way we understand the object(s)?"

ANSWERS: The claims are a, c, and f. The observations or summaries are b, d, and e.

Significant Claims Spark Rather than Extinguish Conversation

Less-experienced researchers might imagine that the most significant claim they could make would present the last word on a scholarly conversation. Though it might seem counterintuitive, experienced researchers do not seek to have the final word in a conversation. Instead, they measure a claim's significance by its capacity to inspire further conversation. Notice, for instance, how business historian Alfred Chandler extends the conversation about the history of American business institutions in his book *The Visible Hand*:

> Historians of the American experience have also moved to the study of institutions. Such scholars as Robert H. Wiebe, Morton Keller, Samuel Hays, and Lee Benson have taken a close look at the changing

nature of political, social, and economic organizations. They have pioneered in what one analyst of recent writing in American history has
called the "new institutionalism." Few historians, however, have tried
to trace the story of a single institution from its beginnings to its full
growth. . . .
   This study is an attempt to fill that void by concentrating on a specific time period and a specific set of concerns. (5)

Before he articulates his intervention—"this study is an attempt to fill
that void"—Chandler offers a good-faith synthesis of numerous historians' research: his predecessors "pioneered" work. Chandler does not
one-up these historians. By displaying his knowledge of the important
work that came before him, he gains the authority to say how he advances their work.

Many scholars feel that Chandler's book represents a significant
contribution to the conversation. In fact, they have cited it over 10,000
times. Does this mean that Alfred Chandler has the last word? Certainly not. Indeed, researchers have identified gaps in Chandler's work
that have motivated new responses. The economic historian Robert E.
Wright, for instance, declares his own intervention:

   Alfred Chandler and other scholars who place greater emphasis on
   the second half of the nineteenth century simply overlooked the
   process of becoming, the precise timing and path by which the US
   economy . . . evolved ever-larger and more efficient modes of production. (149)

Just as Alfred Chandler noted his predecessors' gaps in understanding,
Robert Wright notes how Chandler's focus on the late nineteenth century missed earlier developments. Wright's articulation of this gap is
not a slight to Chandler or other scholars. Indeed, the gap that Wright
proposes to fill becomes visible only because of Chandler's research.

The most important writing promises not only to fill gaps but also
to open new gaps. As Chandler himself wrote about his own work,
"I hope that these facts may also be useful to scholars with other questions and concerns other than those relevant to the generalizations presented here" (6). Chandler reminds readers that they are members of a
community that values progress pursued by many voices. And this idea
takes pressure off our own scholarship: when we make claims, we don't
need to have the last word, only the next word.

Scholars Strive to Be Interesting

If scholars resist having the last word—making the grand, final claim—do they then risk making insignificant or boring claims? While plenty of research carries life-and-death stakes, the stakes of many studies, like Ellen Crowell's study about Oscar Wilde, may not be as immediately apparent. How do researchers measure the significance of their contributions to scholarly conversations? One approach we find helpful hinges on the definition of the word "interesting."

In an essay investigating the problem of defining the "interesting," philosopher Mikhail Epstein begins by considering a tension between a common understanding and a complication: many scholars seem to value the concept of "the interesting," yet few actually define it. Epstein's project, then, is to venture his own definition. He claims that "what makes a certain theory interesting is its presentation of a consistent and plausible proof for what appears to be least probable" (78). His definition relies on two criteria: provability and probability. A claim will be interesting when compelling evidence sustains it (it is provable) and when it is surprising (it is improbable). The most interesting claims are "the least evident and predictable ones" that the writer can support (Epstein 80). We visualize Epstein's definition here:

Table 4.1 A visualization of Mikhail Epstein's definition of "the interesting" shows the relationship between the surprising and the provable in determining whether a project will carry interest for readers (78).

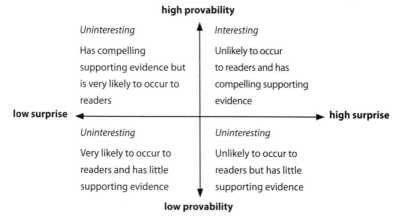

PRACTICE

Distinguish between Interesting and Uninteresting Claims

Task: Revisit Albert M. Bender's "Jobs for Girls & Women" poster. We could generate many claims about it, but not all would be interesting. Choose a quadrant in the preceding grid in which to place each of the following claims.

a. The woman exudes happiness.

b. With his poster, Bender intended to create an image that would launch a new vision of domesticity for working class white women.

c. The woman on the poster is showing that her favorite part of domestic service is dishwashing.

d. The poster's Depression-era depiction of a beaming housekeeper offers women who were struggling to find employment a vision of domestic service as honorable—and even joyful—work that would not diminish their social status.

ANSWERS: A. high probability/low surprise (upper-left quadrant). We could easily prove the claim by analyzing the woman's face, but, given that the poster is promoting housekeeping jobs, depicting a housekeeper as happy is unsurprising; B. low provability/high surprise (lower-right quadrant). The claim is surprising but difficult to prove because Bender is no longer alive to tell us what he intended; C. low provability/low surprise (lower-left quadrant). The poster offers no way to compare the woman's feeling about dishwashing to other tasks, but even if it did, the claim would not surprise us; D. high provability/high surprise (upper-right quadrant). We can prove this surprising claim by analyzing evidence available in the poster itself.

Scholars Value Provable Claims over Unprovable Opinions

Epstein's criterion of provability is helpful for understanding why scholars resist a particular kind of claim: one whose evidence rests on personal opinion or belief. In order to be highly provable, evidence must be easily testable or verifiable rather than dependent on the writer's subjective experience.

Epstein himself critiques scholars who assert that something is "interesting" without defining the term (76). In these cases, the "interesting" is an unverifiable expression of personal taste. Epstein's definition of "the interesting" responds to that shortcoming. He writes, "Our question is not what is interesting to various people, but what constitutes the category of the interesting itself" (77). Once Epstein defines the category, his readers do not have to take on faith that something is interesting merely because he says it is so. They can apply his criteria of improbability and provability to test his claim themselves.

Genre Influences What Counts as Interesting

In keeping with Epstein's project of defining "the interesting," we want to further consider his two criteria, the improbable and the provable, by asking "For whom?" After all, what counts as improbable and provable changes depending on readers' expectations. These expectations come from "genre conventions"—the recurring features of writing specific to certain fields of study. For instance, biology research typically seeks to add to some existing knowledge. Thus, the introductions to biology research start by mapping out the existing knowledge, using a funnel structure that begins with broadly related research and then narrows. The purpose of policy memos, on the other hand, is to help policymakers solve problems. So these memos typically begin by describing the problems they will address. When scholars' writing demonstrates an awareness of genre conventions, it reflects the shared values about what counts as interesting in that discipline.

RESEARCH ON WRITING

Laura Wilder on Learning New Genres

Genre studies researcher Laura Wilder's 2012 book *Rhetorical Strategies and Genre Conventions in Literary Studies* examines the powerful role of genre knowledge for undergraduate writers. This knowledge, she argues, allows students to write their way into insider status (102).

Wilder and her collaborator, Joanna Wolfe, compared two groups of students enrolled in a university's "Writing about Literature" classes: sixty-eight who received explicit instruction in the genre of literary analysis and seventy-seven who didn't. They found that the literary analyses of students who received explicit instruction received higher scores from professors, and the students themselves reported successfully transferring their genre knowledge to literary analyses in subsequent courses

continued

(Wilder 117, 137–38). On the other hand, literature students who weren't explicitly taught genre conventions struggled to transfer their learning about the genre to other literature classes. In particular, they tended to either 1) overgeneralize by imagining that the conventions of the genre were universal features of all good writing or 2) hyper-specify by interpreting genre conventions as merely the personal preferences of a particular professor (162, 168).

Takeaway: What counts as an interesting claim differs from genre to genre. To learn what kinds of claims matter for your writing project, analyze examples of the genre and seek experts' advice.

Read the research: Wilder, Laura. *Rhetorical Strategies and Genre Conventions in Literary Studies*. Southern Illinois UP, 2012.

Tools & Techniques: Moving from Observations to Claims

If you've ever worked as hard as you could on a writing project only to have a reader encourage you to "dig deeper" or "push further," we sympathize. Spending more time and effort on writing doesn't necessarily mean that more interesting ideas will magically occur to us. In this section, we'll share techniques that expert writers use not to work harder but to work more strategically to develop interesting claims.

Claims Develop out of Problems and Projects

In the two previous chapters of this book, we argue that a claim stands on the shoulders of a scholarly problem and a project. Following we offer eight approaches for developing claims. The first six grow out of the kinds of scholarly problems highlighted in Chapter 2; the next two offer alternative approaches. Each approach features templates containing language that scholars commonly use. The templates provide a starting place for generating your own language as you develop claims.

We also include examples of published scholarship that feature claims rising out of scholarly problems. In the examples, we have underlined functional signposts—phrases that signal the function of the words that follow. In these cases, the signposts show writers moving from problems and projects to claims. You can construct your own templates by tracking signposts in any scholarly work that you read.

Common Understanding and Complication

Problem: A tension between the way others have understood the text and some aspect of the text that appears to diverge from that understanding.

Project: An approach to making sense of the problem that asks readers to rethink the common understanding or sheds new light on the complication.

Claim templates:

- While most people think _____, a close examination suggests _____.
- Popular consensus has dictated that _____, but actually _____.
- Scholars have commonly argued _____, but in fact _____.

Example: In his essay "Reinventing Chemistry," George M. Whitesides offers a claim (highlighted in black) about teaching chemistry. His claim makes sense of the tension between the common understanding of the field of chemistry (highlighted in dark gray) and the more complex opportunities the field now faces (highlighted in light gray):

The common understanding	Chemistry is ending an era of extraordinary intellectual growth and commercial contribution to society . . . Although this era is over, the new opportunities that have appeared are, if anything, even greater—both in terms of intellectual challenge and in terms of potential for impact on society—
A new complication	than were those in the rich period now past. . . . These new opportunities are, however, much broader in scope and greater in complexity than the simpler, previous problems,
A claim that addresses the complication	and require new structures and methods. . . . To deal efficiently with these problems, academic chemistry will need to integrate "solving problems" and "generating understanding" better. It should teach students the skills necessary to attack problems that do not even exist as problems when the students are being taught. (3197)

Whole and Part

Problem: A tension between the whole of a text and one part of it that appears to be an outlier.

Project: An approach to making sense of the problem that produces a new understanding of the part or the whole.

Claim templates:

- Because _____ is in tension with the entire text, we must reconsider _____.
- When we consider the whole in light of the divergent part, we realize that _____.
- While _____ appears to diverge from the whole, in fact _____.

Example: Music scholar Arman Schwartz makes a claim (highlighted in black) about Giacomo Puccini's opera *Manon Lescaut* by analyzing a tension between the whole opera (highlighted in dark gray) and a single "peculiar" feature of the performance (highlighted in light gray):

A part of the opera	One of the aria's most peculiar features was, however, never
The whole opera	removed from the score: the offstage flute. Although a seemingly minor detail, it is perhaps worth lingering on this odd device. Even by the meager standards of operatic realism, an offstage flute makes little sense here. . . . American landscapes tend not to be famous for their errant pipers; but it is equally hard to imagine the flute as a "realistic"
A claim that "helps make sense" of the tension	echo of anything occurring onstage. . . . [The] image of unrelenting emptiness helps make sense of the flute's musical and symbolic function. Offstage, onstage, in the pit—the scalar fragment sounds from every location possible, saturating and extending the acoustic space. The melody, like the desert, is undulating, inexpressive, infinite. (55)

Part and Part

Problem: A tension between one part of a text and another part.

Project: An approach to making sense of the problem that generates a new understanding of the parts or their relationship to the whole object.

Claim templates:

- These two contradictory parts makes us realize something new about the whole object, that _____.
- While this part _____, this other part _____, which changes our understanding of _____.
- Although it appears that _____ conflicts with _____, in fact _____.

Example: In their study on selfishness and empathy, the economists James Andreoni and Justin Rao open their paper by articulating two contradictory parts of the scholarly conversation (highlighted in light and dark gray) about selfless giving—altruism—that their claim (highlighted in black) will endeavor to make sense of:

One finding	A common finding is that most subjects [in laboratory experiments] exhibit significant altruism and inequity aversion (Fehr and Schmidt, 1999; Bolton and Ockenfels, 2000; Andreoni and Miller,
A contradictory finding	2002). . . . However, in the United States and other industrialized countries there is vast inequality in consumption, while charitable giving is only 1–2% of income (Andreoni, 2006). How can we reconcile a taste for equality with behavior that indicates people
Claim that resolves the contradiction	generally tolerate a great deal of inequality in their daily lives? In this paper we argue that while humans do have a strong capacity to behave altruistically, selfishness typically predominates. (513)

Form and Function

Problem: A tension between the structure or appearance of the text (its form) and what the text actually accomplishes (its function).

Project: An approach to making sense of the problem that generates a new interpretation of the object's form or its function.

Claim templates:

- Though the text is designed to _____, when we encounter _____, it forces us to realize that _____.
- The formal aspect of the object suggests _____, but its use suggests _____. We must therefore revise our understanding of the object from _____ to _____.
- While the text seems to assert that _____, the formal choice to _____ complicates the way we understand that assertion.

Example: The classics scholar John T. Davis develops a claim (highlighted in black) about a poem by the Latin poet Propertius by analyzing how its form (highlighted in light gray) as an epitaph, a text honoring a dead person, doesn't match its function (highlighted in dark gray):

The text's form	Even though the form of the poem is that of an
The text's function	epitaph, the differences between it and an ordinary epitaph are striking. First, the speaker is neither dead nor buried; for this reason the poem could not be an inscription. Second, the viator [traveler] is a particular
A claim resolving the disjuncture between form and function	man, not just any passerby.... The whole poem is in fact an epitaph only in form. The poet has written the poem in such a way that we, as the audience, hear Gallus dictate his epitaph to a third party, the [traveler] miles saucius. The presentation is dramatic, not epigraphical. (210)

Presence and Absence

Problem: A tension between something you expect to be present and its actual absence.

Project: An approach to making sense of the problem that generates a fresh reading of the text or announces how filling the gap might advance the conversation.

Claim templates:

- Given the presence of _____, the surprising absence of _____ suggests that we must rethink _____.

- Because the text is missing _____, readers must realize that _____.
- Though _____ appears to be missing, in fact we see _____.

Example: Psychologists Jason L. Skues, Ben Williams, and Lisa Wise formulate a claim (highlighted in black) that makes sense of a tension between the presence of *Facebook* friends (highlighted in light gray) and the absence of offline friends (highlighted in dark gray):

The presence of online friends	Given that students who felt lonely reported having more friends [on *Facebook*], it may be that these same individuals are attempting to access and interact with others online to compensate for their lack of offline relationships. . . . It could be that having more friends on *Facebook* also allows individuals to have access, indirectly, to the friends of their friends via status updates, comments and photos, making them feel more connected to others and reducing their sense of isolation. (2417–18)
The surprising absence of offline relationships	
A claim that resolves the tension between presence and absence	

Expectation and Observation

Problem: A tension between what we expect to encounter and what we actually observe.

Project: An approach to making sense of the problem that produces a new interpretation of the object or leads us to question our expectations.

Claim templates:
- Though we expected _____, we observed _____; we can make sense of this discrepancy by _____.
- Where we might expect to see _____, we instead get _____, which leads us to rethink _____.
- By subverting our expectations, the object asks us to question the following assumptions: _____.

Example: Near Eastern studies scholars Ariel and Chana Bloch claim (highlighted in black) that we arrive at a new understanding of divinity in the *Song of Songs*, a book in the Bible, when we make sense of the tension between readers' expectation (highlighted in light gray) that the book would mention God and the observation (highlighted in dark gray) that it actually names two animals instead:

Expectation	In an oath, precisely where we might expect to find the name of
Observation	God, we find instead the names of two animals that are associ-
A claim making	ated with the lovers. This oath makes plain the secular boundar-
sense of expectation	ies of the lovers' world. Divinity lives within them and their
and observation	landscape; the earth is all of paradise they need to know. (9–10)

These templates are designed to help you forward your thinking when proposing a new interpretation of an object. They largely rely on the writer's ability to analyze objects. We want to offer two additional kinds of sophisticated claims that instead rely on the writer's ability to analyze the scholarly conversation: 1) proposing a new scholarly problem, or 2) proposing a new project. Let's look at examples of both.

Claiming a New Scholarly Problem

This type of claim establishes the common way other scholars have formulated a scholarly problem and then argues that, in fact, formulating the problem differently will raise new stakes.

Problem: A gap between the way others formulate the problem and the real problem.

Project: An approach to making sense of the gap that produces a more accurate or useful problem.

Claim templates:

- While others have focused on the issue of _____, a more productive way to define the scholarly problem might be

    _____.
- Framing the problem as a matter of _____, neglects to address _____. Reframing the problem instead as _____ allows us to understand _____.

Example: In his article "'Who Is an Entrepreneur?' Is the Wrong Question," business researcher William B. Gartner contends that the problem that scholars have traditionally addressed (highlighted in light gray) is insufficient to explain what makes someone an entrepreneur (highlighted in dark gray). He claims (highlighted in black) that instead of examining entrepreneurs' personality traits, scholars should instead examine entrepreneurs' actions:

The old problem	Entrepreneurship research has long asked, "Who is an entre-
The limits of the old problem	preneur?" I believe the attempt to answer the question "Who is an entrepreneur?," which focusses on the traits and personality characteristics of entrepreneurs, will neither lead us to a definition of the entrepreneur nor help us to understand the phenomenon of entrepreneurship. The personality characteristics of the entrepreneur are ancillary to the entrepreneur's
A claim proposing a better problem	behaviors. Research on the entrepreneur should focus on what the entrepreneur does and not who the entrepreneur is. (12, 21)

Claiming a New Project

This type of claim establishes how other scholars have approached the problem and then proposes a new approach to making sense of the problem that will produce more meaningful results. A claim proposing a better project might argue for a new theoretical approach, evidence-gathering strategy, or data analysis technique.

Problem: The common approaches for making sense of the problem don't produce the most accurate, meaningful findings.

Project: An approach to making sense of the problem that produces more accurate, meaningful findings.

Claim templates:

- A new research method that entails _____ will account for what the commonly used method cannot account for, namely _____.

- While previous studies have taken the approach of _____, that approach cannot offer insight into _____. Instead, this study takes a different approach: _____.

Example: Chemical engineers Roger Guimera and Luis A. Nunes Amaral propose a new project (passage highlighted in black)—specifically a new data analysis technique—to resolve the tension between the massive amount of data biologists now collect using "high-throughput techniques" (passage highlighted in light gray) and traditional data analysis methods that were not designed to handle such large quantities of data (passage highlighted in dark gray):

A new situation has arisen	High-throughput techniques are leading to an explosive growth in the size of biological databases and creating the opportunity to revolutionize our un-
The old project can't address the new situation	derstanding of life and disease. Interpretation of these data remains, however, a major scientific challenge.
Claim that a new project will address the problem	Here, we propose a methodology that enables us to extract and display information contained in complex networks. Specifically, we demonstrate that we can find functional modules in complex networks, and classify nodes into universal roles according to their pattern of intra- and inter-module connections. (895–96)

Two Pitfalls

Now that you have a sense of the range of claims you might experiment with, we also want to point to two common pitfalls that humanities researchers encounter when crafting claims. These pitfalls—fault-finding and insufficient complexity—can mark someone as not fully belonging to scholarly communities. We'll return to Mikhail Epstein's notion of the interesting to understand why experts consider these pitfalls.

Pitfall #1: Fault-Finding Claims

One common misstep is to formulate a claim that strictly finds fault. Less-experienced writers might be tempted to say, "I notice a contradiction in Milton Friedman's claim; therefore his argument falls apart." Or, "Because Karl Marx's prediction of a workers' revolution didn't come true, the *Communist Manifesto* fails." By finding fault, the writer declares intellectual victory, a tempting claim for a writer who wants to be seen as an expert. This approach, however, can make readers lose interest.

In Epstein's terms, a dismissive claim offers high provability but low surprise. After all, the easiest response to a problem is to characterize it as a failing—in other words, to refuse to make sense of it. If a scholar can instead make sense of a difficult contradiction, they can offer something highly improbable and thus highly interesting.

A passage from Marjorie Garber's book *Shakespeare After All* illustrates how a scholar can generate interest by adopting an *analytical* project rather than a strictly evaluative one. When Garber finds a dissonance between the play *Julius Caesar* and its context—its setting in ancient Rome—she does not dismiss the play; rather she makes sense of the problem:

> Some early editors faulted Shakespeare for the historical "error" in act 2, scene 1, where a clock strikes. Since there were no striking clocks in ancient Rome, this detail was deemed an anachronism, and so it is, but that does not make it a mistake. The presence of a modern clock in Caesar's Rome abruptly reminds the audience of the double time period in which the play is set. Not only a history of the classical past, it is also a story of the present day. The supposed anachronism of the striking clock abruptly jars the audience from any complacency it may be feeling about the difference between "then" and "now." (411)

When Garber analyzes the anachronism, rather than finding fault with it, her project opens up new interpretive possibilities in *Julius Caesar*: we can now see the play commenting not only on ancient Rome but also on the England of Shakespeare's day.

Pitfall #2: Insufficiently Complex Claims

A second pitfall that less-experienced writers may encounter is generating insufficiently complex claims. When faced with a complex text to analyze, writers may imagine that they serve a reader by boiling it down to simpler terms. Yet genre studies researchers find that complexity is a strongly held value, particularly among humanities scholars (Fahnestock and Secor 90).

Epstein's idea of the interesting helps us understand why complexity is so valued. Our first responses to a scholarly problem are usually less surprising: they tend to be simpler and thus more likely to occur to others. When we move past our first responses, we often arrive at thoughts that are new to others and therefore produce greater surprise—all the more so when we string together several linked subclaims, a hallmark of complex thinking. Here, for example, political science scholar Frank Guliuzza strings together "two related arguments" to advance a claim about secular opposition to religious expression in the political sphere:

First subclaim	First, even though religious people are becoming increasingly involved in politics, there is still plenty of bigotry against religious
Second subclaim	faith (particularly among intellectuals). . . . Second, there are several factors that motivate the quest for secularization by academic and cultural elites. Some genuinely believe, akin to religious faith, that society is poisoned by antiquated religious expression. (51)

Notice that the first subclaim addresses prejudice on the part of secularists. The second subclaim, then, will provide several factors that motivate this prejudice. Guliuzza's interconnected claims link an effect to a cause, producing greater complexity and thus greater interest.

Research in composition studies suggests that undergraduate student writers are more likely to pursue their first, most probable thoughts, while seasoned professional writers continue to revise their thinking as they write, grappling with dissonances until they arrive at greater complexity (Faigley and Witte 406; Sommers 380–85; Hayes et al. 176–78). The chapters that follow—on managing research, selecting sources, and reading and note-taking—demonstrate the strategies that seasoned scholars use to cultivate complex thinking even in the earliest stages of their research. These strategies represent anything but passive information gathering; they invite creative thinking.

TURN TO YOUR RESEARCH

Craft an Interesting Claim

Use the chart in Table 4.2 to test how interesting your claim is. For instance, if your claim has a lot of evidence to back it up but seems rather unsurprising, you would place it in the upper left-hand corner. If your claim is highly surprising but lacks evidence, you would place it in the lower right-hand corner.

Table 4.2 A visualization of Mikhail Epstein's definition of the interesting. Which quadrant does your claim belong in?

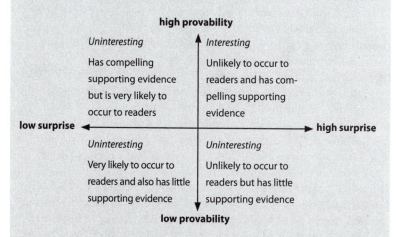

If your claim is not in the upper right corner (and thus it is not "interesting" in Mikhail Epstein's terms), try responding to the following prompts:

1. How can you make sense of the scholarly problem in a way that is more surprising? How would most people respond to the tension you are grappling with? How can you respond differently?

2. As you pursue your project, keep a list of possible claims that make sense of your scholarly problem. Put a check mark next to the ones that you could support using evidence. Of these, which seem most surprising?

Works Cited

Andreoni, James, and Justin M. Rao. "The Power of Asking: How Communication Affects Selfishness, Empathy, and Altruism." *Journal of Public Economics,* vol. 95, no. 7, Aug. 2011, pp. 513–20. *ScienceDirect,* doi:10.1016/j.jpubeco.2010.12.008.

"Article Submission." *American Historical Review,* 2014, www.historians. org/publications-and-directories/american-historical-review/article-submission.

Bender, Albert M. *Jobs for Girls & Women.* circa 1936–1941, *Library of Congress, Work Projects Administration Poster Collection,* www.loc.gov/resource/cph.3b53089/.

Bloch, Ariel, and Chana Bloch. *The Song of Songs: A New Translation with an Introduction and Commentary.* U of California P, 1995.

Chandler, Alfred D. Jr. *The Visible Hand: The Managerial Revolution in American Business.* Belknap Press of Harvard UP, 1977.

Crowell, Ellen. "Scarlet Carsons, Men in Masks: The Wildean Contexts of *V for Vendetta.*" *Neo-Victorian Studies,* vol. 2, no. 1, 2008/2009, pp. 17–45.

Davis, John T. "Propertius 1.21–22." *Classical Journal,* vol. 66, no. 3, 1971, pp. 209–13. *JSTOR,* www.jstor.org/stable/3296468.

Epstein, Mikhail. "The Interesting," *Qui Parle,* translated by Igor Klyukanov, *Critical Humanities and Social Sciences,* vol. 18, no. 1, 2009, pp. 75–88. *Project MUSE,* doi:10.1353/qui.0.0001.

Fahnestock, Jeanne, and Marie Secor. "The Rhetoric of Literary Criticism." *Textual Dynamics of the Professions: Historical and Contemporary Studies of Writing in Professional Communities,* edited by Charles Bazerman and James G. Paradis, U of Wisconsin P, 1991, pp. 76–96. *WAC Clearinghouse,* wac.colostate.edu/books/textual_dynamics/.

Faigley, Lester, and Stephen Witte. "Analyzing Revision." *College Composition and Communication,* vol. 32, no. 4, Dec. 1981, pp. 400–14. *JSTOR,* doi:10.2307/356602.

Garber, Marjorie. *Shakespeare After All.* Knopf Doubleday, 2008.

Gartner, William B. "'Who Is an Entrepreneur?' Is the Wrong Question." *American Journal of Small Business,* vol. 12, no. 4, Mar. 1988, p. 11–32. *SAGE Journals,* doi:10.1177/104225878801200401.

"GSA Bulletin." *Geological Society of America,* www.geosociety.org/GSA/Publications/Info_Services/Author_Info/gsa/pubs/bulletin/home.aspx#overview. Accessed 5 Sept. 2018.

Guimerà, Roger, and Luís A. Nunes Amaral. "Functional Cartography of Complex Metabolic Networks." *Nature,* vol. 433, no. 7028, Feb. 2005, pp. 895–900. *Nature Journals Online,* doi:10.1038/nature03288.

Guliuzza, Frank, III. *Over the Wall: Protecting Religious Expression in the Public Square.* State U of New York P, 2000.

Hayes, John R., et al. "Cognitive Processes in Revision." *Advances in Applied Psycholinguistics,* edited by Sheldon Rosenberg, vol. 2, Cambridge UP, 1987, pp. 176–240.

Marenco, Ricardo, and Concept Arts. *V for Vendetta.* 2005.

McCutchen, Deborah. "Knowledge, Processing, and Working Memory: Implications for a Theory of Writing." *Educational Psychologist,* vol. 35, no. 1, 2000, pp. 13–23. *Google Scholar,* doi:10.1207/S15326985EP3501_3.

Sarony, Napoleon. *Oscar Wilde/Sarony.* 1882, *Library of Congress, Prints and Photographs Division,* www.loc.gov/item/98519733/.

Schwartz, Arman. "Manon in the Desert, Wagner on the Beach." *Opera Quarterly,* vol. 24, no. 1–2, 2008, pp. 51–61. *Project Muse,* doi:10.1093/oq/kbp004.

"Science: Information for Authors." *Science|AAAS,* 31 Jan. 2018, www.sciencemag.org/authors/science-information-authors.

Skues, Jason L., et al. "The Effects of Personality Traits, Self-Esteem, Loneliness, and Narcissism on *Facebook* Use Among University Students." *Computers in Human Behavior,* vol. 28, no. 6, Nov. 2012, pp. 2414–19. *ScienceDirect,* doi:10.1016/j.chb.2012.07.012.

Sommers, Nancy. "Revision Strategies of Student Writers and Experienced Adult Writers." *College Composition and Communication,* vol. 31, no. 4, Dec. 1980, pp. 378–88. *JSTOR,* doi:10.2307/356588.

Whitesides, George M. "Reinventing Chemistry." *Angewandte Chemie International Edition,* vol. 54, no. 11, Mar. 2015, pp. 3196–209. *Wiley Online Library,* doi:10.1002/anie.201410884.

Wilder, Laura. *Rhetorical Strategies and Genre Conventions in Literary Studies: Teaching and Writing in the Disciplines.* Southern Illinois UP, 2012.

Wright, Robert E. "Capitalism and the Rise of the Corporate Nation." *Capitalism Takes Command: The Social Transformation of Nineteenth-Century America,* edited by Michael Zakim and Gary J. Kornblith, U of Chicago P, 2012, pp. 145–68.

CHAPTER 5

Managing Sources

I work inductively, those tend to come first), and my overarching argument. I also ask how my ideas relate to previous and current scholarship. How is what I am saying new? Does it modify or challenge any broadly held ideas? Each idea and question also gets its own index card. If they ever stop making index cards, I may need to stop writing.

Then I sort the cards into categories that roughly correspond to sections of an essay or even to paragraphs. I put like points with like points, and stacks accumulate. Each stack of cards represents a claim plus the evidence for it. I then experiment with different ways of arranging the stacks in sequence; that sequence produces the outline for an essay or book chapter. At this point, I usually discard entire stacks as irrelevant. Once the sequence is established, before I start writing, I pick up a stack and arrange the cards within it, which gives me a sense of how to order ideas and quotes within a paragraph.

I like this method (which I learned from a high school history teacher) because it is tactile, flexible, and separates the act of collecting and ordering evidence from the act of writing. Putting thoughts into words is not easy, and I like being able to concentrate on that without simultaneously trying to order my ideas or search for the perfect quote.

Read the research: Sharon Marcus is a professor in the Columbia University Department of English and Comparative Literature. Her recent books include *The Drama of Celebrity* and *Between Women: Friendship, Desire, and Marriage in Victorian England*. This Scholar's Story is excerpted from an interview by Simon Porzak.

Mindset: Research Systems Are Inventional

We hope that Sharon Marcus's description of her research process proves comforting to newer researchers: the best scholars don't start out as experts on their projects. Instead, they begin as learners and research their way into expertise. Marcus, a literary studies scholar, is known for producing expansive scholarship studying the construction of celebrity, women's friendships in the Victorian era, and the private and public lives of nineteenth-century Parisians and Londoners. Yet when she begins a new project, she doesn't start with a claim. She proceeds inductively, letting her project rise out of what she discovers.

Approaches like Marcus's may seem risky. If one isn't researching in order to find evidence to prove a particular claim from the beginning, will the research be so open-ended that it will never find a focus? This chapter highlights research management systems that scholars use to avoid endless, aimless searching and instead research their way into expertise.

While we'll focus on techniques that might at first seem bland— managing files, citing sources, and so on—we want to emphasize how profoundly a principled approach influences what researchers accomplish. Marcus uses an old-school approach to managing her sources— one that she learned in high school. Yet Marcus's handwritten technique is guided by the same principles as the more technology-driven approaches that you might use. We'll focus on three principles that we see Sharon Marcus and other scholars use to design their research systems: these systems are 1) inventional, 2) efficient, and 3) ethical.

Inventional Research Systems

If scholars often start projects not knowing what they'll claim, they must rely on research strategies that generate new thinking. In other words, they rely upon inventional strategies. When we say that research management is "inventional," we draw from the ancient Roman orator Cicero's term *inventio*, meaning the generation of possible arguments (Cicero 19).

Notice two inventional strategies Sharon Marcus builds into her note-taking system. First, on index cards, Marcus records not only key passages from sources but also her responses to them while they are freshest in her mind. Second, Marcus groups index cards and reshuffles them to experiment with new relationships among ideas.

MYTH VS. REALITY

Myth: Researchers document sources at the final stage of their projects.

Reality: Actually, researchers document sources from the moment they begin working with them.

They document scholarly voices in these early stages for three reasons: 1) to assemble a conversation, 2) to save time while drafting, and 3) to prevent accidental plagiarism.

PHOTO **5.1**
On her desk, Sharon Marcus has sorted her file cards into chunks of related ideas

Research systems like Marcus's capitalize on a habit of mind that cognitive scientists call "chunking." Chunking is characteristically employed by experts engaging in complex activities like chess and writing; it involves organizing many individual facts or ideas by categorizing them into a smaller number of recognizable groups, patterns, or relationships (de Groot 321; Chase and Simon 56; Gobet 185–92). As Sharon Marcus says, "I put like points with like points" (see Photo 5.1).

Chunking makes big research projects manageable. For instance, in her book *Between Women: Friendship, Desire, and Marriage in Victorian England*, Marcus cites 676 sources (317–46). This tidal wave of sources could overwhelm even the most seasoned researcher. Marcus eases the challenge by looking for relationships among the quotes and ideas she records on index cards and grouping related cards together. Then she can begin to experiment with the arrangement of cards within the chunks, a much simpler task than deciding how to arrange each quote or idea in relationship to every single card. The chunks that emerge allow her to focus on *inventio*—to generate new thinking.

In sum, inventional research systems allow researchers to . . .

1. Not only record but interpret sources.
2. Insert their own ideas in response.
3. Chunk ideas and formulate relationships among chunks.

Efficient Research Systems

At first glance, it seems like Sharon Marcus is not overly concerned with efficiency: she writes notes longhand; she takes walks to mull over ideas; she shuffles and reshuffles stacks of index cards. However, another look reveals a systematic approach to managing sources that streamlines her actual writing process. Marcus collects bibliographic information in a numbered works cited page when a source is first in hand, and she cites each passage in her notes as she goes. Using this system, she will never have to interrupt her writing to hunt down a citation.

Notice, too, that Marcus builds interpretive work into her organizational strategy. Her system of taking notes on paper or in individual computer files not only allows her to consider individual passages from the source in relationship to the whole text, but it also invites her to respond to sources. She says, "I push myself to identify my key questions, my subtopics (since I work inductively, those tend to come first), and my overarching argument." This early interpretive work means that Marcus responds to texts when they are freshest in her memory. Then as she drafts, she will not have to revisit texts to reconstruct why she originally thought the passage was meaningful. Experienced researchers anticipate their needs as writers and manage their research in ways that prevent them from rehashing work they've already done.

In sum, efficient research systems allow researchers to . . .

1. Collect bibliographic information about a source upon the first encounter.
2. Save bibliographic information in one central place.
3. Connect passages to their contexts and locations.

Ethical Research Systems

We often hear about the dire consequences that students and professional scholars face when they fail to cite their sources. We don't want to diminish the seriousness of source misuse. Indeed, we devote Chapter 13 of this book to proper citation practices and a thorough discussion about avoiding plagiarism. However, here we are most interested in examining *why* scholars value ethical source use: academic integrity is a hallmark of the desire to forward a scholarly conversation.

Citing sources is the most visible way that scholars map out the voices that constitute the conversation. Thus, tracking sources isn't an afterthought in the research process. It's a commitment from beginning to end. What does this value look like in practice? For Sharon Marcus, it means labeling quotations and paraphrases with their sources, taking all the notes for a source in one document to avoid taking a passage out of context, and distinguishing her own ideas from the source's ideas.

Because Sharon Marcus is a literary scholar, her primary ethical commitment is to represent print texts accurately. Those doing studies involving people or other animals—this includes everything from surveys to surgical procedures—have an additional ethical commitment. They must design their research to protect the well-being of the participants. In 1974, the United States passed the National Research Act in response to a damaging forty-year project known as the Tuskegee Syphillis Study (Centers for Disease Control and Prevention, "Research Implications"). Beginning in 1932, researchers secretly withheld treatment from a group of African American men afflicted with syphillis in Tuskegee, Alabama, in order to study the ravages of the disease (Centers for Disease Control and Prevention, "Tuskegee Timeline"). The National Research Act called for the creation of institutional research boards (IRBs) to prevent abuses like these. Those conducting human or other animal subjects research within American universities or research organizations must secure the approval of their institution's IRB to ensure that their study treats its subjects ethically.

In sum, an ethical research system allows scholars to . . .

1. Connect an idea to its source.
2. Engage with passages in their contexts.
3. Distinguish between quotation and paraphrase.
4. Distinguish between the source's ideas and the researcher's ideas.
5. Map out a scholarly conversation.
6. Protect the well-being of humans and other animals.

Tools & Techniques: Making Your Research Systematic

In this section, we'll share examples of the research management techniques we used for this book to illustrate four organizing strategies of inventional, efficient, and ethical research systems:

1. Collect sources' bibliographic information in one place
2. Create a note-taking system

3. Connect words and ideas to their sources
4. Chunk sources

These strategies appear before the chapters on locating sources and note-taking to reflect the fact that scholars typically establish organizational systems before they begin researching.

Collect Sources' Bibliographic Information in One Place

Efficient researchers designate a single site to store all their sources' bibliographic information. Sharon Marcus enters her sources' information into a numbered document. For this book, we collected ours using reference management software called Zotero (see Figure 5.1). However, we want to stress again that we are not advocating a specific program or technique but rather articulating principles to help you make choices about how to manage your research. Many reference management programs abide by the principles we suggest. To explore options for reference management programs, search the web or an app store for "reference manager."

Most reference managers store sources' bibliographic information at the click of a button. Researchers can then sort the sources to explore various ways of orchestrating a conversation. We knew we wanted to include diverse fields of study in this book, so we sorted sources by discipline in order to assess whether we should extend our searches. In

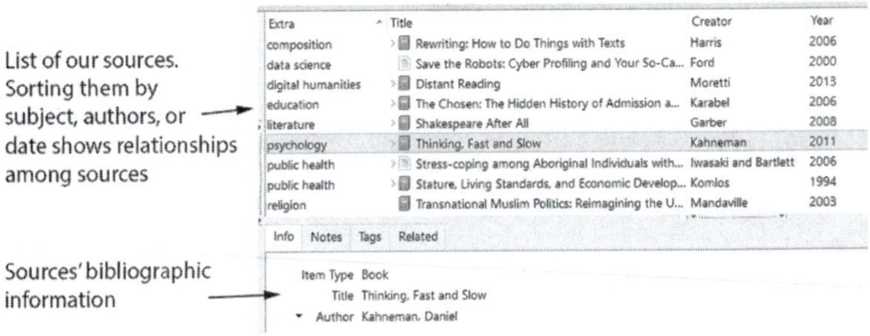

FIGURE **5.1**
We collected the bibliographic information for all of our sources in one place, a citation manager program. The figure shows how our research manager displays our sources from Chapter 3.

Chapter 13, we'll show how researchers can use reference managers to compose citations and bibliographies. As you'll see, no reference manager is perfect, so researchers double-check the accuracy of computer-generated citations.

Create a Note-Taking System

Most researchers have refined a note-taking system that works for them. The system we used for this book allowed us to understand whole texts, identify key passages, and respond to both whole texts and passages. To accomplish these goals, we created a notes document for each source.

For each notes document, we used a template that contains five sections.

1. *Source info*: Here we write the source's bibliographic information.
2. *Context*: In this section, we situate the work in its time, place, and circumstances.
3. *Project*: Here we capture the source's purpose, objects of analysis, methods, and stakes.
4. *Notes*: Under this heading, we paraphrase or quote specific passages and note the pages on which they appear, and we also add our own responses to the text.
5. *Significance*: Here we explain the role this piece might play in our project.

In Chapter 7 you'll find advice for using this note-taking system in your research.

TIME SAVER

Take Notes Right Away

We suggest you write up your notes during your first encounter with a source. This is the moment when the piece will be freshest in your memory. If you delay this step until the drafting phase—or worse, try to hold the text in your memory rather than take any notes—you'll have to waste time refamiliarizing yourself with the source later.

Connect Words and Ideas to Their Sources

Because research gains its significance by contributing to a conversation among scholars, we use research management strategies that highlight who is speaking and in what context. For instance, in our notes on Mikhail Epstein's "The Interesting," an essay featured in Chapter 4, we documented four ways we work with the text: quotation, paraphrase, summary, and our responses. We eliminate the risk of accidentally plagiarizing by distinguishing between the types of notes that we need to cite—quotation, paraphrase, and summary—and the type we don't need to cite—our own responses to the text (see Table 5.1). Chapter 11 explains the differences between quotation, paraphrase, and summary and offers strategies for using each.

TABLE **5.1**

	Page	Note
We cite page numbers for each quote, paraphrase, and summary.	76	"There is a clear discrepancy between the growing popularity of the interesting as an evaluative term and the lack of its theoretical exploration." [This is Epstein's scholarly problem.]
We place Epstein's words, even just one or two words, in quotation marks.	76–77	Asserts that "practically all" academic fields use the term to justify their research. [Broadens the stakes of his definition of the interesting: it can contribute to a lot of fields.]
We omit quotation marks for paraphrases.	78	Historicizes the rise of the term, beginning with Kuhn's *Structure of Scientific Revolutions*.
We place our responses to Epstein in square brackets.	78–79	His definition: "the interest of a theory is inversely proportional to the probability of its thesis and directly proportional to the provability of its argument." [Can we convey this in an equation or a visualization?]

Chunk Sources

As we discussed, cognitive psychologists use the term "chunking" to describe the way that experts group pieces of information into fewer, more manageable units. When researchers chunk sources, they form relationships that help them envision conversations they might orchestrate. For instance, we worked with about twenty-eight sources for Chapter 7 on reading and note-taking. But keeping all those sources in mind as we drafted would have been overwhelming. So we took notes on each and then sorted the notes into ten separate chunks. Figure 5.2 shows one of those chunks that groups together notes about how research generates new thinking.

To create our chunks, we used an app called *Ginko*, which allows users to group together notes under headings and order them. To explore what digital chunking tools might work best for you, we recommend searching "note manager" or "note organizer" in your app store or on the web. You might also consider using a project management program to organize your research notes.

Now that we've considered a principled approach to managing sources, the next question is, "How do we select these sources?" In the next chapter, we'll consider strategies for populating your research with voices you want to include in a scholarly conversation.

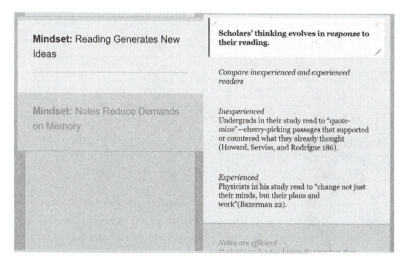

FIGURE **5.2**
This example from our notes shows how we chunked notes from two sources.

TURN TO YOUR RESEARCH

Plan Your Source Management

Sharon Marcus's notecard approach that opens this chapter appears to be quite different than our own approach that used electronic files and resource management software. Both approaches, though, rest on similar principles.

continued

Here we offer space for you to decide how you will address each principle in your research. Perhaps you will use research management software, make your own note-taking system, use the templates we provide, and so on. If you have difficulty completing any of these prompts, we recommend you speak with a research librarian at your institution.

1. In order to collect all my sources' bibliographic information in one place, I will _____.
2. The note-taking system I will use to help me understand whole texts, identify key passages, and respond to whole texts and passages will consist of _____.
3. In order to connect words and ideas to their sources and ensure that I distinguish the source's ideas from my own responses, I will _____.
4. To chunk sources into categories that will help me envision the relationships between my sources, I will _____.

Works Cited

Centers for Disease Control and Prevention. "Research Implications." *U.S. Public Health Service Syphilis Study at Tuskegee*, 22 Feb. 2017, www.cdc.gov/tuskegee/after.htm.

---. "The Tuskegee Timeline." *U.S. Public Health Service Syphilis Study at Tuskegee*, 30 Aug. 2017, www.cdc.gov/tuskegee/timeline.htm.

Chase, William G., and Herbert A. Simon. "Perception in Chess." *Cognitive Psychology*, vol. 4, no. 1, Jan. 1973, pp. 55–81. *ScienceDirect*, doi:10.1016/0010-0285(73)90004-2.

Cicero, Marcus Tullius. *De Inventione. De Optimo Genere Oratorum. Topica.* Translated by H. M. Hubbell, Harvard UP, 2014.

Corporation for Digital Scholarship. *Zotero.* 5.0.66, 2018, www.zotero.org.

deGroot, Adriaan D. *Thought and Choice in Chess.* Amsterdam UP, 2008, www.narcis.nl, dare.uva.nl/aup/en/record/301853.

Epstein, Mikhail. "The Interesting." *Qui Parle,* translated by Igor Klyukanov, *Critical Humanities and Social Sciences,* vol. 18, no. 1, 2009, pp. 75–88. *Project MUSE,* doi:10.1353/qui.0.0001.

Gobet, Fernand. "Chunking Models of Expertise: Implications for Education." *Applied Cognitive Psychology*, vol. 19, no. 2, 2005, pp. 183–204. *Google Scholar*, doi:10.1002/acp.1110.

Kulikov, Aleksey. *Ginko App*. Ginko, Inc, gingkoapp.com/.

Marcus, Sharon. *Between Women: Friendship, Desire, and Marriage in Victorian England*. Princeton UP, 2007.

---. *The Drama of Celebrity*. Princeton UP, 2019.

....

CHAPTER 6

Selecting Sources

SCHOLAR'S STORY

Research Librarian Anice Mills on Supporting Researchers

A graduate student working on his dissertation came to see me, asking about our library's databases of historical newspapers. He was trying to find an obscure publication from early twentieth-century New York. After asking why this publication was important to his project, I realized that he wanted to learn more about a particular socialist author. I realized, too, why he was having trouble finding the article he was looking for: our library holds a collection of historical American newspapers in uncatalogued microfilm, and many early newspapers frequently changed names. We were both thrilled when we found the paper he needed—*The Sun*, from the 1920s—along with other editions of now defunct newspapers published in New York City at that time. These new sources—ones he wasn't searching for originally—proved to be quite helpful for his project, opening up new possibilities in his research.

Researchers like this graduate student often seek out a research librarian with a specific question. I ask them to tell me about their project—where they've already searched, what avenues they haven't yet explored, and what roadblocks they've encountered. I often learn more about the project than the original specific request would indicate. Our conversation usually leads to a deeper conversation about the research process and a more complex answer to the original question.

Though I can satisfy the simple question—"Do you have a database of historical newspapers?"— more enriching and satisfying answers come after a more thorough discussion. Together, we develop new search strategies and find new pathways for research. The researcher leaves not just with answers to specific questions but with strategies for discovering and using meaningful sources on their own.

About the scholar: Anice Mills, now retired, was the Columbia University undergraduate services librarian. Throughout her career, she provided research help to faculty, students, and scholars.

Mindset: Source Selection Shapes the Conversation

Throughout this book, we've used the metaphor of a conversation to indicate the ways that scholars think of their research as speaking with other scholars. Writers who are entering a particular scholarly conversation for the first time often confront one of these three challenges:

1. How do you say something original and significant about a subject that scholars have written about for years? Is it possible to say anything new about *Hamlet?* Water molecules? The Koran?

2. When the problem you're examining has received little attention, how do you find a conversation to enter into? What if no one else has written about a recent event? A new technology? A rare illness?

3. How do you move from writing a report to making a claim? How do you transition from merely explaining what others have said to making your own contributions to the conversation?

To answer these questions, researchers must reject the idea that the exact scholarly conversation they'd like to join is already out in the world, just waiting for them to show up. Instead, researchers generate the conversation they want to join by selecting the participants. As if hosting a party, the writer makes a guest list by looking for people who will spark the most interesting conversation. In this chapter, we examine how scholars locate and choose sources—their guest list—that make for interesting conversations.

This approach—selecting sources based on their potential contributions to a conversation—requires that scholars look beyond the first few sources that appear in their searches of library databases (library databases are electronic catalogs of books, articles, and other media). Why? Databases typically prioritize sources that use keywords frequently; however, they have a harder time measuring a source's influence or its ability to add fresh thinking to a conversation.

To meet the challenges of generating a scholarly conversation, researchers often begin with a *literal* conversation. They speak, for instance, with librarians like Anice Mills who can help guide them to sources they might not have found on their own. Put another way, to be introduced to the scholars who are *not* in the room—the scholars whose publications have shaped the conversation—researchers often begin with the experts who *are* in the room, the librarians and scholars around them.

Sources Serve Specific Functions

To envision source selection as a creative act, we'll go beyond a common question: "Are your sources credible?" This question prioritizes sources that are vetted, or assessed, by experts who ensure that the data are reliable, the methods are valid, and the claims are original and significant. The credibility question is an important one, but it is part of a bigger—and we think richer—question that scholars consider: "Can my source serve the function I am asking it to serve?" In other words, "Can my source do the thing that I want it to do?"

Here we echo writing studies scholar Joseph Bizup's argument that writers should focus "their attention not on what their sources and other materials *are* . . . but on what they as writers might *do* with them" (75). We've isolated four common functions that a source can serve: 1) to be an **object** to analyze, 2) to provide **context** for that object, 3) to offer **critical** commentary on the object, and 4) to provide a **theory** to apply to the object. Once we grasp the functions that sources can play, we clarify how to assess sources and how to search for them.

Let's look at an example. We can see sources serve each of these four functions in English studies scholar Vilja Johnson's 2014 article "'It's What You Do That Defines You': Christopher Nolan's Batman as

KEY TERM

Functional Sources

Functional sources refers to a way of categorizing sources according to the purposes they can serve. While scholars define sources' functions in many ways, we find the following four categories most helpful:

1. An **object source** is anything that can be cited and interpreted in order to raise or address a scholarly problem. Books or articles, events, performances, data sets, images, and so on could all function as object sources.
2. A **context source** provides background information.
3. A **critical source** comments directly on the object source.
4. A **theory source** provides concepts or methods that the writer can apply to the object source in order to see it in a new way.

Moral Philosopher." Johnson confronts two challenges when tackling the subject of Batman movies: first, superhero movies may not seem like fitting objects of scholarly study; and second, readers may not feel that anything new remains to be discovered about such a well-known superhero. We'll examine how Johnson employs sources in strategic ways to overcome these challenges, ways that illuminate how any writer can use sources to construct a scholarly conversation.

1. An **object source** raises the problem a writer wants to study. We use the term "object" rather than "example" or "evidence" to emphasize that the writer's analysis of the object will yield new ideas rather than simply confirm old thoughts. When researchers analyze an object, they often complicate their initial assumptions. Without specific objects to cite and analyze, researchers would be left making only abstract arguments that readers would likely find vague or unconvincing.

Example: Johnson is interested in contributing to a conversation about heroism and villainy. However, readers might struggle to follow an abstract analysis of such broad concepts. How does she instead locate an analyzable, citable object that makes a problem about heroism and villainy visible to readers? She writes the following:

> In 2008, *The Dark Knight*, Christopher Nolan's sequel to *Batman Begins* (2005), smashed box office records, earning over a billion dollars worldwide ("All-Time Box Office"). . . . [Nolan] questions[s] and test[s] Batman's position as a popular hero. This process of questioning forces a re-evaluation of traditional, absolute understandings of heroism, allowing for a variety of new distinctions between hero and villain. (952)

Johnson grounds her analysis in a specific, citable object: Christopher Nolan's film *The Dark Knight* (see Photo 6.1). Her object source raises a scholarly problem: the tension between traditional conceptions of heroism (a common understanding) and "new distinctions between hero and villain" (a complication).

2. A **context source** offers background information. A context source may help readers locate the object source within space and time; within a particular intellectual tradition; within political, scientific, or economic histories; and so on. Context sources may also help readers understand how a scholarly conversation evolves over time.

Example: Most of Johnson's readers are likely already familiar with Batman. So she is careful not to rehash the most well-known context: Batman is a caped crusader, he lives in Gotham, and so on. Instead, she offers context that both feels fresh to many readers and moves them toward the specific conversation about Batman that she wants to generate. She writes:

Photo 6.1
Christian Bale acts out a scene in Christopher Nolan's 2008 film *The Dark Knight*. Photograph courtesy of Warner Bros.

Earlier versions of Batman established some of these foundations for Nolan's eventual representation of his troubled hero. From the time of his initial appearance, Batman has passed through several distinct phases of development. According to creator Bob Kane, the Batman who originally appeared in *Detective Comics* #27 in 1939 was heavily influenced by both noir films and the heroes of pulp magazines (Robertson 52). (Johnson 952–53)

Johnson cites communications researcher C. K. Robertson to give us relevant background information about the roots of Batman's character. Readers will now understand that Nolan's films arrive after a long tradition of reinterpretations, each influenced by its own cultural moment (see Figure 6.1.) This context then primes readers to learn about Nolan's own interpretation within *his* historical moment.

FIGURE 6.1
The character Batman first appeared in this 1939 issue of *Detective Comics* (Kane and Finger). By offering this context, Vilja Johnson is able to demonstrate how, in comparison, Christopher Nolan's 2008 interpretation of the character is unique.

3. A **critical source** offers scholarly commentary on an object. We use the term "critical" not to mean negative judgment but rather to refer to an approach that offers analysis. Critical sources establish how others have interpreted the object. By generating a conversation among critical sources, the researcher identifies places where they can contribute their own ideas. If the critical sources feature a tension (where the sources disagree) or a gap (where the sources have not yet considered something), the researcher can intervene in the conversation to make sense of the tension or gap.

Example: We shared earlier how Vilja Johnson's context sources prepare readers to understand Christopher Nolan's interpretation of Batman. But Johnson hasn't yet stated the stakes of her claim about *The Dark Knight*. How does Johnson use critical sources to show how she can contribute to a scholarly conversation about Batman? We've underlined phrases that Johnson uses to establish the critical conversation and indicate her own contribution:

> The inclusion of a character like the Joker, one who refuses to play by the traditional rules of villainy, has led some critics and scholars to identify *The Dark Knight*'s depiction of violence as a clear allegory for the use of force in response to global threats in post-9/11 America. For example, in a controversial article for the *Wall Street Journal*, Andrew Klavan contends that *The Dark Knight* is "a paean of praise to the fortitude and moral courage that has been shown by George W. Bush in this time of terror and war" (A15). . . . After examining the character of the Joker, J. M. Tyree arrives at a conclusion similar to Klavan's: "Nolan has made a new adaptation to the legend in presenting his Batman movies as oblique but fairly transparent fables of counterterrorism" (32). While the film may act on this level as a pure political allegory in which Nolan either critiques or praises the methods of the Bush administration, this type of analysis misses some of the broader issues Nolan's Batman raises as a hero working within a complex postmodern society. (956)

By using critical sources by political commentator Andrew Klavan and film scholar J. M. Tyree—two writers who have commented on *The Dark Knight*—Johnson generates a conversation that she can contribute to. The final sentence of the paragraph identifies a gap that she can fill: "this type of analysis misses some of the broader issues" (956). Readers now have a motive for reading Johnson's analysis: to address "broader issues."

4. A **theory source** offers concepts or methods for analyzing an object. A theory source does not comment directly on the object. Instead, it provides analytical tools that the researcher can apply to the object to help us understand the object in a new way.

Example: We showed how Johnson uses critical sources to enter a conversation that's focused on Nolan's Batman films. However, she connects that analysis to larger questions about heroism and villainy by turning to a theory source. Here, she uses ideas from the famous nineteenth-century philosopher Friedrich Nietzsche:

> Unable to maintain every "good" value in conflicting dilemmas, Batman acts out the kind of moral critique which Friedrich Nietzsche describes in *On the Genealogy of Morals*: "We need a critique of moral values, the value of these values is for the first time to be called into question—and for this purpose a knowledge is necessary of the conditions and circumstances out of which these values grew, and under which they experienced their evolution and their distortion" (5). . . . In the extreme dilemmas depicted onscreen, Batman tests the utility of various values, prioritizing and even discarding moral codes to achieve what he views as the best possible outcome. (957)

Since Nietzsche wasn't writing about Batman—in fact, he died before Bob Kane created Batman—Johnson has to explain how Nietzsche's theory can advance a conversation about Batman. When Johnson uses Nietzsche to analyze Batman—applying a theory source to help her interpret an object source—she raises the stakes of the scholarly conversation she is generating. Now, her analysis of *The Dark Knight* contributes to a longstanding discussion within Western philosophy about the stability and flexibility of moral values.

Sources Can Serve Multiple Functions

A single source can play many roles. While Nietzsche's *On the Genealogy of Morals* serves as a theory source for Vilja Johnson, it plays other roles in other scholars' projects. For example, when philosopher Walter Kaufman interprets *On the Genealogy of Morals* in the book *Nietzsche: Philosopher, Psychologist, AntiChrist*, Nietzsche's book functions as his object source. And in their book *Theognis of Megara: Poetry and the Polis*, classics scholars Thomas J. Figueira and Gregory Nagy cite

Nietzsche's discussion of the ancient poet Theognis to inform their own discussion of Theognis; Figueira and Nagy thus use *On the Genealogy of Morals* as a critical source (1). The point here is that when scholars consider using a particular source, they focus not on the inherent characteristics of the source but rather on how they will use the source in their own work. In the Tools & Techniques section, we'll offer specific strategies for making sure your sources can credibly play the roles you want them to play.

Scholars Seek Both Established and Fresh Voices

When scholars select sources to use, they strive to show their familiarity with the existing conversation as well as their ability to shape the conversation. One approach that scholars take to fulfill these two tasks is to look for both established voices and fresh voices.

When writers include established voices—prominent thinkers who have shaped the conversation—they demonstrate to their readers that they are insiders who belong to the research community. For instance, when Johnson cites Nietzsche, she indicates her awareness of a moral philosopher who's an established voice in studies of superheroes, cited in thousands of scholarly articles.

When writers invite fresh voices into the conversation, they move the conversation in new directions. Thus, when Johnson cites new articles by Klavan and Tyree, critics who are best known for work that is not about superheroes, she shows that she wants to shift the long-running conversation about Batman toward the moral and political landscape of the 2000s.

Selecting sources based on how you might use them has important implications for how scholars search for sources. Next, we'll examine the strategies that researchers use to find sources that serve specific roles in their projects.

Tools & Techniques: Searching for Functional Sources

Anice Mill's story, which opens this chapter, reminds us that many scholars begin generating a textual conversation by first seeking out live conversations. Here we offer advice for the conversations you might have with people in the order we recommend that you contact them: first a course instructor; then a librarian; and finally, if you still feel dissatisfied with the sources you've found, a specialist scholar. To prepare for each of these conversations, we recommend that you be able to 1) briefly describe the initial scholarly problem you think you want to pursue, or at least describe what issue you want to research and why you think it is interesting, and 2) list a few influential sources that have shaped the conversation about that problem or issue. That way you demonstrate that you are an engaged, prepared researcher who will make the most of thoughtful advice.

1. *Talk to an instructor.* If you're doing a research project for a class, we recommend visiting the instructor's office to ask for advice on which sources to examine. You might ask . . .

   - What key texts are missing from my list?
   - Are any of the texts on my list outdated or not sufficiently relevant?
   - What are the emerging voices that deserve more attention in this conversation?

2. *Talk to a research librarian.* Research librarians act as expert guides through the overwhelming number of resources available. As Librarian Anice Mills reminds us at the top of this chapter, research librarians not only connect scholars with sources; they also teach scholars effective methods for carrying out better searches. The questions scholars ask research librarians include . . .

   - What specialized databases might contain sources relevant to my project?
   - Can you help me locate a source I'm having trouble tracking down?
   - How do I find out who else is citing a source that plays a key role in my conversation?
   - Does the library hold any special collections relevant to my project?

3. *Ask a scholar.* Scholars occasionally answer emails or meet with newer researchers who are seeking advice. In our experience, questions are most likely to get a response when they . . .

   a. Briefly describe who you are and the occasion for your research. "I'm an undergraduate at the University of Texas at Austin doing research for my senior thesis in anthropology."

    b. Briefly explain the scholarly problem you're examining. "My project examines the tension between . . ."

    c. Give a reason for contacting the person. "Your book on ethnographic methods is informing my study design."

    d. Ask for the advice you want. The less you ask for, the more likely you'll receive a response. "What three or four sources would you suggest I start with?"

    e. Acknowledge that the person's time is valuable, and thank them.

Locate Functional Sources

Each source function we've described—object, context, critical, and theory—calls for its own set of search strategies. Here we'll explain some of the most common strategies that researchers use to . . .

Find Object Sources

If you already know the object you're going to examine—say, you're sure you want to analyze the ceiling of the Sistine Chapel or a poem by Emily Dickinson—then you obviously won't need to do a search for an object source. But what if a researcher has in mind only a larger phenomenon rather than a concrete object? Say they want to study the subversive power of Chinese pop music, the way that greeting cards signaled status and desire in the nineteenth century, or how playground design fosters both safety and independence. In these cases, researchers look for citable object sources to analyze (e.g., pop songs, greeting cards, or playground blueprints) so they're not left making vague or unsubstantiated claims.

Strategy: Keyword Search. Keywords are the principal words and phrases that describe the focus of your research. Scholars often start with broad search terms describing the concept they want to study and then zero in on more specific sites, events, people, and texts. Keyword searching can quickly become aimless if you're doing it in the wrong place. We recommend searching databases that specialize in the kind of objects you want to study. For instance, if you're doing market research, you might start by searching the *BMI Research* or *Emerging Markets Information Services* databases. If you are studying high energy physics, you may first try the *INSPEC* or *PHYSICSnet-BASE* databases. If you don't know what specialized databases might best fit your research, a reference librarian can show you your options.

TIME SAVER

Keyword Search Efficiently

Keyword searches in library catalogs and article databases can produce plenty of irrelevant results and waste time. The following search strategies can increase the number of relevant results:

- *Quotation marks.* Placing quotation marks around keywords limits the search results to only entries that contain those exact words in that exact order. For instance, imagine a research project about Mary Peake, a Civil War–era Virginian who was one of the first people to legally teach escaped slaves to read and write in the American South. When we typed the words *Mary* and *Peake* into *Google Scholar's* search box, we found that only one of the first ten results was about Mary Peake. The rest contained *Mary* and *Peake* in separate parts of the descriptions. However, searching *Google Scholar* for *"Mary Peake"* brought up nine of the first ten sources about the Virginia teacher.

- *And.* Search terms linked by *and* produce only sources that contain both terms somewhere in the source's record. For example, imagine a research project studying Jewish World War II refugee Victor Lowenfeld and the years he spent teaching art at Hampton Institute in Virginia. Our search for *Victor Lowenfeld Hampton Institute* in the database *JSTOR* produced over 5,000 hits that contained one or all of the terms. But combining the terms with *and—Victor Lowenfeld and Hampton Institute—*produced 61 entries, almost all relevant.

- *Asterisk.* When searching keywords that have several possible suffixes, using an asterisk in place of the suffixes produces results for all the possible word endings. You avoid having to do multiple searches for different forms of a word. For instance, if you are studying Athenian citizenship, the search terms *Athen* citizen** will yield results that contain *citizens of Athens, Athenian citizens, Athenian citizenship, Athenian citizenry,* and so on.

Find Context Sources

When searching for sources that will provide context, scholars consider two factors:

1. *Relevance.* Researchers ask themselves, "What information is crucial to understanding my project?"
2. *Their audience's ignorance.* Researchers ask themselves, "What will my reader not yet know?" and "What reminders might they appreciate?"

Strategy: Search Specialized Encyclopedias. University libraries offer specialized encyclopedias that scholars frequently use as a first step for gathering context sources. These electronic reference books are arranged by subject (e.g., *The Encyclopedia of Philosophy, Antarctica and the Arctic Circle, Oxford Dictionary of National Biography*). In addition to providing crucial background information written by experts, specialized encyclopedias list established sources that you can turn to as you deepen your search. Fruitful search terms will include the name of the object you're studying; a time period; a place; the names of individuals or institutions associated with the object; and the names of critics who have written about it.

Strategy: Create a Keyword Timeline. A strategy that scholars use to explore the intellectual history of an object involves visualizing the number of sources that cite the object over time. Tools like *Google Books Ngram Viewer* (for books), *ProQuest* (for newspaper articles), and *Gale Primary Sources* (for archival material) offer timelines of how often the search term appears in texts each year. Try searching "Wonder Woman" in these tools, for example, and you'll discover that the term experienced a dramatic jump in the frequency of citations in the 1970s (see Figure 6.2). The context you offer might explain this jump in order to give readers a sense of the character's prominence during various moments in the history of popular culture.

Find Critical Sources

As a first step in locating sources that analyze a specific object, scholars do keyword searches in scholarly databases. Vilja Johnson, for instance, went to *Academic Search Premier*, a database that contains academic journal, magazine, and newspaper articles. When she searched using the keywords "*The Dark Knight*" and "*Batman Begins*," she located

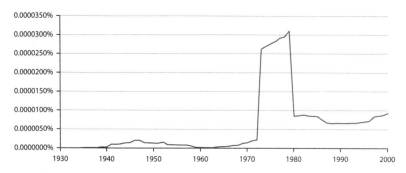

FIGURE 6.2
This timeline, created using *Google Books Ngram Viewer*, charts the appearance of "Wonder Woman" in the text of books catalogued in *Google Books* from 1940 to 2008 (*Google Books*). Mentions of Wonder Woman increase in the 1970s; a researcher might search for context sources to explain this increase.

critical sources that commented on the films: a newspaper article by Andrew Klavan and an academic article by J. M. Tyree.

While a basic keyword search can be a helpful first step, finding helpful critical sources can still be difficult. Scholars face two central challenges: 1) What if the object you're analyzing has received little critical attention? and 2) How can you distinguish established voices from fresh voices when you're new to the critical conversation? To meet these challenges, researchers turn to the following strategies:

Strategy: Review Bibliographies. Sometimes, finding just one source can lead to a whole array of other sources. How is this so? Researchers turn to the bibliographies at the ends of articles and books. By sorting through several bibliographies, researchers can track which authors are commonly cited and thus identify the established voices.

Strategy: Read Literature Reviews. The literature review is the name of a feature that appears frequently in scholarly writing, typically in specialized encyclopedia entries, book reviews, and the introductions to books and journal articles. It is a section that explains which voices the author is including in the scholarly conversation and how their ideas, taken together, call for a response. Literature reviews often identify both established and fresh voices.

Strategy: Refine Keyword Searches. What if Vilja Johnson wanted to study film depictions of the more obscure superhero Squirrel Girl instead of the much-studied Batman? A keyword search for "Squirrel Girl" in an academic database brings up just a couple of journal articles. As a next step, researchers can search broader categories that the object, in this case Squirrel Girl, belongs to:

- Great Lakes Avengers
- Marvel superheroes created in the 1990s
- Female comic book heroes
- The work of writer Will Murray

These searches bring up critical sources that address objects similar to Squirrel Girl. The researcher can then discover whether their ideas could shed light on Squirrel Girl too.

Strategy: Consult Citation Counts. Some research databases, like *Web of Science* and *Google Scholar*, count how many texts have cited a particular source. These citation counts offer one measure of a source's influence. For example, *Web of Science* will show you that if you want to study Nobel Prize winner Gertrude B. Elion's impact on medical research, you should read her article "The Purine Path to Chemotherapy," which has been cited in over 400 studies, rather than her study "Synthesis and Rearrangements of Some N-Methylpurines," which has never been cited (*Web of Science*).

Strategy: Search by date. Scholarly databases allow you to sort search results to put the most recent at the top. You can then view the newest critical sources to examine the latest shifts in the conversation.

Find Theory Sources

When scholars search for theory sources, they seek works whose ideas or methodologies they can use to help them analyze their own object. Unfortunately, keyword searching helps little in locating theory sources because they don't mention the object you want to analyze (Johnson, for instance, wouldn't have found Nietzsche by doing a keyword search for Batman). Experienced researchers can draw on their years of reading to identify methods and theories that they can bring to conversations. How can those who are newer to a conversation select theory sources? In addition to asking experts, we suggest the following strategies:

Strategy: Use Meta-Analysis. Meta-analysis means analyzing the analysis itself. Review the methods and concepts other critical sources have employed to study objects like yours. For instance, if you were researching depictions of female characters in Batman films, you might analyze how other scholars are studying the larger category of gender in film. As you gather articles on the subject and scan for their theory sources, you'll discover that Jacques Lacan's and Laura Mulvey's names appear often in relationship to the key term "the male gaze." You might then go to Lacan's and Mulvey's texts to see whether they might be productive participants in your conversation as well.

Strategy: Make Interdisciplinary Connections. Bring a different discipline into the conversation. By "discipline," we mean branch of scholarship, such as architecture, biology, philosophy, and so on. In a 2014 article, legal scholar Micah Bennett brings a different discipline into a conversation about immigration law to address the United States' definition of who counts as an immediate family member (and is therefore eligible to immigrate) (885–86). The United States' narrow legal definition of immediate family members may conflict with other countries' broader definitions that include grandparents, uncles, aunts, and so on (886–87). Bennett argues in favor of "another solution to the problem: immigration law could look to the discipline of anthropology for its ethnographic methods and informed cultural expertise to obtain answers on how to make both the statutory and judicial analysis of family more flexible" (886). By introducing methods drawn from anthropology, Bennett makes possible a new approach to the existing conversation about immigration law.

Assess Sources' Credibility

Emphasizing the roles we want sources to play in our writing changes how we might typically assess their credibility. Rather than rejecting all sources that do not undergo **peer review** by experts, we recognize that unvetted sources can credibly serve certain functions. For instance, researchers do not use random Tweets as context sources because no expert has verified their accuracy. Yet a researcher could credibly use Tweets as object sources in order to study public responses to a current event. To assess a source's credibility, researchers ask, 1) "What am I asking the source to do?" and 2) "Can the source credibly do what I want it to do?"

Because peer-reviewed work has been so carefully checked by experts, scholars consider it to be authoritative. Scholars use peer-reviewed sources to serve any of the functions we've described: to work as an object to analyze, to supply background context, to offer critical views, and to provide a theory or method to apply.

KEY TERM

Peer Review

When writers submit their work to a publication, editors decide whether or not to publish it. For serious academic work, publication requires an additional step called peer review: before any research is approved by the editor, they send it to experts in the field. These experts assess whether the research is accurate, significant, and original.

How do you know if a source is peer reviewed? Most databases will allow you to filter your results to list only academic journal articles, which are always peer reviewed (sometimes databases use the word "refereed" instead of peer reviewed). Scholarly research books published by university presses are also peer reviewed.

MYTH VS. REALITY

Myth: Researchers never use *Wikipedia* or *Google*.
Reality: Researchers often browse them in the early stages of a project.

You may have been warned that *Wikipedia* entries and *Google* search results aren't credible sources of research. *Wikipedia* itself says that "articles and subject areas sometimes suffer from significant omissions, and while misinformation and vandalism are usually corrected quickly, this does not always happen.... *Wikipedia* is written largely by amateurs. Those with expert credentials are given no additional weight" ("*Wikipedia*: About"). And *Google* sorts search results by ranking how "relevant" webpages seem (*Google Search*). Their measure of a pages' relevance takes into account hundreds of factors beyond its authors' expertise, including a page's popularity, its usability, and the user's location (*Google Search*). Thus, what counts as relevant for most search engine users may not count as relevant to researchers.

While *Wikipedia* entries and many websites that appear in *Google* search results aren't sufficiently vetted to serve as context, critical, or theory sources, they may name key terms or authors that can serve as search terms in academic databases. Some researchers also read *Wikipedia* and search *Google* for another purpose: they treat them as object sources.

Two apt examples are Claudia Wagner et al's 2015 article "It's a Man's *Wikipedia*? Assessing Gender Inequality in an Online Encyclopedia" and Daniel D. Reidpath's and Pascale Allotey's 2018 article "Predicting US State Teenage Birth Rates Using Search Engine Query Data on Pregnancy Termination and Prevention."

Limits to the Functions that Sources Can Credibly Serve

To determine the functions a source can (and can't) play, consider how it was produced. You might chart the means of the source's production using four criteria: timeliness, author's expertise, vetting, and publication standards. Imagine, for instance, that you are researching the public outcry sparked in 2006 when the International Astronomical Union demoted Pluto from a planet to a dwarf planet (see Photo 6.2). What might examining the production processes of a *Facebook* post, a newspaper article, and a scholarly book tell you about the different functions these sources could serve in your research?

PHOTO 6.2
The dwarf planet Pluto, photographed by the National Aeronautic and Space Administration (NASA) spacecraft New Horizons.

Type of source	*Facebook* post	Newspaper article	Scholarly press book
	Sara Azoulay's post: "pluto was my favorite planet. NOW I DONT HAVE A FAVORITE PLANET. *sad*." (Sept. 14, 2006)	Diane Carman's "Pluto Proves Science Is Tentative" (*Denver Post*, Aug. 27, 2006)	Steven J. Dick's *Discovery and Classification in Astronomy: Controversy and Consensus* (Cambridge University Press, 2013)
Timeliness How long does it take to write and publish it?	Seconds	Days or weeks	Years
Expertise Who writes on this platform?	Anybody with web access	Experts and non-experts who meet standards of journalistic integrity	Experts, typically professional scholars
Vetting Who assesses it?	Nobody	An editor who may not be an expert in the subject	An editor, editorial board, and expert peer reviewers
Publication standards What standard must it meet to be publishable?	Determined by the author	Newsworthiness	Scholarly significance and originality

PRACTICE

Determine the Functions Sources Can Serve

Each of the production processes detailed in the preceding chart determines how timely, scholarly, and thoroughly vetted sources are and what standards they must meet. These four qualities determine the functions that each source can serve. Notice that this way of thinking about sources as functional rather than as only credible or noncredible opens up new pathways for research: even a *Facebook* post can be considered serious scholarly evidence.

Task: Which functions could each of the publications listed in the chart above serve? Put a checkmark in the boxes below where you think the source is suitable for the function.

	Object	Context	Critical	Theory
1. *Facebook* post				
2. Newspaper article				
3. Scholarly press book				

ANSWERS:

1. Sara Azoulay is not an astronomy researcher, so her *Facebook* post can't credibly represent the scholarly conversation about Pluto. Nor can it represent the facts, since it hasn't been vetted. It can, however, represent a popular opinion. In this way, Azoulay's post can function as an object source but not a context, critical, or theory source.
2. Diane Carman's newspaper article has been vetted by editors, so it can represent fact and therefore serve as a context source and an object source. However, because Carman's piece hasn't been peer reviewed by astronomy experts, it can't serve as a critical or theory source.
3. Stephen J. Dick's scholarly book—because it has been peer reviewed by experts—can serve any role: object, context, critical, or theory source.

TURN TO YOUR RESEARCH
Make a Research Plan

As you embark on a research project, use this list to set tasks for locating sources you want to explore.
Learn from a librarian:

- A *research librarian* I can work with is [put contact info here]: _____.

continued

Search for object sources:

- To find an object to analyze, I will use the following *keywords*: _____, searching in the following *databases*: _____.

Search for context sources:

- To see how the study of my object has changed over time, I will use the following *data visualizer* [choices include *Google NGram* viewer, *ProQuest, Gale Primary Sources*, and others that your research librarian can help you to find]: _____.
- To find crucial background information, I will consult the following *specialized encyclopedias*: _____.

Search for critical sources:

To see what other scholars have said about my object, I will . . .
- Review *bibliographies* and *literature reviews* from the following sources: _____.
- Refine my *keyword search* with the following terms: _____.

Search for theory sources:

To find sources whose theories or methods I can apply to my object, I will . . .
- Contact the following *experts*: _____.
- Engage in *meta-analysis* using the following sources: _____.
- Look for connections with different branches of scholarship, including the following *disciplines*: _____.

Works Cited

Azoulay, Sara. "Massively Annoyed About Pluto Being Exiled (M.A.A.P.B.E.)." *Facebook*, 14 Sept. 2006, www.facebook.com/groups/2208898183/permalink/10150563264948184/.

Bennett, Micah. "A Family Tradition: Giving Meaning to Family Unity and Decreasing Illegal Immigration through Anthropology." *Indiana Law Journal*, vol. 89, no. 2, 2014, pp. 885–909.

Bizup, Joseph. "BEAM: A Rhetorical Vocabulary for Teaching Research-Based Writing." *Rhetoric Review*, vol. 27, no. 1, 2008, pp. 72–86.

Carman, Diane. "Pluto Proves Science Is Tentative." *Denver Post*, 27 Aug. 2006. *Business Insights: Essentials*, bi.galegroup.com/essentials/article/GALE%7C A150412019/91d7665349351279cd31a541cd0cb0d8?u=columbiau.

Dick, Steven J. *Discovery and Classification in Astronomy: Controversy and Consensus*. Cambridge UP, 2013.

Figueira, Thomas J., and Gregory Nagy. *Theognis of Megara: Poetry and the Polis*. Johns Hopkins UP, 1985.

Google Books. Google Books Ngram Viewer. Google, 2013, books.google.com/ ngrams.

Google Search. "How Search Algorithms Work." *Google Search: How Search Works*, www.google.com/search/howsearchworks/algorithms/.

Johnson, Vilja. "'It's What You Do That Defines You': Christopher Nolan's Batman as Moral Philosopher." *Journal of Popular Culture*, vol. 47, no. 5, Oct. 2014, pp. 952–67. *EBSCOhost*, doi:10.1111/jpcu.12181.

Kane, Bob, and Bill Finger. *Detective Comics no. 27*. May 1939. D.C. Comics. *Detective Comics/Covers*, dc.wikia.com/wiki/Detective_Comics/Covers.

Klavan, Andrew. "What Bush and Batman Have in Common." *Wall Street Journal*, 25 July 2008, p. A.15.

National Aeronautics and Space Administration, Johns Hopkins University Applied Physics Laboratory, Southwest Research Institute. *The Rich Color Variations of Pluto*. 14 July 2015, www.nasa.gov/image-feature/the-rich-color-variations-of-pluto.

Nietzsche, Friedrich. *The Genealogy of Morals*. Edited by Paul Negri, Dover, 2003.

Tyree, J. M. "American Heroes." *Film Quarterly*, vol. 62, no. 3, 2009, pp. 28–34. *JSTOR*, doi:10.1525/fq.2009.62.3.28.

Wagner, Claudia, et al. "It's a Man's Wikipedia? Assessing Gender Inequality in an Online Encyclopedia." *Proceedings of the Ninth International AAAI Conference on Web and Social Media*, Association for the Advancement of Artificial Intelligence, 2015, pp. 454–63. *Google Scholar*, arxiv.org/ abs/1501.06307.

Warner Bros., and D.C. Comics. *The Dark Knight*. 2008, www.warnerbros.com/ dark-knight.

Web of Science. "Citation Report for Elion GB," 19 Oct. 2018, apps. webofknowledge.com.

"Wikipedia: About." *Wikipedia*, 25 Nov. 2017, en.wikipedia.org/w/index.php?titl e=Wikipedia:About&oldid=812,052,332.

CHAPTER 7

....

Reading and Note-Taking

SCHOLAR'S STORY

Musicologist Nicholas Chong on Reading to Discover

My dissertation research on famed German composer Ludwig van Beethoven started with a hunch. I was not entirely convinced by previous scholars who downplayed the influence of Catholicism on his work. Was Catholicism really such a minor factor in Beethoven's composing? If answers existed, I would have to find them in sources like his letters and journal. This terrified me. No figure in music history has been more exhaustively researched than Beethoven. What could I find that was new?

I set aside my fears and started reading the sources with a specific purpose in mind. Though I understand German, I decided to cut myself some slack by using the standard English translations first. It was tedious, lonely work. But one afternoon, while combing through Beethoven's journal, I stumbled upon an awkwardly translated sentence. Intrigued, I ran to find the sentence in the original German. I discovered that Beethoven had actually used an obscure theological term that pointed to his sympathy for a strand of German Catholicism. The respected scholar who had translated the source into English had overlooked this fact—hence the awkward translation. The religious significance of the term had even escaped the notice of German-speaking scholars.

I was thrilled—so thrilled I remember wanting to yell right there in the library! This experience early in my research process gave me the confidence to keep searching for language that offered insight into Beethoven's religious beliefs. I made several more discoveries like the one I just described. Finding something new to say about Beethoven had once seemed overwhelming, but reading with a specific purpose in mind revealed something others hadn't seen.

Read the research: Nicholas Chong is a professor of musicology at Rutgers University. His dissertation is entitled *Beethoven's Catholicism: A Reconsideration*. You can find his article "Music for the Last Supper: The Dramatic Significance of Mozart's Musical Quotations in the *Tafelmusik* of *Don Giovanni*" in *Current Musicology*.

Mindset: Scholars Read Strategically

New researchers might imagine that seasoned scholars are faster readers. However, research on scholars' reading habits suggests instead that they are more *strategic* readers. They adopt approaches to reading that prepare them to write about sources.

Reading Generates New Ideas

What reading strategies did Nicholas Chong use to arrive at a project for his dissertation research on Beethoven? And how did his reading change as his project developed? Notice that Chong practiced "negative capability" at the opening of his project by exploring what he didn't know rather than jumping to a hasty conclusion (see Chapter 1 for more on negative capability). He began reading before he knew exactly what he was looking for. He then read his way *into* a scholarly problem by first making an observation that ran counter to the scholarly consensus. Once Chong had stumbled across a surprising discovery, his reading became more purposeful, his reading practices more refined. He moved from a typical question that scholars begin with—What can I find that is new?—to a specific search for "language that offered insight into Beethoven's religious beliefs." His reading became a way for him to generate new ideas.

Scholars are motivated by the desire to learn something new, to advance or complicate their initial assumptions. So they read in order to find the unfamiliar, the new, the surprising, or the challenging. To do this successfully, their ideas must evolve *because of* their reading.

Photo 7.1
A research physicist at work: Russian physicist Natalia Zaitseva grows crystals and manufactures plastics that can distinguish between different kinds of radiation (Zaitseva). Photo courtesy of Lawrence Livermore National Laboratory.

This push in new directions requires seasoned scholars to employ a different set of reading practices than less-experienced researchers do. In a study on reading practices, Rebecca Moore Howard, Tricia Serviss, and Tanya K. Rodrigue find that less-experienced researchers tend to read in order to "quote-mine": to dig for short passages that either affirm or counter their claims (186). In other words, they start with fixed claims and read for passages that agree or disagree with the claims but do not advance or complicate them. In a study of the reading practices of professional research physicists (see Photo 7.1), Charles Bazerman observed a quite different approach. Physicists in Bazerman's study primarily read in order to "change not just their minds, but their plans and work" as a result of their reading (22). While we might imagine that experienced researchers are more certain of their initial ideas than newer researchers, these studies suggest the opposite. Seasoned scholars read for concepts and approaches that change their ideas.

Notes Reduce Demands on Memory

Annotations—the notes that a reader makes on a page's margins—offer a way for scholars to record their immediate responses to a source. When they return to the source later, they don't have to struggle to remember their earlier thinking. Had they only highlighted or underlined passages,

MYTH VS. REALITY

Myth: Scholars need to read texts only once.
Reality: Scholars rely on rereading.

Novelist Vladimir Nabokov argued that "Curiously enough, one cannot read a book; one can only reread it. A good reader, a major reader, an active and creative reader is a rereader" (3). For Nabokov, the physical act of a first reading—of moving our eyes across the page to find out what a book is about—requires enough effort that we miss the nuances of a text. We can make more sophisticated observations when we reread.

But there is a subtler reason that scholars reread: it has to do with a phenomenon called the hermeneutic circle. The hermeneutic circle—an idea discussed by thinkers like Wilhelm Dilthey, Martin Heidegger, and Hans Gadamer—says that 1) we cannot understand a whole text until we understand its component parts and 2) we cannot understand any single part of a text unless we place it within our understanding of the whole text. The hermeneutic circle presents us with a paradox that we can solve by rereading. When we reread the opening of a text, for instance, with knowledge of how the text will unfold, we can better understand how the opening contributes to the meaning of the whole text. Rereading allows researchers to interpret sources by keeping in mind the relationships between a whole source and each of its parts.

they would know that those passages had seemed important but would have to tax their memories to recall why. While annotating makes for slower initial reading, it actually saves time in the long run. Indeed, a study by Carol Porter-O'Donnell found that annotating texts helped students understand their texts more quickly (87).

In addition to annotating sources, scholars typically take more detailed research notes in separate documents. Let's look at the way that historian Judith Walkowitz takes notes during her research. In the following account, she describes how she engages with documents in an archive. As you read her description, consider what her practices accomplish for her that strictly annotating in the margins of the source could not:

> I then take careful summary notes of what seem to be the most significant documents, with careful attention to their place in the sequence of the file, how much space they take up, and their rhetorical ordering

and sequencing. I back up my files religiously on the external hard drive. I also open a second Word file, which I call "Idea File." This is a space of free association, a form of uncensored writing that might well not see the light of day in any final text. This second file is intended 1) to engage in an active cognitive process or "engaged reading," 2) to move to generalization while still staying very close to the textual particulars, and 3) to start the writing process as early as possible.

In this second file, I sometimes include a running commentary on what I think is going on in this document and how it might connect to other sources. I also write memos to myself about secondary or theoretical texts I need to consult in relation to this material. Most important, I record the details or features that strike me as surprising or telling: whether there are significant silences or elements that seem to be missing. (38)

Walkowitz views her notes as necessary to both remembering the text (through "summary") and to advancing her own thinking (through "free association"). Both of these functions prepare her to write about her sources. The archives of published writers reveal similarly meticulous note-taking. To see an example, search the web for the digitized archives of philosopher Rose Rand at the University of Pittsburgh Library.

Why do writers put such effort into their research notes? A study by cognitive psychologists Annie Piolat, Thierry Olive, and Ronald T. Kellogg demonstrates that note-taking while reading requires about twice the cognitive effort of reading alone (299). This increase in cognitive effort carries two benefits for note-taking readers: 1) when they're reading, note-taking helps them engage more deeply with texts, and 2) later, when they're writing, their notes help them more efficiently recall their initial thoughts about the texts (296). The second benefit leads to a third benefit: because researchers can remember their initial thoughts, they now can complicate those initial thoughts.

Writers Emulate Texts They Admire

When creative writing professor Rachel Toor interviewed well-known scholars about their writing practices, a number of them explained that they emulated writing that they admired, using it as a model for their own writing. Economist Deirdre McCloskey, for instance, says, "I noted how the best writers in economics did it: Robert Solow, for example, who lets his personality through. I had the advantage over many economists of reading outside of economics: Willa Cather, A. N. Wilson, Martha

Nussbaum, Richard Rorty, Howard Becker, and Wayne Booth" (*Scholars Talk Writing*). And philosopher Steven Pinker responds, "I lingered over passages of writing I enjoyed and tried to reverse-engineer them." McCloskey and Pinker describe a reading practice that focuses on how texts are composed—"reverse engineering." Reverse engineering means taking apart a finished object in order to understand how its components were assembled. What does reverse engineering look like for writers? It means looking at writing with an eye toward the specific techniques that a writer uses and adapting similar techniques in one's own writing.

Tools & Techniques: Reading to Write

Scholars use various reading strategies depending on what they want to achieve in their writing. Here we focus on four common reading goals and the strategies scholars use to achieve them:

1. Reading to select sources
2. Reading to populate a conversation
3. Reading to generate a scholarly problem
4. Reading to emulate

Chapter 12 is dedicated to a fifth goal: reading to analyze sources.

Reading to Select Sources

Many reading strategies we recommend require slow, careful attention to entire sources. However, in the earliest stages of research, scholars often review a lot of sources quickly in order to identify the smaller number that they will analyze in depth.

Strategy: Read from the Outside In

The English studies scholar John Guillory observes that researchers often vet sources by starting with the material at the front and back of a text and reading their way in: "Scholarly books are often read from the peripheral matter inward, from the table of contents, the index, the notes, the introduction and conclusion, then to the chapters themselves" (14).

Example: Reading Deirdre McCloskey's book *The Rhetoric of Economics* from the outside in, we encounter at the front the book's title, publication year, publisher, table of contents, and introduction. Together, these give us a picture of the book's timeliness, the level of expert vetting it has received, the questions it addresses, and its structure (see Figure 7.1). At the back, we find a bibliography and an index. The bibliography lists the participants in McCloskey's scholarly conversation, while the index offers a list of key thinkers, institutions, events, and terms that appear in the book. The index can be a quick way to determine how deeply a book addresses a particular subject (see Figure 7.2). If, for instance, you were studying the application of ancient Roman thought to contemporary economics, the index would tell you that the poet Catullus appears on just one page while the orator Cicero appears on seven pages (*The Rhetoric of Economics* 219).

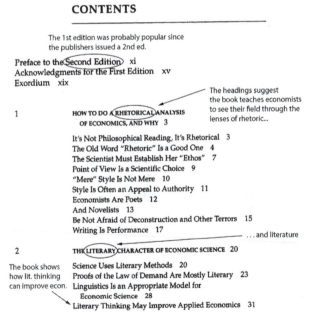

Figure 7.1
When using the "read from the outside in" strategy, scholars scan tables of contents like this one from Deirdre McCloskey's *The Rhetoric of Economics* for an overview not only of the subjects that the book addresses but also how it addresses them (vii).

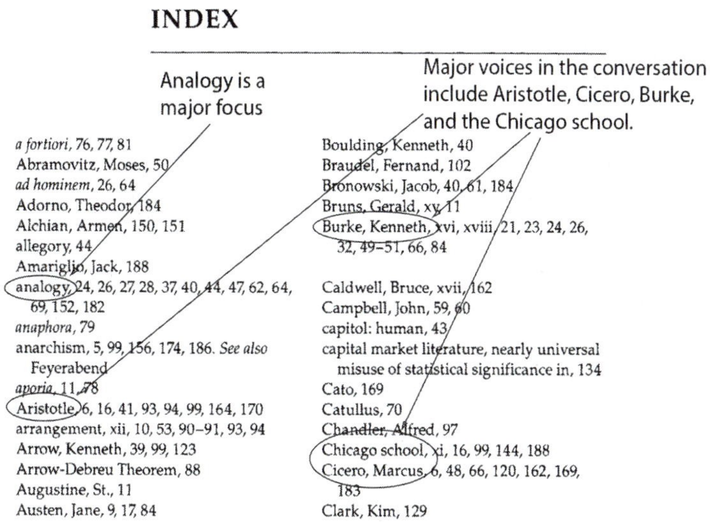

INDEX

Analogy is a major focus

Major voices in the conversation include Aristotle, Cicero, Burke, and the Chicago school.

FIGURE 7.2

When reading "from the outside in," researchers scan indexes like this one from *The Rhetoric of Economics* to identify the entries that appear on many pages (219). These entries give readers a sense of the focus of the book and indicate the major voices in its conversation.

Strategy: Read Information-Rich Components of a Source

To determine quickly whether a source is useful to them, researchers target features that tend to be rich with information. For main ideas, summaries, and key findings, they look for abstracts (a paragraph-length summary typically appearing at the beginning of a scholarly article), headings, charts and graphs, introductions, and conclusions. Book introductions typically include brief summaries of each chapter.

Reading to Generate Conversation

In their study, "Rhetorical Reading Strategies," composition studies researchers Christina Haas and Linda Flower argue that we can best make sense of sources when we relate them to other sources rather than understanding them in isolation (168). Creating what Haas and Flower call "complex networks" of sources (168) requires practicing strategies for reading *across* sources. We feature here three such strategies: source tracking, mind mapping, and keeping an idea file.

TIME SAVER

Skimming and Scanning

Sometimes, a preliminary search for sources can yield so many sources that the results are overwhelming. In these cases, it can be helpful to think about not only what to read carefully but also what to read quickly and what not to read at all.

John Guillory makes the point that scholarly reading is a specialized practice. He distinguishes between "skimming" and "scanning" (13). When readers *skim* text, they read quickly, aiming to get only the gist of a text. When scholars *scan* text, on the other hand, they focus their attention on specific "keywords, names, dates, or other features of a text" (13). They delay slow, intensive reading of the text until they find the feature they were looking for, at which point they stop scanning and begin reading in a slower, more narrowly focused way. This practice allows researchers to move through many pages of text efficiently.

Strategy: Track Sources

In scholarly texts, literature reviews and bibliographies give researchers clues about which voices have contributed most to the conversation. Literature reviews, which appear toward the beginnings of many academic books and articles, are sections of studies that describe how the scholarly conversation has evolved, which thinkers have influenced it most, and how the researcher's project builds on what has come before. Bibliographies appear at the ends of texts to list all the sources the study has cited. Scholars regularly glance through them to observe which texts commonly appear in many studies. Literature reviews and bibliographies help a researcher envision the network of voices that make up the conversation they want to shape.

Strategy: Mind Map

A mind map helps you visualize relationships among sources that will prepare you to generate a scholarly conversation. You might map texts' overlapping problems, key terms, methods, claims, or evidence. You may visualize sources on a timeline to chart the intellectual history of an area of inquiry.

As an example, the mind map in Table 7.1 visualizes the network of thinkers who participated in the Macy Conferences. The Macy Conferences were a series of meetings in the 1940s and 1950s among academics whose scholarship forms the foundation of the area of study called cybernetics. Cybernetics is the study of systems that govern animals (including humans) and machines—systems of communication, cognition, social relationships, and so on.

Faced with a dizzying number of scholars who participated in the conferences, we created this mind map to cluster them by their areas of specialization. The map makes visible one of the things that made the Macy Conferences so remarkable: it was a rare space where academics from diverse fields came together to define an area of study. And yet it also shows that more science and social science scholars shaped the conversation than humanities scholars. Different groupings would make different interpretations of the Macy Conferences possible. Mind maps that instead group the participants by gender, nationality, race, ethnicity, or religion would allow us to visualize new scholarly problems.

TABLE 7.1

Fields of study that shaped cybernetics at the Macy Conferences. By grouping the participants by their academic fields, we can see that cybernetics evolved out of richly interdisciplinary conversations. For a different approach to mind mapping the Macy Conferences, see Katherine Hayles's book *How We Became Posthuman* (16).

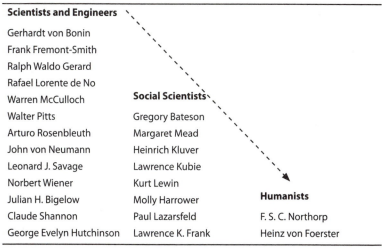

Scientists and Engineers	Social Scientists	Humanists
Gerhardt von Bonin		
Frank Fremont-Smith		
Ralph Waldo Gerard		
Rafael Lorente de No		
Warren McCulloch		
Walter Pitts	Gregory Bateson	
Arturo Rosenbleuth	Margaret Mead	
John von Neumann	Heinrich Kluver	
Leonard J. Savage	Lawrence Kubie	
Norbert Wiener	Kurt Lewin	
Julian H. Bigelow	Molly Harrower	Humanists
Claude Shannon	Paul Lazarsfeld	F. S. C. Northorp
George Evelyn Hutchinson	Lawrence K. Frank	Heinz von Foerster

Strategy: Keep an "Idea File"

As she researches, Judith Walkowitz, who narrated her reading strategies earlier, records the connections she makes among texts in a document she calls her "Idea File" (38). Dedicating a document to articulate relationships across sources ensures that you are actively formulating a scholarly conversation at the moments when texts are freshest in your mind: as you are reading them.

Reading to Generate a Scholarly Problem

As we discussed in Chapter 2, scholars seek out scholarly problems—difficulties that arise from gaps in understanding. These problems take the form of tensions or dissonances that scholars can make sense of. For instance, our common understanding of an issue might exist in tension with a new complication we discover, or a pattern we see might exist in tension with a sudden break in that pattern. Like a rubber band that can be stretched only when both sides are pulled, a tension must have two elements. The following reading strategies are designed to help you find specific kinds of scholarly problems by discovering and articulating both elements of a tension.

Here are reading strategies for finding tensions between ...

Common Understanding and Complication

Strategy: Read for the accepted view and for conflicts with that view

First, research the common understanding. Consider how others have typically described and responded to the problem you are studying. Then complicate your understanding by reading sources to identify specific aspects that this common understanding cannot account for.

Whole and Part

Strategy: Re-read (or re-view, re-listen, and so on)

Study the source(s) first to grasp the big picture. In your notes, describe your overall sense of its claim, structure, and style. Then read again, this time annotating parts that don't conform to your sense of the whole.

Part and Part

Strategy: Label the parts of the source

In your annotations, name the components or attributes of each section, such as types of evidence, stylistic features, and so on. Then read your labels. Notice any incongruities among the component parts.

Pattern and Break

Strategy: Read for repetition

Annotate patterns you see in language, structure, imagery, and so on. Then read again, this time looking for places that don't adhere to the pattern.

Presence and Absence

Strategy: Read for what is there and what is not

First list the aspects of the source that typically appear in similar sources or that the source itself suggests will be present. Consider the style of language, the types of evidence, the approach to analysis, kinds of claims, and so on. Next, read the source and notice what items on your list are absent from the source itself.

Expectation and Observation

Strategy: Anticipate, and then annotate

First note your expectations. Before reading a source for the first time, describe the approach you expect the source to take (and why) based on what you know about the author, the publication, the type of writing, the date of publication, the subject, and so on. When you read, annotate any passages that don't conform to your expectations.

PRACTICE

Anticipate, and Then Annotate

If you have trouble anticipating how a text might appear, we recommend a hands-on approach. Before you read or view your source, actually compose (write or draw) a portion of the text as you anticipate it to be. Then note observations that differ from what you composed.

Task #1

a) Anticipate. Picture what a typical cemetery monument for a late nineteenth-century writer might look like. Now draw it.

b) Annotate. Search the web for photos of Oscar Wilde's tomb in Paris's Père Lachaise Cemetery. How does it differ from your drawing? What scholarly problems might the differences present?

continued

Task #2

a) Anticipate. Imagine how an ecologist might begin an essay arguing that it is our ethical obligation to preserve the environment. Write the first four sentences of the essay you imagine.

b) Annotate. Turn the book to read the following passage: the opener to ecologist Aldo Leopold's "The Land Ethic," a classic 1949 essay on ecology. How does it differ from your sentences? What scholarly problems might the differences present?

THE OPENER TO ALDO LEOPOLD'S "THE LAND ETHIC":

When god-like Odysseus returned from the wars in Troy, he hanged all on one rope a dozen slave-girls of his household whom he suspected of misbehavior during his absence.

This hanging involved no question of propriety. The girls were property. The disposal of property was then, as now, a matter of expediency, not of right and wrong. (201)

Text and Context

Strategy: Research, then compare

Before you read, briefly research the source, author, and time period. If you're reading a book, you might look at book reviews, which typically place the book within the author's body of work and within an intellectual tradition. Then find aspects of the source that don't seem to fit the context.

PRACTICE

Read to Generate Scholarly Problems

What reading strategies might you use to find scholarly problems in this passage from Arlette Farge's book *Allure of the Archives*? The book explores how historians learn about people who lived long ago by studying dusty documents left behind in library archives. Farge, a prominent French historian, is especially interested in the emotional connections researchers make to their subjects. In this passage, she imagines how a scholar might feel when opening brittle papers from a French police archive that haven't been read since the eighteenth century.

Task: Choose two reading strategies for identifying scholarly problems from among the ones described earlier. Practice both strategies on Farge's passage. (We recommend trying the "read for repetition" strategy in particular.) Several strategies may require you to take some notes before you read. For instance, if you choose the "anticipate, then annotate" strategy, you'll first want to jot down what you expect of the passage before annotating it for elements that go against your expectations. No matter which strategies you choose, you will want to annotate the passage carefully.

It is as if some material traces had returned from this departed world, traces of moments that were the most private and the least often expressed. . . . The archive preserves these moments at random, chaotically. Each time, the person who reads, touches, or discovers them is at first struck by the feeling of certainty. The spoken word, the found object, the trace left behind become faces of the real. As if the proof of what the past was like finally lay there before you, definitive and close. As if, in unfolding the document, you gained the privilege of "touching the real." And if this is the case, what's the point of scholarly debate, why come up with new words to explain what is already there on these sheets of paper (or between them)?

These overwhelming feelings never last; they are like mirages in the desert. . . . The physical pleasure of finding a trace of the past is succeeded by doubt mixed with the powerless feeling of not knowing what to do with it. (11)

Annotation and Note-Taking Strategies

In 1844, the famous American writer Edgar Allan Poe wrote about his love of reading books that had space on the page for him to record his own thoughts: "In getting my books, I have been always solicitous of an ample margin; this not so much through any love of the thing in itself, however agreeable, as for the facility it affords me of penciling suggested thoughts, agreements and differences of opinion, or brief critical comments in general" (176). For Poe, as for researchers, annotations provide a low-stakes way to imagine possible responses to sources. In this way, annotations prepare writers to begin writing about sources not only efficiently but also with greater sophistication.

Scholars typically use two kinds of annotations: 1) personal shorthand made up of markings and 2) worded responses.

Shorthand Annotations

Researchers typically develop their own symbols that act as shorthand for common interactions with sources. Here are some common ways that researchers mark up sources:

- Underline or circle key ideas, terms, and thinkers
- Use asterisks or vertical lines to mark crucial sections and passages to reread
- Use question marks to note a question, a place of potential disagreement, and words to look up in a dictionary
- Use numbers to indicate the development of a source's ideas and the steps in an argument

Worded Annotations

While less-experienced scholars typically make use only of shorthand annotation, seasoned scholars rely more heavily on worded responses; worded notations act as a transitional step toward responding to the source in one's own project. Scholars write in the margins to paraphrase the source's argument, to note the source's structure and language choices, to question (or answer), and to make connections to other sources.

Here is an example of our own annotations on a book by psychologist Daniel Kahneman. In this passage, Kahneman explains that the mind is made up of two systems (System 1 and System 2) that deal differently with doubt. Our annotations include underlining and an asterisk we used to signal a crucial phrase, alongside key terms that would tell us why we thought this phrase was crucial. Notice, too, we made an annotation connecting Kahneman's argument about doubt to John Keats's notion of negative capability. When we returned to this source later, we were reminded of this connection to Keats.

* System 1 vs system 2 re: doubt Sounds like Keats's negative capability	As I described earlier, *System 1 is not prone to doubt*. It suppresses ambiguity and spontaneously constructs stories that are as coherent as possible. Unless the message is immediately negated, the associations that it evokes will spread as if the message were true. *System 2 is capable of doubt*, because it can maintain incompatible possibilities at the same time. However, *sustaining doubt is harder work than sliding into certainty*. The law of small numbers is a manifestation of a general bias that favors certainty over doubt, which will turn up in many guises in following chapters.

Note-Taking

In Chapter 5, we discussed setting up an organizational system that includes a template for taking notes. Our template has the following sections:

- *Source info*. Here we write the source's bibliographic information.
- *Context*. In this section, we describe the source in relationship to its historical moment, place, and circumstances.
- *Project*. Here we capture the source's purpose, objects of analysis, methods, and stakes.
- *Notes*: Under this heading, we paraphrase or quote specific passages and note the pages on which they appear. We also add our own thoughts in brackets.
- *Significance*: Here we explain the role this source might play in our project.

We used this template in our own research for this book. An example of the reading notes that resulted appear in Figure 7.3. You can see that we carefully distinguished the source's ideas from our own by placing our responses in square brackets.

We did, in fact, use Kahneman in the following passage from Chapter 1:

Many writers recognize how difficult it is to push toward ignorance. Nobel Prize-winning psychologist Daniel Kahneman writes, "sustaining doubt is harder work than sliding into certainty" (114). It is no easy task to remain unsettled and open-minded, especially when you know that your eventual goal may be to make a confident, convincing claim.

Source info: Kahneman, Daniel. *Thinking Fast and Slow.* Farrar, Straus, and Giroux, 2011.

Context: Daniel Kahneman, Psychology Prof Emeritus at Princeton, Nobel Prize; famous for work w/ Amos Tversky on decision-making: challenged long-held ideas that "people are generally rational"(176); major contributor to fields of psych. and behavioral econ.

Summary/project: Big book about how humans think, focused on "judgment and decision making" (4); explains two-system model to describe mind: System 1 → quick, intuitive, unconscious; System 2 → deliberate, rational, conscious (13); humans have difficulty thinking statistically and acknowledging ignorance; cites hundreds of pieces of research from dozens of years, mostly in field of psych.

Notes: Interested in places where Kahneman talks about writing as conversation (6); concision and working memory (30); on working memory: "We normally avoid mental overload by dividing our tasks into multiple easy steps, committing intermediate results to long-term memory or to paper rather than to an easily overloaded working memory" (38) [can explain how writing is a way to advance thinking by freeing up memory so writers can come up with more complex thoughts, etc.; might also help us say why researchers break big projects into small, manageable tasks]; on ignorance: "sustaining doubt is harder work than sliding into certainty" (114) [Love this quote; seems to fit exactly w/ idea of negative capability that we'll use in ch. 1.]

Significance: I can see us using the book in two ways: 1) to get a researcher from field of psychology who occasionally reflects on his own writing; 2) to get insights from Kahneman's research about human brain that relate to writing.

Figure 7.3
An excerpt from our reading notes on Daniel Kahneman's book *Thinking Fast and Slow.*

We were able to write these sentences using only our notes rather than having to reread Kahneman's almost-500-page tome or search our memories to recall our initial thoughts about the source. Working from our notes prepared us to bring Kahneman into our writing efficiently.

RESEARCH ON WRITING

Should You Read Texts in Digital or Paper Form?

While several studies have found that readers tend to prefer reading on paper over screen reading (Spencer 41), research is mixed on whether that preference translates to faster reading or better comprehension. In their literature review of that research, Jan M. Noyes and Kate J. Garland note that pre-1992 studies typically gave paper the edge over digital texts (1354–56). However, as digital display technologies have improved and readers have become more accustomed to them, some studies favor one over the other, and other studies show little difference (1358–60).

A small but interesting 2010 study by Norwegian media studies scholar Terje Hillesund looks more specifically at scholars' strategic choices in reading media. He examined the reading habits of ten expert readers: all social science and humanities researchers. Hillesund found that the researchers tended to choose different reading media for particular purposes. When they were reading longer sources or sources that they wanted to analyze in depth, they preferred to read on paper. But when they were reading to get an overview, they were more likely to seek out digital texts and less likely to take notes. Hillesund writes that, of the different digital reading technologies (e-readers, pdfs, and so on), "Web browsers are probably the least suited for immersive reading." Instead, the researchers tended to skim and jump around on web pages.

Takeaway: When you want to closely analyze a text, try working on paper. If you choose to do analytical reading on a digital text, make use of electronic annotation tools.

Read the research: Hillesund, Terje. "Digital Reading Spaces: How Expert Readers Handle Books, the Web and Electronic Paper." *First Monday*, vol. 15, no. 4, 2010. *Google Scholar*, uncommonculture.org/ojs/index.php/fm/article/view/2762/2504.

Noyes, Jan M., and Kate J. Garland. "Computer- vs. Paper-Based Tasks: Are They Equivalent?" *Ergonomics,* vol. 51, no. 9, 2008, pp. 1352–75. *Google Scholar*, doi:10.1080/00140130802170387.

Spencer, Carrie. "Research on Learners' Preferences for Reading from a Printed Text or from a Computer Screen." *Journal of Distance Education,* vol. 21, no. 1, 2006, pp. 33–50.

Annotated Bibliography

Using annotation strategies, researchers zoom in on specific passages in their sources. However, this zooming in can make scholars lose sight of whole texts or larger conversations. One strategy they use to zoom out again is to create an annotated bibliography. Annotated bibliographies alphabetically list sources' bibliographic entries, with each entry followed by a paragraph describing the source. An annotated bibliography allows researchers to review descriptions of all their sources in a single document so that they can consider how the sources might interact. In addition to the source's bibliographic information, annotations frequently include some combination of the following information about the source:

- *The scholarly problem.* What gap in understanding does the source address?
- *Its project.* What is its purpose? What object(s) does it analyze? What methods does the source use to address the scholarly problem? What are the stakes?
- *Its claims.* What are its findings or conclusions?
- *The quality or value of the source.* Is the research credible? Is it significant?
- *The role it might play in one's research.* Will I use the source as an object to analyze? To provide context? To offer critical analysis of the object I am investigating? To offer a theory or method that I can apply to my study?

As you read the following example from Colin Lewis's "Annotated Bibliography: Work and Faith," note how the annotation addresses several of these questions (Lewis 240). This annotation of is one of twelve sources listed in Lewis's annotated bibliography. Together, they give readers an overview of the existing scholarly conversation about Christian understandings of work.

Imagine that you were researching Christian conceptions of labor, and you created an annotated bibliography similar to Lewis's. How might you use it to generate new ideas for your writing? One approach would be to read all the annotations to identify gaps in the research that you could fill. For instance, you might observe that sources focus heavily on the writings of clergymen but shed little light on the writings of clergywomen and lay people. Another approach might be to look for trends in the existing research that you could extend or complicate. Perhaps, for example, you notice that most studies rely on older treatises as evidence. You might, then, propose to look at the most recent treatises on work

Bibliographic entry: Lewis uses APA style	Ranft, P. (2006). *The Theology of Work: Peter Damian and the Medieval Religious Renewal Movement*. New Middle Ages. New York: Palgrave Macmillan.
The source's scholarly problem	In this treatment of what she calls "medieval work theology," Ranft contends that a more robust look at the Middle Ages—and, in particular, the religious renewal of the eleventh through thirteenth centuries—helps to answer the question of whether Christians in the West developed a theology of work before the Ref-
The project: its method (historical survey) and object of analysis (Peter Damian)	ormation. She begins with a brief historical survey of early Christian attitudes towards work before delving into her primary topic, namely the life and thought of the Benedictine monk and Cardinal Peter Damian.
The source's claim	Ranft contends that Damian's treatment of work was the first of its kind and formed a significant part of his larger reform of the religious life. In the final part of
The stakes of the project	the book, she draws out the implications of Damian's vision both on the monastic world and the rest of society, noting that he helped to create what was, by the end of the Middle Ages, a view of work as a way of
The source's significance: what it adds to the conversation	imitating Christ. Ranft's book thus stands apart from the historiographic mainstream in its willingness to debunk the myth that only with the advent of the Reformation did work once again find its proper place in Christian theology and spirituality.

and Christianity in order to see how contemporary thinking compares to older thinking. Or you might study how other kinds of evidence—private journals or monasteries' financial records—complicate what we understand from treatises. Annotated bibliographies give researchers the big picture of a scholarly conversation so that they can locate places to intervene.

Reading for Emulation

What does a film director pay attention to when they watch a movie? How might it differ from what a casual viewer pays attention to? The casual viewer will likely get wrapped up in the story and the characters.

The film director, however, will also observe *how* the film was shot: How did the camera angles create suspense? How did the lighting direct the audience's gaze? How did the music interact with the visuals? When scholars annotate sources, they take a similar approach. They pay attention not only to *what* the source says, but also *how* it says it. They annotate writing strategies that they can emulate—that they can adopt and adapt.

Here are annotation strategies that identify three aspects of sources' writing that you might emulate: structure, source use, and the author's presence.

Structure

How is the text structured? What would an outline of the text look like? What function do the opening and closing sections serve?

Strategy: Reverse-outline

Reconstruct a "says/does" outline of the piece by 1) numbering each paragraph, 2) annotating what each paragraph conveys (what it *says*), and 3) annotating the function of each paragraph within the piece (what it *does*). For instance, the opening paragraph of this chapter *says* that Nicholas Chong was searching for something new about Beethoven. What the opening paragraph *does* is use an anecdote to introduce a key concept.

Source Use

What counts as evidence? Where is the evidence located throughout the piece? How much evidence does the author use? How does the author introduce evidence? How does the author analyze evidence? How much summary, paraphrase, quotation, and synthesis of sources is typical?

Strategy: Code the text for source use

Using different colored markers for each, mark the places in the text where you see context, summary, paraphrase, quotation, or synthesis (for descriptions of each of these uses of evidence, see Chapter 11).

The Author's Presence

How do readers experience the writer's persona? How does the writer reveal their presence in the text? What is the writer's relationship toward their sources?

Strategy: Annotate for indications of *ethos* (the author's character)

Underline language like first-person pronouns such as "I" and "me" that make the writer's presence explicit. Look for anecdotes or other narratives that show the writer's presence as a researcher. Mark language that reveals the kinds of relationships the writer has with their sources. For example, do they evaluate one text as "crucial" and another as "vexing," or do they resist assessing the sources they cite?

You might start actually drafting your own text by gathering and rereading the annotations and notes you took using the methods in this chapter. When scholars use the techniques described in this chapter, moving from research to drafting should feel like a small step. The next chapter helps you make that step.

TURN TO YOUR RESEARCH

Part 1: Design Your Annotation Key

Researchers typically adopt their own annotation strategies. For instance, one writer might draw a box or a circle around key terms; another might put a star next to them. Creating your own set of annotation strategies saves you time. Note how you will annotate each item listed here when you identify it in a reading:

Within the body of a text, how will I note . . .
- Key terms and their definitions?
- Main ideas?
- Passages that speak to my own research?
- Patterns in word choice or word order?
- Things to learn more about?
- Other features _____?

In a text's margins, how will I annotate . . .
- My summary of the text's ideas?
- My response to the text's ideas?
- Connections between the text and things outside the text?
- The text's structure?
- The function a passage is serving (for instance, a section could be laying out the scholarly problem, the project, and so on)?
- Writing strategies that I want to emulate?
- Other annotations _____?

TURN TO YOUR RESEARCH

Part 2: Design Your Reading Notes Template

We shared with you our note-taking template. It is a word processing document that has sections we populate each time we read a text that we anticipate writing about. Ours consists of the following section headings: "source info," "context," "project," "notes," and "significance." Create your own by opening a new word processing document. Save it as "Reading Notes Template," and write the section headings that will guide your notes as you read a text that is important to your research.

Ideally, you will work directly from your notes in the drafting process. Consider, then, what kind of notes will allow you to do the writing you'd like to do. For instance, your headings might prompt you to describe the whole text, connect specific ideas to their locations in the text, respond to individual passages, make connections to things outside of the text, and so on.

Works Cited

Bazerman, Charles. "Physicists Reading Physics: Schema-Laden Purposes and Purpose-Laden Schema." *Written Communication*, vol. 2, no. 1, Jan. 1985, pp. 3–23. *SAGE Journals*, doi:10.1177/0741088385002001001.

Dilthey, Wilhelm. *Wilhelm Dilthey: Selected Works, Volume IV: Hermeneutics and the Study of History*. Princeton UP, 2010.

Farge, Arlette. *The Allure of the Archives*. Translated by Thomas Scott-Railton. Yale UP, 2013.

Gadamer, Hans-Georg. *Truth and Method*. A&C Black, 2013.

Guillory, John. "How Scholars Read." *ADE Bulletin*, no. 146, 2008, pp. 8–17. *CrossRef*, doi:10.1632/ade.146.8.

Haas, Christina, and Linda Flower. "Rhetorical Reading Strategies and the Construction of Meaning." *College Composition and Communication*, vol. 39, no. 2, 1988, pp. 167–83. *Google Scholar*, doi:10.2307/358026.

Hayles, Katherine. *How We Became Posthuman: Virtual Bodies in Cybernetics, Literature, and Informatics*. U of Chicago P, 1999.

Heidegger, Martin. *Being and Time: A Translation of Sein Und Zeit*. State U of New York P, 1996.

Hillesund, Terje. "Digital Reading Spaces: How Expert Readers Handle
Books, the Web and Electronic Paper." *First Monday*, vol. 15, no. 4,
2010. *Google Scholar*, uncommonculture.org/ojs/index.php/fm/article/
view/2762/2504.

Howard, Rebecca Moore, et al. "Writing from Sources, Writing from Sentences."
Writing & Pedagogy, vol. 2, no. 2, 2010, pp. 177–92.

Kahneman, Daniel. *Thinking, Fast and Slow*. Farrar, Straus and Giroux, 2011.

Lawrence Livermore National Laboratory. *Natalia Zaitseva*. 4 Feb. 2015.
Lawrence Livermore Laboratory News, www.llnl.gov/news/lawrence-
livermore-physicist-be-inducted-alameda-county-women%E2%80%99s-
hall-fame.

Lewis, Colin. "Annotated Bibliography: Work & Faith." *The Christian Librarian*,
vol. 61, no. 2, Dec. 2018, pp. 236–40.

McCloskey, Deirdre N. "Scholars Talk Writing: Deirdre McCloskey." Interview
by Rachel Toor. *Chronicle of Higher Education*, 20 Mar. 2016, www
-chronicle-com.ezproxy.cul.columbia.edu/article/Scholars-Talk-Writing
-Deirdre/235767.

---. *The Rhetoric of Economics*, 2nd ed. U of Wisconsin P, 1998.

Nabokov, Vladimir. *Lectures on Literature*. Houghton Mifflin Harcourt, 2017.

Noyes, Jan M., and Kate J. Garland. "Computer-vs. Paper-Based Tasks: Are They
Equivalent?" *Ergonomics*, vol. 51, no. 9, 2008, pp. 1352–75. *Google Scholar*,
doi:10.1080/00140130802170387.

Pinker, Steven. "Scholars Talk Writing: Steven Pinker." Interview by Rachel Toor.
Chronicle of Higher Education, 1 Aug. 2016, www-chronicle-com.ezproxy
.cul.columbia.edu/article/Scholars-Talk-Writing-Steven/237315.

Piolat, Annie, et al. "Cognitive Effort during Note Taking." *Applied Cognitive
Psychology*, vol. 19, no. 3, Apr. 2005, pp. 291–312. *Wiley Online Library*,
doi:10.1002/acp.1086.

Poe, Edgar Allan. *The Complete Works of Edgar Allan Poe*. Vol. IX, Cosimo, 2009.

Porter-O'Donnell, Carol. "Beyond the Yellow Highlighter: Teaching Annotation
Skills to Improve Reading Comprehension." *English Journal*, vol. 93, no. 5,
2004, pp. 82–89. *JSTOR*, doi:10.2307/4128941.

Spencer, Carrie. "Research on Learners' Preferences for Reading from a Printed
Text or from a Computer Screen." *Journal of Distance Education*, vol. 21,
no. 1, 2006, pp. 33–50.

Walkowitz, Judith R. "On Taking Notes." *Perspectives on History*, vol. 47, no. 1,
Jan. 2009, pp. 38–39.

....

CHAPTER 8

Getting Things Written

Mindset: Scholars Write to Think

Jack Kerouac explained that he wrote his famous novel *On the Road* by inserting long rolls of paper into his typewriter and typing furiously (Flood 13). When one roll ran out, he taped it to a new one and kept writing. In all, Kerouac said that he composed the entire novel over the course of three weeks in April of 1951 using six rolls of paper (Flood 13). What's more, he explained, in the final published version he revised very little of what appeared on those roles—a remarkable feat (Flood 13). In a 1968 interview, Kerouac explained why he resisted revising: "By not revising what you've already written you simply give the reader the actual workings of your mind during the writing itself: you confess your thoughts about events in your own unchangeable way" (Kerouac). He suggests that a writer's first thoughts are more honest and authentic, especially if that writer is blessed with talent like Kerouac's.

What Kerouac didn't mention is that once the six rolls were typed up onto standard 8½ by 11-inch pages, he spent years going over the pages, cutting, reorganizing, and rewriting (Flood 13). You can see a typical page of his revisions in Figure 8.1. How does this page help you interpret Kerouac's claims about not revising? For our part, we don't think that puncturing Kerouac's myth diminishes what he accomplished in

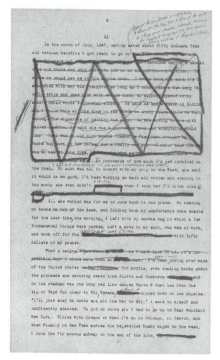

FIGURE 8.1

Manuscript page from *On the Road* by Jack Kerouac. Copyright Jack Kerouac, used by permission of The Wylie Agency LLC.

On the Road. Instead, we hope to demonstrate that skillful writing is the product of deliberate practices that we can all use rather than a form of genius that only some are born with.

The seeming messiness of Kerouac's revisions—he's crossed out or rewritten as much as he's left alone—is typical of expert researchers as well. When we examine their materials, we find piles of notes and drafts full of clunky sentences and half-formed ideas. Experts' messy writing represents thinking that is evolving on the page, becoming more complex, more original, and more interesting. This rather counterintuitive reality—more-experienced writers tend to produce messier drafts than less-experienced writers—underscores a truth that runs through this book: successful, published writers aren't necessarily smarter, faster, or more talented than less-experienced writers. Instead, they are better at recognizing their limitations and adopting strategies for *working around* these limitations.

Scholars Recognize the Limits of Their Memories

Composition researchers who compare the drafting and revising habits of college students and professional writers find surprising differences (Crowley; Faigley and Witte; Sommers). Early in their college careers, undergraduates are more likely to begin writing only after they have envisioned in their minds what the completed text will say. Because their thinking feels fully formed before they begin a draft, they are reluctant to revise their ideas once they begin writing. Instead, they focus on what researchers Lester Faigley and Stephen Witte characterize as "surface changes" to individual words, revisions that do not change the meanings of the sentences (Faigley and Witte 408). Most frequently, early undergraduate writers' revisions involve swapping out a word for a better-sounding synonym (Faigley and Witte 408). As one first-year undergraduate told researcher Nancy Sommers, "I go over and change words around" (Sommers 381). Faigley and Witte argue that this focus on "surface changes" frequently does not make texts better and sometimes makes them worse (411).

When Nancy Sommers interviewed expert writers about their processes, they described a different approach; they emphasized using writing to think and rethink ideas rather than only to reword ideas. Said one, "My first draft is usually very scattered. In rewriting, I find the line of argument. After the argument is resolved, I am much more interested in word choice and phrasing" (Sommers 384). While we might expect that professional writers start projects feeling even surer of what they want to write, they typically start writing *before* they know what they want to say. They jot down their early, partially formed ideas. Then, through the act of writing and rewriting those ideas, they shape them into fully formed thoughts. Thus, expert writers do more dramatic rethinking of their drafts on the page than less-experienced writers (Faigley and Witte 408).

Cognitive psychologist Ronald Kellogg and educational psychologist Deborah McCutchen find that the differences between the writing practices of professionals and less-experienced writers can be explained by the different ways that writers rely on their working memories—the system the brain uses to hold and process information over a short

TIME SAVER

Refine Sentences Last

The more time a writer has put into crafting the most elegant phrasing or finding the perfect word, the less willing they will be to revise or delete those words. In the earlier stages of a writing project, when the project develops the most from thinking and rethinking on the page, writers benefit from being willing to omit, revise, or move sentences. Thus, experienced writers typically wait to refine sentences until the later stages of their processes.

period of time (Kellogg; McCutchen, "A Capacity Theory of Writing"). Less-experienced writers tend to overload their working memories—for instance, attempting to hold too many thoughts in their heads before writing them down or attempting to do too many revision tasks at the same time. Experienced writers, on the other hand, employ practices that sometimes look messy on the page but place fewer demands on their working memories. As one of Sommers's expert writers explains, "I can only conceptualize so much in my first draft—only so much information can be held in my head at one time; my rewriting efforts are a reflection of how much information I can encompass at one time" (Sommers 384).

These different writing practices produce different results on the page. By reducing the demands on their working memories, experienced writers can focus more attention on developing more complex ideas.

RESEARCH ON WRITING

Deborah McCutchen's "Knowledge, Processing, and Working Memory"

When novice writers try to juggle too many writing tasks at once—when, say, they try to generate new ideas, structure their texts, and polish their sentences at the same time—they overwhelm their working memories. Educational psychologist Deborah McCutchen finds that writers with overtaxed working memories have difficulty performing complex writ-

continued

ing tasks. When asked to analyze a text, for instance, these writers will instead revert to strictly summarizing the text ("Knowledge, Processing, and Working Memory" 20). It's not necessarily that novice writers don't know how to analyze, but rather that their memories are too overloaded to perform analysis.

McCutchen also highlights certain writing situations that can even further overburden writers' memories and limit their thinking. These situations include . . .

- Tackling unfamiliar types of writing—for instance, writing a policy memo or an engineering research report for the first time.
- Writing about unfamiliar subjects—perhaps writing about the Brazilian banking system or the science of tornadoes for the first time.

Writers in these challenging situations—which require new structures of thought and new language—can overburden their working memories so much that they instead turn their full attention to a more familiar task: crafting individual sentences ("Knowledge, Processing, and Working Memory" 18). This tight focus on single sentences prevents writers from attending to higher impact concerns like developing sophisticated ideas that evolve across paragraphs ("Knowledge, Processing, and Working Memory" 18).

Takeaways: 1) Writers produce more sophisticated thinking when they focus on just one writing or revision goal at a time. 2) Writers working on unfamiliar projects and subjects should use strategies for developing their ideas across paragraphs rather than strictly dealing with each sentence in isolation.

Read the research: McCutchen, Deborah. "Knowledge, Processing, and Working Memory: Implications for a Theory of Writing." *Educational Psychologist*, vol. 35, no. 1, 2000, pp. 13–23. *Google Scholar*, doi:10.1207/S15326985EP3501_3.

Scholars' Writing Processes Are Goal-Driven

You may have received advice to break down your writing process into steps: first prewriting; then outlining; then drafting; followed by revising and editing; and, finally, proofreading. These lists of steps are helpful in the sense that they show writers the range of tasks they might perform in their writing processes. However, such lists seldom reflect how most scholars actually write. Research in composition studies demonstrates that instead . . .

- *Scholars don't follow a single set of steps in their writing processes.* Not only do scholars practice a wide range of writing processes, but individual scholars' practices also change from project to project (Harris 54–55; Faigley and Witte 410). In reality, experts experiment with their processes. When one approach doesn't work, they try new ones.
- *Scholars tend to draft and revise recursively, returning to earlier tasks before moving forward.* As experts begin drafting one paragraph, for instance, they may discover something that leads them to go back and revise an earlier paragraph (Sommers 378).

If scholars don't follow any single, fixed, linear writing process, how do they actually determine what writing tasks to perform? In their classic study "A Cognitive Process Theory of Writing," Linda Flower and John R. Hayes demonstrate that experienced writers choose tasks based on their "own set of self-made goals" (379). Flower and Hayes find that the less-experienced writers they studied were likewise goal-driven. However, they selected goals that tended to be more rigid and harder to execute. For example, a less-experienced writer might seek to write in a way that appeals to readers. This is certainly a worthwhile goal, but it may be too broad to translate into specific tasks targeting specific passages. A more experienced writer might approach a similar aim differently by . . .

1. Identifying well-defined goals (Flower and Hayes 377–78).

    Goal: Make difficult concepts accessible to readers.

2. Setting narrower subgoals that would help them achieve their larger goal (Flower and Hayes 377–78). Notice that each subgoal translates into a practical task:

    Subgoal #1: Identify key terms that would be unfamiliar or challenging to most readers.
    Subgoal #2: Define the key terms.

3. Revising their goals in response to what they discovered while writing (Flower and Hayes 378–79). As they write, perhaps

the experienced writer discovers that some difficult terms still remain too abstract, so they add a third subgoal:

Subgoal #3: Offer examples of how one might apply abstract terms.

Given the research about expert writers' processes, our advice in the Tools & Techniques section will help you decide which writing tasks you might choose based on your goals for writing.

Tools & Techniques: Writing to Think and to Polish

German studies scholar and writing teacher Rebecca Schuman is a prolific writer; she published two books and several articles in just a few years. But, she points out, her writing habits are ones that anybody can practice:

> I cannot possibly overemphasize the fact that I am neither unusually gifted nor very industrious nor really disciplined. I finished all of that writing with a deceptively simple system of doing just a little bit of work, mostly every day, and trusting that the "brilliance" (or acceptability) of the whole would come together through the drudgery of many, many, many (many) smaller, less-brilliant parts (Schuman).

Schuman's approach, to do "just a little bit of work, mostly every day" on "smaller, less-brilliant parts," is an effective one. In what follows, we offer techniques for tackling this sort of steady, manageable work efficiently.

PRACTICE

Reduce Demands on Your Memory

Consider the research comparing more-experienced and less-experienced writers' approaches to drafting. Which group would you consider more efficient? Inexperienced writers tend to keep more of the ideas and structures that they initially draft (Faigley and Witte 407–08). Does this mean that they don't have to work as hard or as long as experienced writers to produce the same results? Not necessarily.

To explore your assumptions about efficient writing habits, try the following two drawing exercises. For each exercise, try to produce an image that looks as close as possible to the photograph of the Mexican bean beetle (see Photo 8.1). Spend no more than ten minutes on each drawing.

Task #1: Beginning in the top left corner of the grid below, draw the beetle image one square at a time. Do not move on to a new square until you complete the previous one.

Task #2: Draw the beetle image by first loosely, lightly sketching a rough outline of the big shapes and then the smaller shapes. Next draw a more refined outline on top of your rough outline. Then, add light shading where needed. Finally, add darker shading where needed.

Drawing #1

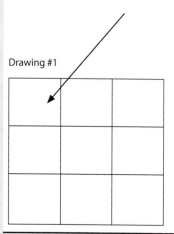

Drawing #2

Photo 8.1
A Mexican bean beetle on a soy plant leaf. Photo by Stephen Ausmus, courtesy of the Agricultural Research Service.

continued

Compare your two drawings. 1) Which looks most like the photograph? 2) Which was faster to draw? 3) Which was more difficult to draw (and therefore more likely to encourage procrastination)?

produces more-satisfying results.

later moving to fine-tuning tasks. This approach demands less and, at the same time, ers who focus on one writing task at a time, starting with larger conceptual tasks and harder to produce less-satisfying results. Drawing task #2 echoes the practices of writ- effective whole. It also overloads the working memories of writers, who thus work produces sentences that may sound strong on their own but may not connect in an sentences in sequence, and polishing each before moving on to the next. This approach efficiency, tackle multiple writing tasks at the same time: generating ideas, composing

TAKEAWAY: Drawing task #1 echoes the practices of writers who, in the name of

Writing Efficiently

Efficient writing practices can feel counterintuitive because they tend to generate a lot of ideas, structures, and words that won't appear in the final draft. Yet, as the drawing exercise demonstrates, experts' seemingly messy practices are more efficient because they require less memory-intensive effort to produce more complex and polished thinking in the end. When less-experienced writers, in the desire to be efficient, mistakenly take on too many writing tasks at one time, they often create a further problem. They become more likely to procrastinate or experience writer's block.

MYTH VS. REALITY

Myth: Procrastination stems from a lack of character or work ethic.
Reality: Procrastination stems from habits that writers can change.

When writers procrastinate, it is often because they employ habits that create difficult, high-pressure, memory-taxing situations. No wonder they want to put it off. Habits that can lead to procrastination include attempting to . . .

- Write a whole draft in a single sitting.
- Make the first draft the final draft.
- Write in sequence, starting with the first sentence, then the second, and so on.

- Polish each sentence before moving on to the next.
- Write without forward-looking feedback.

Not only do these habits increase pressure on writers, they also tax memories and shut down revision. Writers are thus stuck with their first thoughts.

The following habits help writers avoid procrastination by lowering pressure and easing demands on memory. Crucially, they also help writers produce more complex thinking. To avoid procrastination, writers can . . .

- Break down large writing projects into a series of small, manageable tasks.
- Do low-pressure composing in the early stages. Try freewriting, recording, talking out ideas, drawing, listing, and so on.
- Draft from easy sections to hard sections rather than from beginning to end. In other words, start with the section that feels easiest to write. Save the most daunting sections—typically the introduction and conclusion—for last.
- Overproduce, writing sentences you won't mind revising or deleting.
- Save polishing prose until the later stages of writing. Generate early; edit late.
- Seek out feedback along the way. In Chapter 9, you will find strategies for getting the feedback you need.
- Do multiple drafts, each focusing on just a few goals at a time.
- Write in multiple sittings over multiple days.

Choosing Tasks Based on Your Goals

Research in cognitive psychology emphasizes the power of doing *fewer* writing tasks at one time. But how do scholars choose which writing tasks to focus on? They choose based on their goals and subgoals for writing. Linda Flower and John R. Hayes emphasize that successful writers are able to define specific, feasible subgoals (377-78). How do you know if your subgoals are feasible? Ask yourself whether you can define a task that would achieve them. Here we name different tasks that can help you achieve your goals in drafting and revising.

Write to Download Your Memory

Professional researchers use writing to download from their brains all the ideas they have about a project. Getting ideas down on paper—even in the form of quick notes—can free up your memory to come up with new, more complex thoughts.

- Make a bulleted list. List all your thoughts on a project; worry about structuring those thoughts later.
- Freewrite for a set amount of time. Write without stopping or going back to reread.
- Record yourself talking out your ideas. Use an audio recorder or a speech-to-text program. (If you are using *Google Docs*, try the "voice typing" tool.)
- Talk it out. Ask a writing center consultant or a friend to take notes on what you are saying.

Write to Generate New Thinking

As we described in Chapter 1, experienced writers have a number of techniques that help them write their way into "knowledgeable ignorance" (Firestein 11). Often they write as quickly as they can, not worrying about editing their prose until later.

- Start writing before you know what you want to say.
- Freewrite, not worrying about grammar or correctness.
- Record yourself talking out your ideas.
- Talk it out with others.
- Start writing whatever section you know the most about.
- Resist editing. To focus your attention on new thinking, resist going back to polishing old thinking. Move forward.
- Blind type. To resist editing your language too early, cover your laptop screen with a piece of paper or make the font color the same as the background color while you draft.

Revise to Complicate and Extend

After generating initial thinking, writers return to their drafts to identify opportunities to complicate their ideas or extend them further. One of the most efficient ways to do this is to disrupt your existing assumptions by considering others' perspectives—whether those perspectives come from other texts or a reader.

- Revisit your reading notes. Look for ideas that bring greater nuance to your thoughts.
- Add a complicating source. Introduce a text or idea that your claim cannot make sense of right away; how might you revise your claim to account for this new source?
- Get feedback. Share your draft with a trusted reader, a writing center consultant, or an instructor. See the next chapter for advice about seeking feedback.

Revise to Better Incorporate Sources

Throughout their project, as their ideas develop, writers consider which voices they want to incorporate into the scholarly conversation to serve various functions: context, object, critical, and theory sources (which we explain in Chapter 6).

- Reread your reading notes. Notice what remaining key ideas might enliven the conversation you create in your text.
- Give readers context.
- Explain the source's project.
- Describe sources' relationships to each other.

Revise to Structure

Writers look for the relationships among the parts of the piece they are writing. They ask themselves how the parts are connected, what order makes the most sense for their readers, and which parts might no longer be necessary.

- Describe what your draft says and does. For each paragraph of your draft, list what it says (in other words, summarize) and what it does (in other word, describe the function it plays in the text, such as "sets up a problem" or "describes my method"). Try out different structures, focusing on approaches that alternately heighten and satisfy readers' curiosity, as we explain in Chapter 10.
- Reverse-outline. After drafting, make an outline that describes your draft to get a snapshot of your existing structure. Then experiment with alternatives.
- Talk through different structures with others. Get feedback on the approaches that feel the most enlightening and clear to them.

Revise to Polish and Present

In the final stages of the writing process, expert writers typically concern themselves with sentence-level matters of style that will help their readers. We'll offer some specifics in Chapter 15.

- Read your draft aloud.
- Have someone else read your draft aloud.
- Add signposts. Chapter 10 describes signposting strategies.
- Read for redundancies.
- Revise for concision.

Revise to Correct Sentence-Level Mistakes

After other revisions, seasoned scholars carefully review their work to correct any mistakes in grammar, punctuation, syntax, and formatting.

- Read the draft multiple times, looking for a single error each time.
- Use the "find" command in your word processor to locate your common mistakes.
- Read backward. Start with the last sentence of your draft. Read it aloud to spot errors. Then move to the second-to-the-last sentence and so on. Reading backward increases the likelihood that you will read what is actually on the page rather than what you think is on the page.
- Use spell checkers and grammar checkers cautiously. These tools catch some mistakes, but they create others (Lunsford and Lunsford 795–96). Grammar apps carry the same limits as the checkers built into word processing programs (Dembsey 67, 84-85).

Notice that the tasks we've listed move from writing and revision that explores to revision that polishes (see Figure 8.2). Early in their processes, writers seek to generate new thinking. At these moments, they choose tasks that record their initial thinking and then complicate or question it. These tasks deliberately employ unpolished, provisional writing that writers won't mind revising or crossing out as their thinking evolves. Later in the process, writers seek to refine and clarify their thinking. At these moments, they choose tasks that help them envision how readers will experience the text.

Earlier: Explore new thinking and structures

Use strategies that produce unpolished writing, which invites rethinking.

Later: Polish thinking with a reader in mind

Use strategies that polish, making your thinking accessible to readers.

Figure 8.2
In order to lessen demands on their memories, expert writers typically think of sentence refining as a separate—and later—task than generating new ideas.

TURN TO YOUR RESEARCH

Define Goals, Subgoals, and Tasks

When composition studies scholar David Bartholomae writes, he uses two notepads: "one to write on," he explains, and "one for making plans, storing sentences, and taking notes" (193). This second note pad serves as a designated space for Bartholomae to formulate goals while he writes. This strategy echoes Linda Flower and John R. Hayes's research showing that expert writers 1) set specific goals, 2) identify feasible subgoals, and 3) revise their goals as they write (379, 381–82).

To try Bartholomae's method, create your own planning document. Use this document to . . .

1. List specific goals and subgoals that you can translate into tasks.
2. Revise your goals as your project evolves.
3. Focus on accomplishing no more than two or three goals at once. Check them off when they are completed.
4. Accomplish goals related to generating your ideas before turning to goals related to fine-tuning sentences.

Works Cited

Ausmus, Stephen. *Mexican Bean Beetle, Epilachna Varivestis.* 18 Aug. 2016. *United States Department of Agriculture, Agricultural Research Service,* www.ars.usda.gov/oc/images/photos/jun06/d496-82/.

Bartholomae, David. *Writing on the Margins: Essays on Composition and Teaching.* Palgrave Macmillan, 2005.

Crowley, Sharon. "Components of the Composing Process." *College Composition and Communication*, vol. 28, no. 2, 1977, pp. 166–69. *JSTOR*, doi:10.2307/356106.

Dembsey, J. M. "Closing the *Grammarly*® Gaps: A Study of Claims and Feedback from an Online Grammar Program." *Writing Center Journal*, vol. 36, no. 1, 2017, pp. 63-100. *JSTOR*, www.jstor.org/stable/44252638.

Faigley, Lester, and Stephen Witte. "Analyzing Revision." *College Composition and Communication*, vol. 32, no. 4, 1981, pp. 400–14. *Google Scholar*, doi:10.2307/356602.

Firestein, Stuart. *Ignorance: How It Drives Science.* Oxford UP, 2012.

Flood, Alison. "On the Road Just as Jack Kerouac Wrote It." *The Bookseller*, no. 5290, July 2007, p. 13.

Flower, Linda, and John R. Hayes. "A Cognitive Process Theory of Writing." *College Composition and Communication*, vol. 32, no. 4, 1981, pp. 365–87. *JSTOR*, doi:10.2307/356600.

Harris, Muriel. "Composing Behaviors of One- and Multi-Draft Writers." *Concepts in Composition: Theory and Practice in the Teaching of Writing*, edited by Irene L. Clark, Routledge, 2011, pp. 52–69.

Kellogg, Ronald T. "A Model of Working Memory in Writing." *The Science of Writing: Theories, Methods, Individual Differences and Applications*, edited by C. Michael Levy and Sarah Ransdell, Routledge, 2013, pp. 57–71.

Kerouac, Jack. *On the Road.* 1955. Jack Kerouac Papers, Berg Collection, New York Public Library.

---. "The Art of Fiction No. 41: Jack Kerouac." Interview by Ted Berrigan. *Paris Review*, no. 43, summer 1968, www.theparisreview.org/interviews/4260/jack-kerouac-the-art-of-fiction-no-41-jack-kerouac.

Lunsford, Andrea A., and Karen J. Lunsford. "'Mistakes Are a Fact of Life': A National Comparative Study." *College Composition and Communication*, vol. 59, no. 4, 2008, pp. 781–806.

McCutchen, Deborah. "A Capacity Theory of Writing: Working Memory in Composition." *Educational Psychology Review*, vol. 8, no. 3, Sept. 1996, pp. 299–325. *SpringerLink*, doi:10.1007/BF01464076.

---. "Knowledge, Processing, and Working Memory: Implications for a Theory of Writing." *Educational Psychologist*, vol. 35, no. 1, 2000, pp. 13–23. *Google Scholar*, doi:10.1207/S15326985EP3501_3.

Schuman, Rebecca. "A New Series on Scholarly Productivity: 'Are You Writing?'" *Chronicle of Higher Education*, Oct. 2018, www.chronicle.com/article/A-New-Series-on-Scholarly/244689.

Sommers, Nancy. "Revision Strategies of Student Writers and Experienced Adult Writers." *College Composition and Communication*, vol. 31, no. 4, Dec. 1980, pp. 378–88. *JSTOR*, doi:10.2307/356588.

CHAPTER 9

Feedback

Read the research: Elsa Olivetti is a professor of materials science and engineering at the Massachusetts Institute of Technology. She studies how to make materials more recyclable and sustainable. For an example of her research, we recommend "Lithium-ion Battery Supply Chain Considerations: Analysis of Potential Bottlenecks in Critical Metals" in *Joule*.

Mindset: Scholars Seek Feedback That Keeps Them in Control

Elsa Olivetti's early experience as a researcher in materials science is common for junior scientists: she received plenty of feedback on her writing. And it is easy to understand why she might have needed feedback at this early stage of her scholarly development. She was still learning what it means to produce professional research. Yet now that she is a professor and has started her own research group, Olivetti continues to seek out feedback. Is that because she struggles to write? Not at all. Olivetti regularly publishes her research: she has authored or co-authored over 110 published articles. Still, in the 2017 article by Olivetti that we cite earlier, she and her three co-authors thank five readers who gave them feedback. In this chapter, we'll explain not only why scholars like Olivetti seek out feedback, but we'll also talk about the specific kinds of feedback they value and how they get it.

Scholars Are Hungry for Feedback

In order to understand why expert writers seek feedback, we return to the point we made in Chapters 1 and 2: seasoned writers begin by seeking out what they don't know—"knowledgeable ignorance," in neurobiologist Stuart Firestein's words (7). The very act of writing allows scholars to see what they do and don't understand and to find new questions to ask. They write their way into discovering new scholarly problems, pursuing new projects, and offering new claims. When they seek feedback, scholars are again searching for knowledgeable ignorance, testing their assumptions against reader's feedback. When writers see the places where readers understood or didn't understand their work, they discover gaps and possibilities in their own writing.

Elsa Olivetti offers an additional reason why she seeks feedback: forming her thoughts in conversation with others makes her "a part of the community" of her fellow scientists. We find it reassuring that even seasoned writers seek out feedback. Expert researchers like Olivetti don't just arrive at original and significant ideas because of their unique brilliance but because they practice a habit any writer can emulate: seeking out feedback from other members of their scholarly communities. What counts as a scholarly community? For some researchers, scholarly communities consist of a network of thinkers who have collaborated with each other (see Figure 9.1). For less-experienced writers, communities can consist of classmates, peer workshop groups, writing center consultants, and so on.

Writers Stay in Charge of Their Work

In "Responding to Student Writing," the researcher Nancy Sommers argues that the most valuable feedback for undergraduate writers helps them rethink their initial ideas in order to pursue their own goals in

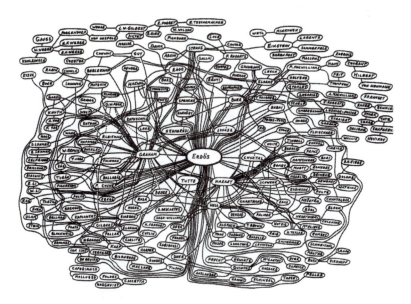

FIGURE 9.1
Collaboration among researchers is common. This visualization of a scholarly community shows the network of mathematicians who coauthored research papers; each line represents a scholarly collaboration (Odda 167). At the center of the drawing is Hungarian mathematician Paul Erdős, who coauthored papers with over five hundred researchers. We can see that an entire field of research is driven by cooperation among scholars.

writing (153–54). Sommers found that student writers were more motivated to revise when their instructor's feedback aimed at fulfilling the student's vision of the project rather than the instructor's vision (149–50). What can writers take away from Sommers's study? Writers who adopt a sense of ownership over their writing—that is, they take responsibility for deciding how to develop a project—are more likely to make the kinds of meaningful revisions that experts regularly make in their own writing.

This mindset might seem paradoxical: we've argued that the best writers are hungry for feedback, yet we also argue that expert writers stay in charge of their work. This paradox suggests that writers who feel ownership seek *particular kinds* of input that allow them to advance their own projects. They look for readers who won't dictate how to revise (which would give the reader the power to determine the project) but will instead describe their reading experiences. With a clear picture of what their readers experience, writers can then make more informed decisions about how to pursue their own projects. In Tools & Techniques, we offer examples of the kind of feedback that motivates and helps writers.

Tools & Techniques: Asking for, Using, and Giving Feedback

Elsa Olivetti's experience seeking feedback goes against the common myth that only struggling writers need help. When people become more experienced at writing, they don't seek out less feedback; they tend to seek out more. And the nature of the feedback they seek may change as well. Here, we'll offer strategies to 1) ask for feedback that improves your immediate project, 2) use feedback to improve more broadly as a writer, and 3) give feedback that helps other writers make their own choices.

Ask for Feedback That Improves Your Immediate Project

How do writers receive feedback that lets them stay in charge of their projects? They ask for it. In particular, seasoned writers ask for feedback that is appropriate for where they are in the writing process. For instance, while generating ideas, writers often seek feedback on whether their project seems interesting and feasible. While structuring their thinking, writers may seek feedback on the logical progression of their ideas. Only after they solidify their projects do writers seek sentence-level feedback that helps them polish their language.

How, specifically, do writers ask for feedback? What do they ask their readers to do? Nancy Sommers's research suggests that asking for evaluative feedback like "Is it good?" or "Do you like it?" or prescriptive feedback like "What do I need to revise?" or "Tell me what to fix" can shut down productive revision. These prompts make the reader responsible for defining what counts as a successful project. Such prompts can encourage writers to edit only the sections that readers mention, therefore limiting the kind of major rethinking that experts use to push their ideas forward.

Instead, Sommers recommends that readers use **descriptive feedback** to narrate the experiences they have while reading: Where did they experience confusion, boredom, surprise, or curiosity? (148) Not only does Sommers's approach retain writers' ownership of their projects, it takes the pressure off of readers. No longer do readers have to worry about hurting writers' feelings with criticism or propping them up with praise. Their task is not to evaluate but to describe.

The following prompts can help you receive descriptive feedback that tells you how your writerly choices impact a reader.

To learn whether your draft gets your ideas across, ask for . . .

- A *"say back"* response. Ask the reader to "say back" to you the scholarly problem they think you're addressing, the project you're pursuing, and the main claim you're making.

KEY TERM

Descriptive Feedback

Descriptive feedback is a form of responding to others' writing that recounts one's experiences rather than evaluates. Descriptive feedback does not say whether a text is good or bad or whether it works or doesn't work; instead, it narrates the reader's experience (for instance, "Here I was confused," "Here I felt excited," "This section made me wonder . . ."). Such feedback helps writers identify gaps between what they intended and what the reader experienced. The writer can then work to close those gaps by revising.

Do differences emerge between what the reader says and what you intended to communicate? How can you revise your writing to minimize those differences?

- *A says/does response.* At the end of each paragraph or section, ask your reader to note what the section says (summary) and what it does (the function it serves in the text). For example, the opening paragraph of this chapter *says* that the more writing experience Elsa Olivetti gained, the more she valued feedback, and it *does* work to introduce a tension that drives the chapter. The "says/does" strategy can help you see if you are getting your ideas across (says) and whether those ideas seem to serve your project (does).
- *An expect/experience response.* Before your reader reads a particular section of your writing, ask them to jot down what they expect it to accomplish. Then, after they've read the section, ask them to tell you what they actually experienced. The differences between the two will show you places where a writer was surprised. You can then decide if that feeling of surprise advances or interferes with your project.

To test whether the draft is creating your desired impact, ask readers to . . .

- *Narrate their reading experience.* Ask "Where do you find yourself slowing down?" "Where do you find your energy/interest going up or down?" "Where do questions come up?"
- *Name takeaways.* After reading the whole draft, ask your reader to describe what they take away from the experience. What will stay with them?

To learn where your reader needs more or less analysis and context, ask your reader to . . .

- *Code each passage* with one of these four categories: 1) "already knew," 2) "didn't know but didn't want to know" (or "TMI"), 3) "wanted to know," 4) "want to know more." You can then discover which parts of your work need elaboration and which parts need trimming.

Use Feedback to Improve as a Writer

Feedback can do more than help you decide how to revise individual passages. Even if you receive feedback on only a portion of your work, you can use that feedback to strengthen an entire draft and, better yet, to develop more broadly as a writer. The kind of feedback that is most likely to develop your writing skills looks forward rather than backward. While backward-looking feedback pronounces a final judgment on a finished piece of writing, forward-looking feedback assumes that the writing process is ongoing. Forward-looking feedback is future-focused and meant to prompt a writer both to revise a specific piece of work and to work more broadly on their writing development.

We recommend three strategies for using forward-looking feedback to promote your writing development:

1. *Notice patterns.* Does the feedback you receive on one passage describe something that also occurs in other places in your writing? If so, use that feedback to motivate revisions of each occurrence. For instance, perhaps a reader notes that a particular transition befuddled them. If you use that transition strategy often, apply the reader's feedback to the entire draft and also to future projects.

2. *Prioritize high-impact revisions.* Composition studies scholars Lester Faigley and Stephen Witte found that less-experienced writers are more apt to make "copy-editing adjustments" to their drafts rather than more substantial "meaning changes" (402–03). In other words, inexperienced writers can feel tempted to concentrate on less-impactful revisions. Instead, prioritize issues that most influence a reader's understanding of your ideas and your credibility as a writer. For instance, rather than focusing first on comma placement, you might prioritize analyzing evidence.

3. *Use feedback to gain insight into what readers generally expect and appreciate.* If a reader describes their experience of a specific passage of your work, can you characterize the readerly desire behind that description? For instance, a reader might say, "I found myself intrigued by the quote you used, but I wasn't sure what you wanted me to take from it." From this feedback, you could draw a conclusion that might guide your future writing: readers expect writers to analyze quotations.

Give Feedback That Helps Writers Make Their Own Choices

Like other aspects of the writing process, giving helpful feedback is a learned skill, not a talent you're born with. Peer reviewers sometimes imagine that the best way to help writers is to offer a version of tough love—to be both a fierce critic who points out errors as well as a cheer-leader who acknowledges effort and gives praise. However, the role that maintains the writer's ownership of their project is that of *reader*. Playing the role of reader means simply offering the writer a clear-eyed description of what you experience while you read. Writers can then decide if their writing is producing the effect they intended.

In the following chart, we list several ways that readers can make their feedback more effective by revising evaluative language (language that judges) or prescriptive language (language that tells the writer what to do) into descriptive language (language that narrates the reader's experience).

Instead of evaluating or prescribing, such as . . .	Try describing, such as . . .
Expand.	Here, I didn't understand the connection between the study you cite and the claim you're making about it. I was wanting some explanation of how the study connects to the claim.
Move this paragraph up so that it follows the question you raise in the first paragraph.	This section answered a question that I've been waiting for an answer to since the first paragraph. Do you want to keep readers in suspense this long?
I like this quote!	A light bulb went on for me when I read this quote. It helps me see that . . .
Vague.	I read this passage twice to see if I could find a definition for this term. I've seen it used in different ways—which definition are you intending?
This is a great draft.	I walk away from this draft with a new understanding of . . . which matters to me because . . .

What does descriptive feedback look like on an actual writer's draft? Figure 9.2 shows the first paragraph of a rough draft of a research essay that one of our students, Eileen Gao, wrote as a first-year undergraduate. In the essay, Gao explores the relationship between data collection and social power by engaging with ideas from Michel Foucault, Ian Hacking, Richard Thompson Ford, and Sun-ha Hong. You will notice that Gao's draft is rough; its punctuation and wording aren't polished and her ideas and structure are not yet fully articulated. This is because her course assignment asked her to do low-pressure writing to explore her ideas rather than high-pressure polished writing. In accordance with that assignment, Gao's peer reviewers, Morgan Navarro and Mari Husain, focused not on punctuation or grammar but instead on Gao's ideas.

Husain and Navarro both describe moments of confusion they experienced while reading Gao's essay. Further, they offer reasons for their confusion. Many scholars have noted that one of the most difficult challenges for writers is to imagine how readers will experience their texts (Ong 19; Kellogg 3–4, 7–10; Sommers 148). Will readers be confused? Challenged? Invigorated? Descriptive comments like the examples here address that challenge by creating an image of a reader that Eileen Gao or any writer can carry in their minds as they decide how to revise.

Excerpt from Eileen Gao's draft of
"The Panopticon: Now Available on Mobile Devices"

. . . Foucault points out that surveilling people to collect data has been a source of social power . . . Hacking supports this idea, that classification can be used as a means of control. After enough data is collected, we can fit individuals into stereotypes that we can better understand. However, at some point data collection itself developed into something larger than the creators and diverges from the data according to Ford and Hong. Data collection and analysis have been ceded to machines and algorithms and with it, the power of data. While I agree that information is power, is any amount of information enough? How much data does a single person hold? Hacking points out that people "are moving targets because our investigations interact with them, and change them" (23). Does this mean that enough data collection will result in enough change to fully control someone?

Mari Husain: I'm having some trouble understanding how this question relates to your beginning (the part about empathy).

Morgan Navarro: This question confused me because I am not sure what is meant by "enough" and I am not sure how it relates.

FIGURE 9.2
Rough draft of Eileen Gao's essay with feedback from two classmates.

PRACTICE

Revise Prescriptive and Evaluative Feedback

Task: Try revising the following three comments on another excerpt from Eileen Gao's draft in Figure 9.3 into descriptive feedback. We understand that this rough draft might feel a little difficult to comprehend, but we think you'll still be able to revise these comments so that they are better able to prompt Eileen Gao to make changes while still retaining ownership of her project.

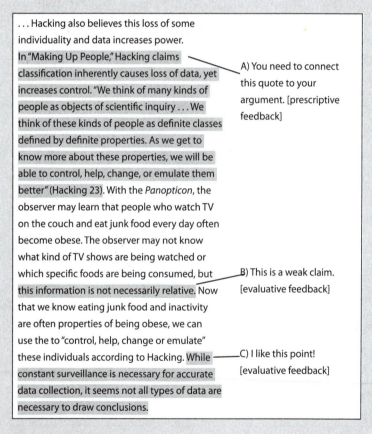

... Hacking also believes this loss of some individuality and data increases power.

In "Making Up People," Hacking claims classification inherently causes loss of data, yet increases control. "We think of many kinds of people as objects of scientific inquiry ... We think of these kinds of people as definite classes defined by definite properties. As we get to know more about these properties, we will be able to control, help, change, or emulate them better" (Hacking 23). With the *Panopticon*, the observer may learn that people who watch TV on the couch and eat junk food every day often become obese. The observer may not know what kind of TV shows are being watched or which specific foods are being consumed, but this information is not necessarily relative. Now that we know eating junk food and inactivity are often properties of being obese, we can use the to "control, help, change or emulate" these individuals according to Hacking. While constant surveillance is necessary for accurate data collection, it seems not all types of data are necessary to draw conclusions.

A) You need to connect this quote to your argument. [prescriptive feedback]

B) This is a weak claim. [evaluative feedback]

C) I like this point! [evaluative feedback]

Figure 9.3
A second excerpt from Eileen Gao's rough draft.

POSSIBLE ANSWERS: Mari Husain's actual descriptive feedback on Gao's draft is as follows:

A. I expected this quote to support the preceding statement, but I had trouble understanding how the two related to one another.

B. I'm not really sure I understand what you're saying here. If you're trying to say it's irrelevant, which would be my guess (am I reading that right?), I'm not entirely sure I'd agree that what TV shows these people watch are irrelevant necessarily. I'd want more support to believe that statement.

C. This really helped me to understand how more data might not necessarily be more power.

COMMON PITFALL

Empty Feedback

Peer reviewing—the act of giving another writer feedback on a draft—becomes unproductive when reviewers imagine that their task is to evaluate their peer's work. Playing the role of evaluator can be uncomfortable because you risk hurting a peer's feelings. To avoid being hurtful, we see many peer reviewers offer either unearned praise ("Your claim is really strong." "I like the examples you use.") or critiques that focus on aspects of writing that feel less personal, like punctuation.

Rather than evaluating, we suggest reframing your task: simply describe your experience reading the draft. Shifting from evaluative to descriptive feedback requires some practice. If you find yourself evaluating a writer's text, ask yourself, "What experience did I have while reading that led me to this evaluation?" Then simply describe that reading experience.

TURN TO YOUR RESEARCH

Part 1: Ask for the Feedback You Need

Fill in this template to ask a reader for feedback that responds to this moment in your writing process and moves you toward what you want to accomplish next.

Dear [reader's name],

This is an [early, middle, or almost-finished] draft of a project I'm planning to complete on [date]. In my next draft, I plan to focus on

continued

[one or two aspects of the draft]. At this point, I want to learn how
a reader experiences this aspect of my project. You could help me
most if you would [name one or two of the following tasks: a) say
back what you understand to be my scholarly problem, project,
and claims; b) articulate what each paragraph says and does; c)
explain what you expect a paragraph will say and then what you
experience it as actually saying; d) narrate your reading experience;
e) name key takeaways; or f) code each passage to show me where
you wanted more or less explanation]. Thanks for your feedback.

Sincerely,

[your name]

TURN TO YOUR RESEARCH

Part 2: To Improve Your Current Project, Write a Revision Plan

To make the most of the feedback you receive on a draft, review your
reader's comments and create a to-do list for yourself by completing these
three steps:

1. *Restate each piece of feedback as a revision task.* If you have
   trouble understanding how to translate the reader's experience into a task, ask yourself, "What desire is behind the
   reader's response?" For example, if a reader writes, "In the
   third paragraph, I lost the thread of your ideas," you might
   tell yourself that the reader desires to understand how each
   paragraph builds on what came before. Thus, you can restate
   their feedback as a task: "In paragraph three, indicate how
   the ideas build on paragraphs one and two."
2. *Identify feedback that could apply to your whole text.* Restate
   revision tasks about specific passages as tasks to address on
   the entire draft. For instance, if the reader writes, "Here this
   historical context about this source really helps me envision
   where it fits within the conversation," you might add an item
   to your to-do list that reads, "Each time I introduce a new
   source, determine whether to add historical context that
   would help readers place it within the larger conversation."

3. *Prioritize higher-impact tasks.* Sort your list of tasks according to the order you plan to do them, placing higher-impact issues first and lower-impact issues later. For example, you might place "analyze each quotation" toward the top of your to-do list and "delete unnecessary adjectives" toward the bottom.

TURN TO YOUR RESEARCH

Part 3: To Improve as a Writer, Keep a Revision Log

Because writers tend to take similar approaches to much of their writing, they can often apply feedback on one project to their other projects. Writers improve quickly when they translate feedback on individual drafts into larger principles and tasks that they continue to work on in future writing projects.

An efficient strategy for using feedback to develop as a writer is to keep a revision log. A revision log is a place to chart the feedback you receive on all your writing projects. Writers return to their logs to guide their revisions each time they tackle a new project. Using the following example as a model, create a revision log with three columns: feedback, principles, and tasks. Find two recent drafts that you received feedback on. In the first column, record your readers' feedback. In the second column, identify principles—or underlying ideas—that inform the readers' feedback. In the third column, give yourself a revision task that fulfills the principle. The next time you revise a draft, return to your revision log to select tasks that might improve your draft. For example,

Readers' feedback	Principles that apply to all my writing	Revision tasks
My peer reviewer says, "I'm not sure what 'This' refers to. I re-read the previous sentence to try to figure out which noun it stands in for, but I can't tell."	Readers look for a clear indication of what nouns like "this" and "that" stand in for.	On the last draft, use the "Find" command in my word processor to locate all instances of "this" and "that." Clarify which nouns they refer to.

continued

Readers' feedback	Principles that apply to all my writing	Revision tasks
My editor writes, "Your ideas about justice come alive for me when you apply them to this particular court case."	Readers can best understand abstract concepts when the writer examines how they play out with a concrete example.	In early drafts, identify places in my drafts that address abstract concepts. Explore how I might clarify these concepts by applying them to specific instances.
My professor writes, "This title tells me what you're writing about but doesn't yet make me excited to read the draft."	Readers expect titles not only to name the focus of the text but also to suggest why the reader might care.	In the middle drafts, test out different titles and get feedback from readers about which best launches my text.

Works Cited

Faigley, Lester, and Stephen Witte. "Analyzing Revision." *College Composition and Communication*, vol. 32, no. 4, 1981, pp. 400–14. *Google Scholar*, doi:10.2307/356602.

Firestein, Stuart. *Ignorance: How It Drives Science*. Oxford UP, 2012.

Hacking, Ian. "Making Up People." *London Review of Books*, 17 Aug. 2006, pp. 23–26.

Kellogg, Ronald T. "Training Writing Skills: A Cognitive Developmental Perspective." *Journal of Writing Research*, vol. 1, no. 1, 2008, pp. 1–26. *Directory of Open Access Journals*, doi:10.17239/jowr-2008.01.01.1.

Odda, Tom. "On Properties of a Well-Known Graph or What Is Your Ramsey Number?" *Annals of the New York Academy of Sciences*, vol. 328, no. 1, June 1979, pp. 166–72. *Crossref*, doi:10.1111/j.1749-6632.1979.tb17777.x.

Ong, Walter J. "The Writer's Audience Is Always a Fiction." *Publications of the Modern Language Association of America*, vol. 90, no. 1, 1975, pp. 9–21. *JSTOR*, doi:10.2307/461344.

Sommers, Nancy. "Responding to Student Writing." *College Composition and Communication*, vol. 33, no. 2, 1982, pp. 148–56. *Google Scholar*, doi:10.2307/357622.

CHAPTER 10

Structure

Mindset: Different Structures Serve Different Purposes

In a classic study, linguists Charlotte Linde and William Labov asked one hundred New Yorkers a question: "Could you tell me the lay-out of your apartment?" (925). Before you continue reading, we invite you to pause and answer their question yourself. If you don't live in an apartment, you might instead describe the layout of your childhood home.

Linde and Labov argue that answers to their question reveal how people structure their thoughts in language. The hundred responses they collected fell into two groups:

- "Tour" strategy. An overwhelming number of respondents, 97 percent, gave a verbal tour of their apartments (930). They described what someone would see as they entered the front door, then walked into the first room, and then the next room, and so on (927).
- "Map" strategy. Just 3 percent of respondents described a map of their apartments (930). They started with an overview of the floorplan: "It's laid out in a huge square pattern, broken down into four units" (929).

Which approach did you take? Linde and Labov argue that the map strategy is more likely to help listeners draw an accurate layout of the apartment (927–30). So why did most people use the tour strategy instead? Linde and Labov argue that the tour strategy served as a memory tool for the respondents: it helped them describe each room without forgetting or repeating any (930).

Composition studies researcher Linda Flower extends Linde and Labov's study of apartment layouts to the logic of structuring writing. When writers talk about "structure," they mean the sequence of a text's components—the order of sentences, paragraphs, and sections. To describe the structure of your writing is to describe its layout. Flower equates the tour strategy with what she terms "**writer-based structure**" and the map strategy with "**reader-based structure**" (28–29).

Writers strive for reader-based structures in their final drafts to clearly communicate their ideas to readers. Yet Flower argues that writer-based structures still serve a purpose: "The structures which fail to work for readers may be powerful strategies for retrieving information from memory and for exploring one's own knowledge network" (28). Because writer-based structures help writers think, they are particularly effective in the stages of a project when writers are generating ideas.

Flower's argument reveals a surprising reality of writing: structures that help scholars generate ideas are seldom the same structures that help readers understand those ideas.

Writer-Based Structures Generate New Ideas

In the idea-generating phases of writing, scholars rely on writer-based structures for the same reason that most people give tours rather than maps of their apartment layouts: these structures help writers download

---

KEY TERM

Writer-Based Structure and Reader-Based Structure

Writer-based structure is an order determined by what is most helpful for writers themselves while they're drafting, as they try to remember to include everything important (Flower 29).

Reader-based structure is an order determined by what is most helpful for readers as they encounter new ideas (Flower 20).

PRACTICE

Experiment with Writer-Based and Reader-Based Structure

Try this experiment to test Linde and Labov's claim that the map strategy is easier for listeners to follow than the more common tour strategy.

Task: Ask a friend to make two attempts at drawing the floor plan of the Bronx apartment shown in Figure 10.1 based only on your verbal descriptions. In your first description, use the tour strategy by starting with the entryway in the lower right corner of the image and describing each room as though you were walking through the space. In your second description, use the map strategy by beginning with the overall (roughly) rectangular shape of the apartment and then describing where the rooms fit into that shape.

Which one of your friend's drawings is more accurate?

FIGURE 10.1
The layout of an apartment on Independence Avenue in New York City.

all of their ideas without repeating them. Typical writer-based approaches to structure include . . .

- *A story of discovery.* A writer organizes ideas in the order that those ideas occurred to them: "At first I thought that . . . Then I realized that . . ."
- *A chronology.* When the writer is analyzing a source, they start with the beginning of the source (the opening scene of a film or the beginning of a historical event, for example) and then move sequentially through the source: "When the character first appears, she is . . . However, in the next scene, she shifts her perspective. . . ."
- *Responses to questions in the order they're posed.* When responding to a series of questions, the writer answers them in order. For instance, in response to a prompt to compare and contrast two texts, the writer begins by asserting that "The texts are similar in several ways" and then shifts to "Yet they also differ with respect to . . ."

In each case, writer-based strategies ensure that the writer has recorded all of their ideas. However, each of these structuring strategies

TIME SAVER

Avoid Writer's Block by Restructuring

Writer's block—the inability to generate writing despite the writer's effort—can feel maddening. Composition studies researcher Mike Rose suggests that certain structuring strategies can be one source of writer's block. In particular, the writers that Rose studied became blocked when they imagined that they had to stick to their initial plans (398–99). When their original writing plans—their writer-based structures—seemed not to be working, they got stuck, and writer's block set in.

Writers who avoided blocks, on the other hand, tended instead to see their plans as evolving over the course of a project (Rose 397). Why is this so? Through the act of drafting, writers complicate initial ideas in ways that call for new structures of thought. Thus, fluid writers reorganize their writing multiple times, first to advance their own thinking and later to guide a reader.

relies on experiences that the writer and reader do not share. The writer, like the person giving a tour of their apartment, draws from their memory of discovering ideas, analyzing a source, or reading questions in a prompt. The reader lacks these memories. Therefore, the writer must arrive at a structure that makes sense to someone encountering their ideas for the first time.

Reader-Based Structures Tell Stories

Later in the writing process, scholars shift their attention from structures that help them think to structures that make readers *want* to read. What makes a structure reader-based? Less-experienced writers might imagine that they help readers most by employing a reporting structure: listing the findings or conclusions of their research ("I will argue three points. First . . . Second . . . Third . . ."). And indeed, this approach helps readers by giving them a map of how the text will arrive at a claim. With this map, they are less likely to get lost along the way. However, it neglects something that readers need first: a reason to care about the claim. We call this reason for caring the "stakes."

How do writers create stakes? You'll recall that in Chapter 2 we quoted the playwright and screenwriter David Mamet, who gave the following writing advice to the writers of *The Unit*, a television series about military operatives: "Start, every time, with this inviolable rule: *The scene must be dramatic*. It must start because the hero has a problem, and it must culminate with the hero finding him or herself either thwarted or educated that another way exists" (qtd. in Haralovich 302). For Mamet, no television viewers would stay tuned just to receive a report; the audience needs drama. And the source of that drama comes from the hero facing a problem.

If dramatic problems keep viewers hooked on a television show, scholarly problems keep readers motivated to keep reading a piece of research. In drawing this comparison, we are suggesting that academic writing is a form of storytelling. In fact, scholars in the humanities and social sciences frequently talk about their research in these terms because they study people and events they want to bring to life on the page. But even scientists who study soil samples or neurotransmitters ask themselves, "What's the story of my research?"

In interviews with 106 scientists, writing studies researcher Lisa Emerson found that the more senior the science writer, the more likely they were to move away from writing as a form of reporting and embrace writing as a creative, storytelling act (12, 195–96). One senior neurobiologist explained it this way: a typical short story character "is confronted by a situation that raises the question of how will they resolve it, and has an outcome . . . that takes the character to a new state of being . . . The same may be said of scientific writing . . . In both situations, we (the readers) are taken on a journey" (qtd. in Emerson 157).

Let's look at one common way scholars take readers on a journey by comparing the structure of a story with the structure of a scholarly text:

Beginning of a story	Introduction to a scholarly text
The writer introduces characters and sets the scene.	**Context:** The writer introduces background information and the scholarly conversation.
The writer presents a dramatic problem.	**Scholarly problem:** The writer presents a difficulty arising from a gap in understanding.
Characters confront the problem.	**Project:** The writer describes an approach to confronting the problem.
Characters set off on a path toward resolving the problem.	**Claim:** The writer promises a path toward resolving the problem.
Middle of a story	**Body of a scholarly text**
Characters grapple with the problem.	**Evidence and analysis:** The writer analyzes evidence to grapple with the problem.
Characters develop as the problem becomes more complex with new characters and new events.	**Complication:** The claim develops as the problem becomes more complex with new scholars and new evidence.
Ending of a story	**Conclusion of a scholarly text**
The problem resolves in a way that offers readers new understandings of the characters to take away.	**Takeaway:** The problem resolves with a claim that offers readers a new understanding to take away.

Notice that story writers as well as scholarly writers create structures that emphasize complexity and tension: hurdles to arriving at a resolution. These structures sustain readers' curiosity, and when readers reach the conclusion, they feel the text accomplished something challenging and meaningful by overcoming the hurdles it presented.

Three Common Reader-Based Structures

Our outline of a scholarly structure is not a formula but rather one common model that cultivates readers' curiosity. Of course, writers structure stories in many ways. Some stories lack a traditional beginning, don't have clear action, or don't resolve the problem in the end. Similarly, not all scholarly research has a clear introduction, body, or conclusion. For each new project, the writer must choose a structure that best tells the story of their research. They must decide how to organize the elements of academic writing that alternate between heightening and satisfying readers' curiosity. Those elements include the following:

Curiosity-heightening elements	Curiosity-satisfying elements
• Problem	• Claim
• Project	• Evidence
• Complication (an idea that calls for rethinking a previous understanding)	• Analysis
	• Takeaway

Here we offer three variations on the common structures that appear frequently in academic writing. They differ according to where the claim appears. As you read about each, think about where they heighten or satisfy readers' curiosity.

    a. *The front-loaded claim.* The introduction previews the claim and maps out the steps it will take to arrive at that claim.

        Introduction: Context, problem, project, and *claim*
        Body: Evidence and analysis
        Conclusion: Takeaway

Writers choose this structure when they anticipate that readers will have questions about the study's methods. Social scientists and scientists commonly use it to report the results of data-driven research. Their readers want to discover the claim early so that they can then assess whether the method of analysis that follows is sufficient to justify that claim. This structure satisfies readers' curiosity early.

b. *The back-loaded claim.* The writer unveils the claim in the conclusion.

Introduction: Context, problem, and project
Body: Evidence and analysis
Conclusion: *Claim* and takeaway

Writers choose this structure when they want readers to have the experience of discovering the claim, an especially effective approach when readers may at first resist the claim. Essayistic, reflective writing in any field may favor this structure because it sustains curiosity until the end.

c. *The complex claim.* The introduction offers an overarching claim or the promise of a claim. The body then complicates the overarching claim and addresses those complications with subclaims.

Introduction: Context, problem, project, and claim (or the promise of a claim) that the text will develop
Body: Series of complications that prompt subclaims, alongside evidence and analysis
Conclusion: *Fully developed claim* and takeaway

Writers choose this structure when complications at many points in the body will sustain readers' curiosity. Writing across all disciplines often follows this structure when conveying complex claims.

MYTH VS. REALITY

Myth: Academic writing structures are governed by rigid rules.
Reality: Writers must choose the structures that best present their ideas.

You might have encountered what felt like "rules" for structuring academic writing: place claims in the last sentence of the first paragraph, place main ideas in the first and last sentences of paragraphs, use five paragraphs, and so on. When we examine published research, we discover quickly that expert researchers do not hold tightly to any rules of structure. For instance, many students are taught to present data-driven research using an introduction-methods-results-discussion (IMRD) structure. Applied linguists Kathy Ling Lin and Stephen Evans set out to study whether published scholars actually adhere to the IMRD structure themselves. They examined 433 published articles from the sciences, engineering, the social sciences, and the humanities and found that just 12 percent of the articles followed the IMRD structure (152–54). The other articles they studied employed a remarkably wide variety of structures (154).

Before we dismiss structure rules entirely, however, we might consider some common-sense readerly habits that inform them. For instance, readers won't feel motivated to continue reading until they understand the stakes of the piece, so writers typically explain the stakes in the introduction. Likewise, readers are interested in claims, so if writers place claims where readers' attention is highest—typically at the beginnings and endings of paragraphs and sections—readers will have an easier time locating the main ideas they can take away from the text.

Of these three structures, the third is perhaps the most common because it dramatizes the value of complexity that we described in Chapter 4. For this reason, we'll pay particular attention to it in the Tools & Techniques section to follow.

Tools & Techniques: Structuring to Serve Writers and Readers

Different techniques produce writer-based and reader-based structures. Writers deploy these techniques strategically depending on whether they want to generate new ideas or present a logical structure to readers.

Writer-Based Strategies for Structuring

In the Mindset section, we named three writer-based structuring approaches that scholars commonly use in the earliest stages of a project to efficiently download their thinking: a narrative of discovery, a chronology, and responses to questions in the order they're posed. Writers experiment with these approaches at moments when they want to generate new thinking. Common structuring strategies that we see writers employ for this purpose include listing and sorting, outlining, mind mapping, and reverse outlining.

The first three of these strategies help writers capture their initial thoughts and then experiment with their order to discover possible projects they might pursue. Each strategy relies on visualizing ideas and then experimenting with different ways of grouping them.

1. *Listing and sorting.* Bullet-point every idea that might go into your text. Then group related bullet points. Take notes on the relationships you see among your ideas. This strategy helps produce an initial, low-stakes structure.

2. *Outlining.* List everything that might go into your text. Identify main ideas. Then place supporting or complicating ideas under main ideas. This technique helps prioritize key ideas and determine the available supporting evidence and analysis.

3. *Mind mapping.* Visually diagram a structure by placing each idea on a field and drawing lines among related ideas to create a visual network. Maps might take the form of clusters, trees, timelines, Venn diagrams, and so on. Mind maps help visual learners and those working with nonlinear ideas. For an example of a mind map, see Chapter 7.

While listing and sorting, outlining, and mind mapping each help writers envision different structuring possibilities, they also present a limitation. They can force writers to commit to a structure before they

TIME SAVER

Mind Mapping Tools

You can find many free mind mapping tools on the web and also built into your word processor. The mind mapping tools in *Microsoft Word* appear within the "SmartArt" feature. In *Google Docs*, they appear in the "Drawing" feature. To find diagramming apps, we recommend doing a web search for "mind mapping app." You might add "outline" to your search if you're interested in tools that convert mind maps into outlines. Of course, paper and a pencil are also effective mapping tools.

have fully explored their ideas. As we discussed in Chapter 8, writing is a powerful form of thinking. If you don't do enough writing before trying to structure your ideas, you won't have a rich set of ideas to work with. The fourth strategy, reverse outlining, addresses this problem by building in a step for more fully exploring one's thinking before structuring.

> 4. *Reverse outlining.* First, freewrite or write an initial rough draft. Label each paragraph or chunk of text with its main idea. Then number the labels in the order you may want the paragraphs or chunks to appear. Reorder the labels according to any groups, patterns, or tensions that emerge.

Reader-Based Simple and Complex Structures

In Chapter 4 on claims, we explained that academic communities value complexity of thought. Complex claims, which consist of a group of sub-claims that build on one another to arrive at a main claim, signal writers' belonging in their scholarly communities (Wilder 119; Fahnestock and Secor 91). Scholars value complex claims because they are more likely to be new and, therefore, more interesting. A simple claim, on the other hand, is more likely to have already occurred to many people and therefore seem less interesting. These differences between simple and complex claims are visible in texts' structures as well. Simple claim structures often look something like Figure 10.2.

TIME SAVER

Reverse-Outlining Tools

Most word processing programs have tools to create reverse outlines. Simply create labels for each passage using the "Headings" feature in the program's "Style" menu. You can format major ideas as "Heading 1," subideas as "Heading 2," and so on. Then go to the word processor's "View" menu. In *Microsoft Word*, select the "Navigation pane" option, and in *Google Docs* select "Show document outline" option. Each will display headings as items in an outline. The navigation pane in *Microsoft Word* is especially powerful: merely dragging and dropping a heading in the navigation pane allows users to move a whole section of text.

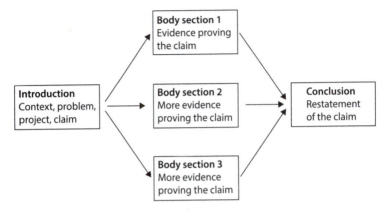

Figure 10.2
The elements of a simple claim structure. Each body section adds evidence to support the initial claim. The conclusion, then, arrives at the same place the text started: with the main claim.

A simple claim structure repeatedly argues one main claim throughout without breaking it down into subclaims. Each body section connects to the introduction and the conclusion but not to each other. The body sections each serve the same function: to add more evidence to prove the main claim. Thus, transitions between body paragraphs emphasize addition. Common transitions include "In addition," "Also," "Similarly," "Furthermore," "Likewise," "Along the same lines," and so on.

The simple claim structure can provide an efficient way to deliver a single claim. However, it also creates three challenges for readers:

- *Simplicity of ideas.* The structure features a single claim that, because it lacks complexity, will likely have already occurred to readers.
- *Repetition.* Since each body section reiterates that it is proving the main claim, readers may wonder if all the sections are necessary.
- *Few opportunities to heighten readers' curiosity.* Body sections don't offer complications that would make readers want to keep reading.

The body sections of simple claim structures function like episodic television series: shows whose episodes stand alone and whose characters don't evolve. Think, for instance, of a classic series like *The Simpsons*, whose characters never age or develop in response to the experiences they have. You could skip episodes or watch them out of order and still understand everything. Likewise, in simple claim structures, readers could skip body sections or encounter them in any order without missing anything: they still arrive at the same claim.

An alternative to the simple claim structure—the complex claim structure—overcomes the simple structure's challenges. Instead of reiterating a single claim throughout, the introduction previews a main claim, and then each body section complicates the claim and offers a subclaim in response. Each subclaim takes a new step toward the main claim (see Figure 10.3). Complex claim structures allow writers to offer a series of subclaims that become increasingly complicated and interesting.

In complex claim structures, the order of the body sections isn't random: each body section raises a complication that creates a need for

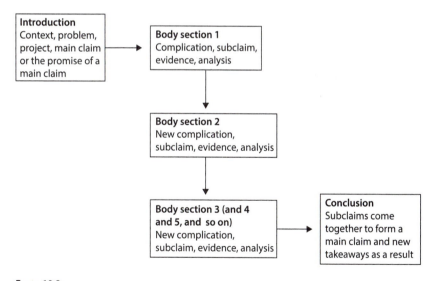

FIGURE 10.3
The elements of a complex claim structure. Notice that each body section has a unique role to play in moving readers through subclaims that lead to the main claim.

a new subclaim, a step toward the main claim. Complex claim structures allow for . . .

- *A sense of progress.* Each body section serves a unique function, offering a new subclaim that builds toward the main claim.
- *Many opportunities to heighten readers' curiosity.* Each body section raises readers' curiosity by introducing a new complication.
- *Complexity of ideas.* New subclaims in each body section highlight the complexity of the writer's thinking.

The body sections of complex claim structures function like serial television series—those that only make sense when you watch each episode in order. Think of classic series like *Mad Men* or *Game of Thrones*, for example, in which events lead to characters' development. One episode raises a problem (sometimes called a "cliffhanger") that motivates readers to tune in to the next episode to see how it will resolve.

Elements of a Complex Claim Structure

Because the complex claim structure is a common and valued approach in many academic settings, here we'll take a close look at one example. In the following table we've reverse-outlined excerpts from the introduction, body, and conclusion of "Taking on *Turnitin*: Tutors Advocating Change," an academic journal article published by a team of undergraduates and a graduate student. The article's authors—Renee Brown, Brian Fallon, Jessica Lott, Elizabeth Matthews, and Elizabeth Mintie—were featured in the Scholars' Story in Chapter 2. They were tutors in their university's writing center, and they found themselves unsure of how to help students who came to the writing center concerned that *Turnitin.com* had flagged their writing as plagiarized. Their article reviews the research on source use and examines *Turnitin*, software that some university faculty require students to use in order to check for plagiarism. They propose that writing center tutors take on new roles to teach students and faculty how to handle source use ethically.

In the reverse outline, the annotations on the left 1) pose questions you might ask yourself as you approach each section of your text and 2) offer commentary on the approach these authors took.

Introduction. Like the opening of a story designed to make a reader curious, the opening of academic writing typically begins with context that ushers readers into the world of the text. It then introduces a problem and a project that make readers curious to read on. It follows with a claim, or in this example, the promise of a claim, which assures readers that their curiosity will be rewarded.

For many writers, introductions are the most challenging sections of texts to write. We recommend writing this section after you write the body section, once you have explored the subclaims you want to make.

I. Context and problem

Context: Assuming that readers haven't had your experience, what background information would set the scene for them?

Problem: What gap in understanding exists that merits making sense of? *Here, the authors describe a tension between how writing center tutors respond to plagiarism and how faculty who use* Turnitin.com *respond to plagiarism. The opener dramatizes the tension with the story of a student coming to the writing center with a problem they didn't know how to solve. That unsolved problem raises readers' curiosity, and it carries stakes because this student's experience was part of a larger trend.*

Like many writing centers, ours trained us to respond to writers whose papers might involve plagiarism; we learned to show students how to use various paraphrasing techniques and how to cite sources. In staff meetings, we talked about why it was more important to understand the causes of students' plagiarism than to judge them for it. Then one day, a student walked into our writing center and said that she had submitted a paper to her professor online, as required, only to learn a little later that her paper had been reported to her professor as plagiarized. Visibly upset, this student asked that we help her with this paper so that she could resubmit it and avoid failing the course. She also showed us this statement in the course syllabus: "Students agree that by taking this course all required papers/reports/tests may be subject to submission for textual similarity review to *Turnitin. com* for the detection of plagiarism." This was the boilerplate language recommended to professors at our institution who chose to use *Turnitin.com*, a web-based plagiarism detection service, in their courses (Sherwood). Before our tutors had time to decide how best to respond to this experience, other panicked students came in with similar stories. We felt helpless to do anything for these students because we understood so little about *Turnitin* or their professors' literacy expectations and values. (7–8)

II. Project (the text's approach to making sense of the problem)

Purpose: What might making sense of the problem accomplish?

Method: How will you analyze the objects you study? *Notice that method most often follows a description of the object(s) of analysis. In this article, method comes before.*

Object of analysis: Which texts or data will you analyze?

Stakes: Why does making sense of the problem in this way matter for readers? *The authors argue their study carries stakes for how writing tutors approach tutoring.*

A. Purpose

We began our mission with two goals: What did our writing center staff need to know about *Turnitin*? and, How could tutors help students who must deal with *Turnitin* and the professors who require it? (8)

B. Method

We combed through websites and talked to students and faculty, collecting evidence that was sometimes technical, frequently changing, and often confusing. (8)

C. Object of analysis Our aim was to learn as much as we could about *Turnitin*. . . . (8)

D. Stakes [W]e felt that our findings were best used when we considered the pitfalls and possibilities for tutoring involved. (8)

III. Promise of a claim

Promise of a claim: How will you foreshadow making sense of the problem?

Our research began with the practical challenge of what to say to students who brought papers to us that had been identified by *Turnitin* as containing plagiarized material. . . . This challenge, though, soon led us in a number of directions that would help us to offer the best advice possible to students and to discover what kinds of roles we as tutors and the writing center play in campus conversations on plagiarism. (9)

Body. The body section develops the story of the research. The authors explore the scholarly conversation about plagiarism. The excerpts we've selected highlight complications created by the appearance of new thinkers and evidence. These complications raise readers' curiosity and create the need for subclaims, which the writers then support with evidence and analysis.

As you read, notice the places where the text heightens readers' curiosity with complications. This strategy is characteristic of complex claim structures. We suggest paying particular attention to the way that the authors use sources. When they want to heighten readers' curiosity, they cite other scholars—but not merely to offer evidence which would support their claims. Instead, they cite scholars either to complicate what has come before or to establish an idea that they will then complicate.

I. Review of the scholarly conversation (sometimes called the "literature review")

Review of the scholarly conversation: What's already known about this problem? How might this knowledge advance your thinking about the problem? *They begin with research by Rebecca Moore Howard.*

In order to find the right words to say to students who visit with *Turnitin* concerns, we had to understand plagiarism better, the stance writing center literature takes on plagiarism, and what kinds of institutional roles tutors can play. (9)

As students, we began to feel that our own perceptions on plagiarism, mainly that it is academic dishonesty, were problematic because what *Turnitin* had flagged as plagiarism didn't seem to suggest that students were intentionally being dishonest. With the help of our assistant director, we looked to composition studies for some answers and considered some of Rebecca Moore Howard's thoughts on plagiarism. Through an exploration of her work, we began to expand our understanding of plagiarism by taking into account Howard's attention to patchwriting. . . . (9)

Complication: How might other research complicate the conversation? *Bouman shows how Howard's conclusions differently impact international students.*

In addition to Howard, Kurt Bouman has strongly suggested that differences in cultural and academic expectations can lead some students, particularly international students, to make choices that would be deemed wrong by an American academic audience. . . . (9)

With a better sense of how experts in the field define plagiarism, we began to think carefully about what the writing center's stance is when it comes to plagiarism. . . . Our response

Complication: *A third piece of research by Shamoon and Burns complicates how the previous two pieces might apply to writing center tutoring.*

to such a situation had to be informed by what scholars were saying about the writing center's tempestuous past and present relationship to plagiarism. In their "Plagiarism, Rhetorical Theory, and the Writing Center: New Approaches, New Locations," Linda Shamoon and Deborah H. Burns provided not only a history of this relationship, but some answers to the questions we had about how the writing center might approach the issue of plagiarism in general. (10)

II. First subclaim, then complication: How tutors should educate writers about plagiarism

Subclaim: How does the preceding complication prompt rethinking? *As a result of the research, they claim tutors should take a certain approach to their work.*

In line with their recommendation to approach tutoring from this perspective, we believe that our job as tutors is to help students come to new meanings, understandings, and ideas through their writing and to do so while situating themselves in the kinds of disciplinary conversations their teachers expect of them.

Complication: How does the sub-claim require rethinking? *Two complications arise: 1) the subclaim is difficult to carry out, 2) yet it is important to carry out because the problem is widespread.*

This is not an easy task, but what we've learned about plagiarism, particularly in Howard's explanation of patchwriting, tells us that complicated plagiarism issues most likely happen in the writing center more frequently than we may have thought. (10–11)

III. Second sub-claim, then complication: How tutors should educate faculty about plagiarism

Source that advances the conversation: *Here, a source adds a new idea. It argues that writing centers should take part in larger conversations about plagiarism within academic disciplines.*

... [quoting Shamoon and Burns, who argue that writing centers should take part in larger conversations about plagiarism among academics] "rather than side step the issue of plagiarism by claiming to build a fence around collaboration and tutoring, such a writing center inserts itself into a conversation about the rhetorical and social nature of the disciplines" (Shamoon and Burns 192). . . . (11)

Complication prompted by a source: *A complication emerges in carrying out the subclaim: being heard in these larger conversations proved difficult.*	Of course, the time we spent researching *Turnitin* was extensive, and we had the opportunity to present our findings both locally and nationally, but the persistent issue of who is really listening to us, the tutors, kept nagging us throughout this project. . . . (11)
Subclaim: *The preceding complication leads to a new subclaim: in order to be heard, the authors had to take on a new role.*	In considering a political and pedagogical space for our research, we found it necessary to step outside the traditional roles of writing center tutors in order to make claims about how *Turnitin* was influencing teaching on our campus. (11–12)

We've outlined the first body section to illustrate the interplay between curiosity-heightening complications and curiosity-satisfying subclaims. The body sections that follow examine the "technological, legal, and ethical" implications of *Turnitin.com*, study students' reactions to the software, and uncover *Turnitin's* influence upon faculty when they teach ethical source use (12–24).

Conclusion. The concluding paragraphs of an academic text have the tricky job of bringing the story to a satisfying close. They usher readers from the world of the text to the world outside the text and give them something to take away. Thus, a crucial question to answer is "What do you want readers to take with them?" Put another way, what should readers now do/think/feel/believe as a result of your text that they didn't grasp before? What are the implications of this new understanding? For whom?

I. Main claim

Main claim: Taken together, what overarching stance do the subclaims in the body section lead to?	Believing that *Turnitin* will function as a "cure all" detracts our attention from asking why or how students plagiarize and places an emphasis on what they plagiarize. The danger in such a focus is that the teaching of proper paraphrasing may be overlooked for the simplest solutions to preventing plagiarism. . . . The

point is that we cannot and should not forget about the kinds of responsibilities we have to young writers as tutors and teachers just because we now have the ability to compare cases of textual similarity. (24)

Takeaways: Above all, what should readers walk away with? What are the implications of the text's claims? How should readers' thinking or actions change based on these takeaways? *Here, the authors argue for three actions writing center tutors should take.*

II. Takeaways

[First] Writing center staff should press their faculty and administration to offer all students the opportunity to learn how to document their sources before they require them to use *Turnitin*. Second, writing center staff should promote in-service education for all instructors who use *Turnitin* so that they are familiar with the program and learn to use it in limited, pedagogically sound ways. And, finally, we believe that all members of the writing center community need to keep up with technological innovations related to plagiarism detection so that faculty can be warned against and tutors can be prepared to deal with programs that are potentially detrimental to the educational process in composition. (27)

"Taking on *Turnitin*: Tutors Advocating Change" demonstrates how researchers who are new to a conversation can create a sophisticated complex claim structure by responding to sources. If you would like to further examine the structure of the article, you can find it in *Writing Center Journal*.

Making Structure Visible to Readers

Researchers not only have to decide how to structure their writing but also how to guide readers through the logic of that structure. Cities' public transportation systems provide an apt metaphor: buses and subways run on highly structured timetables and routes, but individual riders waiting at a stop inevitably feel antsy if they don't know when the next bus or subway is arriving. In response, some public transportation systems have installed countdown clocks that display real-time information about when the next train or bus will arrive (see Photo 10.1). Urban planning researchers find that these real-time updates increase passengers' satisfaction (Gooze et al. 101). Riders who get real-time information are more likely to use public transportation, and they are more likely to feel

PHOTO **10.1**
A countdown clock at the Times Square subway station in New York City tells riders how long they will have to wait for subway trains.

safe when they ride (Gooze et al. 101). In short, when people know what to expect on their journey, they can relax and enjoy the ride.

When we apply this same psychology to the structure of texts, we can imagine that readers will have better experiences when writers map out the overall structure of their texts using **signposts**. Signposts 1) reassure readers that they are on a clear path, 2) show them where they are on that path, and 3) motivate them to continue traveling the path. We see scholars use three common strategies to map their texts' structures for readers: sequencing signposts, functional signposts, and complicating signposts.

Sequencing Signposts Map a Clear Path

A bus rider wants to know how many stops they have before they reach their destination. If they have to get off in two stops, they may sit near the door. If they have to ride for ten stops, however, they may get comfortable, set down their bag, and open a book. Readers likewise will adjust their reading experiences based on how many main ideas or sections they anticipate coming up. Sequencing signposts—language that

---

KEY TERM

Signpost

A signpost consists of words that offer information to readers about the structure of a text. Signposts give readers cues for how to approach a text so that they can plan where and when to focus their attention.

explains how many points to expect and in what order—help readers envision the path they will travel and settle in accordingly.

The excerpt that follows from the introduction to Benjamin Meiches's article "Non-Human Humanitarians" uses three common kinds of sequencing language—numerical (highlighted in light gray), chronological (highlighted in dark gray), and listing (highlighted in black). Meiches uses these signposts to map the path that readers will follow through his research about the ways that nonhuman things (mine-detecting dogs, peacekeeping drones, and maps of refugee camps) help during humanitarian crises.

Numerical signposts quantify the number of ideas to expect ("three contributions") and often number each idea ("First," "Second," "Third").

The article makes three contributions to the existing critical literature on humanitarianism and non-human theories. First, attending to the role of non-humans in humanitarian practices provides new insights into why specific humanitarians practices are successful . . . Second, focusing on the material effects of non-humans also moves the debate over humanitarian intervention away from abstract questions about ethical principles and refocuses it on the implications of humanitarian practices. . . . Third, raising the figure of the non-human provides a different avenue for exploring the limits and benefits of humanitarian ethics . . .

Chronological signposts preview the order of ideas that the reader will encounter as they move through time. Signposts include phrases like "To begin this study," "Then," "Next," "Following that," "Lastly," and "Finally."

The next section outlines the theoretical approach of the article and explains why investigating the relations formed between humans and non-humans is valuable for International Relations (IR). From there, the article examines three different cases of non-human humanitarians: dog deminers, peacekeeping drones, and refugee camp diagrams. . . . The final section of the article returns to the theoretical and political problems posed by non-human humanitarians and explores the potential of a non-human humanitarianism. (2–3)

Listing signposts list ideas in the order that the text will address them. Meiches's readers will expect sections on dogs, drones, and diagrams in that order.

Functional Signposts Signal Where Readers Are on the Path

While sequencing signposts give riders a sense of the path they are on, riders often need more information along the way. To help, bus drivers announce the landmarks riders will find at a particular stop ("This is the stop for City Hall") or the routes they can transfer to there ("Transfer here for airport shuttles"). In other words, they signpost not just the name of the stop but what passengers will encounter there. Certain kinds of signposts, called functional signposts, act like bus drivers' announcements: they tell readers the function or purpose of a particular section. These types of signposts often draw from the language you have encountered throughout this book to name the elements of scholarly texts: language like "context," "problem," "project," "claim," "complication," and so on. Functional signposts tell readers why arriving at this point in the structure will be useful to their understanding of the text.

Take, for instance, these functional signposts (highlighted) from Janine Remillard's study of elementary school math teachers, "Mapping the Relationship Between Written and Enacted Curriculum: Examining Teachers' Decision Making." Here Remillard introduces her research on the moments when teachers decide not to follow their written lesson plans while teaching actual lessons in the classroom:

The focus of the analysis	The analysis presented in this paper is particularly concerned with examining the relationship between curriculum resources and the performance of teaching. My
The methods	
	approach draws on Brown's (2009) and others' idea that
Objects of analysis	teaching is a design activity . . . Using video recordings of elementary teachers' mathematics lessons, together with interviews and artifacts detailing their reading of
Question the study will address	the teacher's guide, I consider the following conceptual question: How can enacted lessons be conceptualized and represented for the purpose of analyzing the design work teachers do during enactment? . . . As described later in
Original contribution to the conversation	the results section, I introduce the concept of instructional design arcs to model instructional episodes . . . that require the teacher to make instructional design decisions in the
Purpose of the study	moment. . . . My aim in this analysis is to build a tool to examine empirical questions about the relationship between the enacted and written curriculum. (484–85)

Even if you don't fully grasp Remillard's study in this short excerpt, her functional signposts give you a lot of information about the purpose of each section of her text. Functional signposts operate under the common-sense logic that readers are more likely to understand what a section is trying to accomplish if you name its function in advance.

Complicating Signposts Motivate Readers to Keep Following the Path

You might be familiar with the idea of a "topic sentence," a sentence that begins a paragraph and summarizes what the paragraph is about. Many student writers are taught to start each paragraph with a topic sentence because it prepares readers for what is to come, in the same way that describing the overview of an apartment layout helps someone imagine the space. We find, however, that published scholars tend to rely on a different strategy for introducing new paragraphs that does more than describe the topic of the paragraph. They write introductory sentences that complicate what has come before. These sentences feature **complicating signposts.**

Complicating signposts come in many varieties, but they all begin by revisiting what has come in the previous paragraph(s) and then suggesting that it requires rethinking. We offer here a few examples from published research. Each of these examples comes from the opening of a paragraph; notice how each takes steps toward creating a more complex

---

KEY TERM

Complicating Signposts

Complicating signposts are words that point out a problem or gap raised by the preceding paragraph(s). This complication creates a need for the sentences that follow: they promise to make sense of the complication. Complicating signposts are a common feature of complex claim structures, particularly at the beginnings of body paragraphs, because they spell out for readers how each body section takes a new step toward a main claim.

main claim. We've underlined the signposting language that indicates to readers the purpose of the forthcoming passage.

Narrow implications → broader implications. This strategy argues that the implications for the claim established in the previous section can apply more broadly. Here's an example from Emma Coombes et al.'s "The Implications of Climate Change on Coastal Visitor Numbers: A Regional Analysis":

> "Although this study has focused on the implications of climate change for coastal recreation within East Anglia, the issues identified are relevant to other coastal regions" (989).

Claim → counterclaim. This strategy raises a new subclaim that calls for rethinking the subclaim established in the previous section. This example comes from Susanne Diekelmann et al.'s "The Whats and Whens of Sleep-Dependent Memory Consolidation":

> "Together these results speak for the notion that sleep enhances weak associations in memory to a greater extent than strong associations. . . . However, two recent studies report divergent results, i.e., greater sleep benefits for strong memories" (313).

Conversation → gap. This strategy notes a gap in the scholarly conversation that the previous body section laid out. Here's an example from Jianguo Liu et al.'s "Effects of Household Dynamics on Resource Consumption and Biodiversity":

> "Human population size and growth rate are often considered important drivers of biodiversity loss, whereas household dynamics are usually neglected" (530).

When scholars use complicating signposts to write the opening sentences of paragraphs, they don't address the question, "What is the topic of this paragraph?" but instead "How does this paragraph make my project more complex and more interesting?" As you saw in the example of "Taking on *Turnitin*: Tutors Advocating Change," scholars often rely on other researchers' voices to complicate their own thinking. In the next chapter, we'll detail strategies for integrating sources into your writing that drive your ideas forward.

TURN TO YOUR RESEARCH

Part 1: Move from Writer-Based to Reader-Based Structure

Try this exercise to move from writer-based structures that generate ideas to reader-based structures that present ideas to readers. Start by sitting down with a source you will be analyzing. This source could be a novel, film, journal article, data set, piece of art, event, or another text.

Task #1. Capture all of your observations about the source. Start at the source's beginning and move in sequence to its end. As you go, use the following prompts to list your observations about the text. You will likely write down multiple observations for each prompt.

1. At the beginning of the source, I first observe . . . Then I observe . . .
2. In the next section, I observe . . . (Repeat this prompt for each section of the source)
3. At the end of the source, I observe . . . Then I observe . . .

Because you have "toured" the source, you can feel confident that you have a thorough list of observations. However, the observations are ordered according to the logic of the source's structure rather than the logic of your analysis.

Task #2. To structure according to the logic of your own analysis, try one of the four writer-based structuring strategies we mentioned in this chapter: 1) listing and sorting, 2) outlining, 3) mind mapping, or 4) reverse outlining. Generate at least three different structures that follow the logic of your own analysis rather than the logic of the source's structure. You might try structures that . . .

- Group observations that represent the common understanding or expectations and then group observations that complicate the common understanding or expectations
- Identify main ideas or claims and place related subideas or subclaims underneath them
- Group observations around related themes or subjects
- Group observations that echo other scholars' ideas and then group observations that differ from other scholars' ideas

You may discover from this task that you actually generated new thinking as you restructured your observations. The next step is to adjust the structures you have generated into reader-based structures.

Task #3. To shift to a reader-based structure, now restructure the groupings you made to fill out the following storytelling structure:

I. Introduction
    A. Context
    B. Scholarly problem
    C. Project
    D. Claim or promise of a claim

II. Body
    A. Complication, subclaim, evidence, and analysis
    B. Complication, subclaim, evidence, and analysis
    C. Complication, subclaim, evidence, and analysis
    D. Etc.

III. Conclusion
    A. Fully developed main claim
    B. Takeaways

TURN TO YOUR RESEARCH

Part 2: Test Whether Your Structure Is Simple or Complex

Test #1. The shuffle test. Print out your draft, and, using a pair of scissors, cut each body section so that each is on its own piece of paper. Shuffle the body sections into a new random order. Read the draft with the body sections in this new order, and ask yourself the question posed in Figure 10.4.

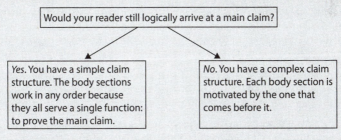

FIGURE 10.4
The shuffle test determines whether a text contains body paragraphs that raise complications about what's come before—and therefore won't make sense when structured out of order.

Test #2. The transition test. On your draft, highlight the sentences that introduce each body paragraph. Then label each as either "additive" or "complicating." Additive introductory sentences, those that emphasize the addition of more evidence to prove a single main claim, are typical of simple claim structures. They may use words like "also," "additionally," "another reason," and "similarly." Complicating introductory sentences, those that signpost a complication about what comes before and call for a subclaim to make sense of it, are typical of complex claim structures. If you find that your introductions to paragraphs are additive, we recommend returning to Chapter 4 on claims to revisit strategies for complicating your claim.

Works Cited

Brown, Renee, et al. "Taking on *Turnitin*: Tutors Advocating Change." *Writing Center Journal*, vol. 27, no. 1, 2007, pp. 7–28.

Coombes, Emma G., et al. "The Implications of Climate Change on Coastal Visitor Numbers: A Regional Analysis." *Journal of Coastal Research*, vol. 25, no. 4, July 2009, pp. 981–90. *ProQuest*, doi:10.2112/07-0993.1.

Diekelmann, Susanne, et al. "The Whats and Whens of Sleep-Dependent Memory Consolidation." *Sleep Medicine Reviews*, vol. 13, no. 5, Oct. 2009, pp. 309–21. *Crossref*, doi:10.1016/j.smrv.2008.08.002.

Emerson, Lisa. *The Forgotten Tribe: Scientists as Writers*. UP of Colorado, 2017.

Fahnestock, Jeanne, and Marie Secor. "The Rhetoric of Literary Criticism." In *Textual Dynamics of the Professions: Historical and Contemporary Studies of Writing in Professional Communities*, edited by Charles Bazerman and James G. Paradis, U of Wisconsin P, 1991, pp. 76–96. *WAC Clearinghouse*, wac.colostate.edu/books/textual_dynamics/.

Flower, Linda. "Writer-Based Prose: A Cognitive Basis for Problems in Writing." *College English*, vol. 41, no. 1, 1979, pp. 19–37. *JSTOR*, doi:10.2307/376357.

Gooze, Aaron, et al. "Benefits of Real-Time Transit Information and Impacts of Data Accuracy on Rider Experience." *Transportation Research Record*, no. 2351, Jan. 2013, pp. 95–103. *SAGE Journals*, doi:10.3141/2351-11.

Haralovich, Mary Elizabeth. "Those at Home Also Serve: Women's Television and Embedded Military Realism in *Army Wives*." In *A Companion to the War Film*, edited by Douglas A. Cunningham and John C. Nelson, Wiley & Sons, 2016, pp. 289–304. *Crossref*, doi:10.1002/9781118337653.ch17.

Lin, Ling, and Stephen Evans. "Structural Patterns in Empirical Research Articles: A Cross-Disciplinary Study." *English for Specific Purposes,* vol. 31, no. 3, July 2012, pp. 150–60. *Google Scholar,* doi:10.1016/j.esp.2011.10.002.

Linde, Charlotte, and William Labov. "Spatial Networks as a Site for the Study of Language and Thought." *Language,* vol. 51, no. 4, 1975, pp. 924–39. *JSTOR,* doi:10.2307/412701.

Liu, Jianguo, et al. "Effects of Household Dynamics on Resource Consumption and Biodiversity." *Nature,* vol. 421, no. 6922, Jan. 2003, pp. 530–33. *Biology Database,* doi:10.1038/nature01359.

Meiches, Benjamin. "Non-Human Humanitarians." *Review of International Studies,* vol. 45, no. 1, Jan. 2019, pp. 1–19. *Cambridge Core,* doi:10.1017/ S0260210518000281.

Remillard, Janine. "Mapping the Relationship Between Written and Enacted Curriculum: Examining Teachers' Decision Making." In *Invited Lectures from the 13th International Congress on Mathematical Education,* edited by Gabriele Kaiser, et al. Springer International Publishing, 2018, pp. 483–500. *Springer Link,* doi:10.1007/978-3-319-72170-5_27.

Rose, Mike. "Rigid Rules, Inflexible Plans, and the Stifling of Language: A Cognitivist Analysis of Writer's Block." *College Composition and Communication,* vol. 31, no. 4, 1980, pp. 389–401. *JSTOR,* doi:10.2307/356589.

Street Easy. *Floorplan, 3901 Independence Avenue.* 2018, streeteasy.com/ sale/387670.

Wilder, Laura. *Rhetorical Strategies and Genre Conventions in Literary Studies: Teaching and Writing in the Disciplines.* Southern Illinois UP, 2012.

Integrating Sources

Legal Scholar Richard Thompson Ford on Using Sources in Good Faith

My 2008 book, *The Race Card*, examined misunderstandings about racial bias. I wrote the book because for years I had listened to the same arguments about racism over and over again: every few months a fresh racial scandal (police violence, racial profiling, employment discrimination, Oprah Winfrey being snubbed at a Parisian luxury goods store, Jay-Z being snubbed by a champagne house) produced the same kind of media firestorm, the same accusations, denials, indignation, and recrimination, often with the same talking heads making the same points they had made the last time around. Even though many of the arguments were valid, it seemed that little progress was being made: the antagonists were talking—or yelling—past each other. As a lawyer, I have some experience with how difficult it is to define "bias"—much less prove it. So I hoped to use legal analysis to clarify the debates around racism more generally. I also wanted to cut through the bad faith, denial, and political correctness around race—rhetorical strategies and displacement mechanisms designed to score points and win arguments at the expense of an honest account of the stakes of conflicts.

The challenge was to do all of this without getting mired in precisely the kinds of dead-end debates I wanted to disrupt and to reach people on "both sides" of the debates: anti-racist activists and people who were skeptical of racial bias claims, people who were victims of racism and people who felt they had been wrongly accused of racial bias. I tried to do it with humor—to draw people in and puncture the reflexive posture of righteous indignation on all sides—and by telling stories in such a way that the reader could sympathize with all parties. For instance, I tried to tell of Oprah Winfrey's experience in the Paris store so that one could understand how she would feel snubbed and humiliated but also how the shop clerk might not have intended a racial insult. By some accounts, I succeeded: the book got lots of positive reviews, including one in *The Nation*—a left/liberal publication—and one in *National Review*—a conservative magazine.

Read the research: Richard Thompson Ford is the George E. Osborne Professor of Law at Stanford University. His books include *The Race Card: How Bluffing about Bias Makes Race Relations Worse* and *Rights Gone Wrong: How Law Corrupts the Struggle for Equality.*

Mindset: Scholars Advance Their Projects by Responding to Others

Richard Thompson Ford wrote *The Race Card* neither to take a side in seemingly unproductive debates about race nor to appease all the participants. Rather, he wanted "to clarify the debates around racism." To advance his project, Ford had to generate a productive conversation where he didn't see one before, translating voices from either side of the debate into language that the other side could understand. In other words, he strove to present others' voices fairly, fully, and even generously. At the same time, Ford needed to use sources in ways that would serve his own project. He used strategies for integrating sources in order both to create a scholarly conversation and to advance that conversation. In this chapter, we explain five such strategies: **contextualization, summary, paraphrase, quotation,** and **synthesis.**

All five strategies appear in the following passage from Ford's *The Race Card.* Ford contextualizes, summarizes, paraphrases, quotes, and synthesizes—all for the purpose of advancing his own project. The passage appears in a chapter that critiques analogies between racism and

KEY TERMS

Strategies for Integrating Sources

Contextualization: Offers information external to the source that explains the intellectual or historical circumstances surrounding the source and its author.

Summary: Distills the main takeaways of a whole source using your own language. Effective summary often focuses on the source's project (a concept we describe in Chapter 3).

Paraphrase: Captures the meaning of a passage without using the language or structure of the original.

Quotation: Repeats the exact language from a source and places that language in quotation marks.

Synthesis: Brings together the ideas of multiple sources to develop a concept that any one of the sources couldn't convey individually.

other forms of discrimination. The passage examines the arguments that conservative supporters of gay marriage advanced in the early 2000s. In particular, Ford focuses on an article by writer Jonathan Rauch called "Power of Two." As you read the passage, notice the strategies that Ford uses to situate Rauch's ideas:

Context	Gay marriage advocate Jonathan Rauch published several articles de-
Synthesis	fending gay marriage in explicitly conservative terms. He insisted that
Quotation	"marriage is the ultimate commitment for all: the destination to which
Paraphrase	loving relationships naturally aspire," and he suggested that society should not only allow but "expect" marriage of all romantic couples. For Rauch, a virtue of gay marriage was that it would stop the "proliferation of alternatives: civil unions, domestic-partner benefits and socially approved cohabitation." This argument echoed those of other conservative advocates of gay marriage whose positions had split the gay
Summary	community in the previous decade. Andrew Sullivan, for instance . . . Gabrielle Rotello was even more explicit, insisting that . . . (111)

Even though this passage represents the ideas and words of others, Ford controls the conversation. He frames Rauch's quotations in the **context** of who Rauch is, "a gay marriage advocate," and what he's written on the topic, "several articles." Ford then **synthesizes** Rauch's larger project, "defending gay marriage in explicitly conservative terms," so that readers understand the quotations in light of his articles. Ford goes on to **quote** two passages from Rauch's article. Notice the way that Ford places those quotations within **paraphrases** that reveal the role Rauch plays in Ford's project: to show that supporting gay marriage was not strictly a liberal cause. In the next sentence, Ford **synthesizes** Rauch's article within the larger conversation among conservative supporters of gay marriage. He goes on to **summarize** the arguments of two of those supporters.

Certainly, as Ford wrote this passage, he could have saved himself time by strictly selecting a few quotes from Rauch that best represent the conservative support of gay marriage. However, by embedding quotations in other forms of source use—contextualization, paraphrase, summary, and synthesis—Ford demonstrates his credibility. Rather than cherry-picking quotations that serve his project, he examines the whole texts and contexts that make up the conversation. In this way, he shows that he's acquired the expertise to represent the conversation and respond to it. These choices about source use earn readers' trust.

Writers Address Whole Texts Rather than Only Individual Sentences

The Race Card represents the conversation about racism in ways that satisfied both liberal and conservative reviewers. To accomplish this feat, Richard Thompson Ford had to represent others' ideas honestly and resist using sources as **straw men**.

We might say that Ford tried to stay true to the Latin roots of the word "conversation": *com* "with, together" + *versare* "to turn," "turning toward," or "keeping company." But if scholarship is a form of conversation, it is a rather odd kind of conversation—the participants can't respond in real time. Thus, Ford strives to represent an "honest account" of others' thinking, just as he would want his fellow scholars to represent his writing. We can think of this as the golden rule of scholarly writing: represent others' texts as generously as you would want others to represent yours. When presented in their full complexity, sources bring

KEY TERM

Straw Man Fallacy

The straw man fallacy is a form of unethical source use in which the writer simplifies or misrepresents someone's ideas in order to make them easier to oppose. Envision a figure made out of straw (see Photo 11.1); it's easy to push over. Scholars avoid the straw man fallacy by presenting others' ideas fully and accurately.

Photo 11.1
A scarecrow stuffed with straw, scaring birds from a pumpkin patch in Maryland. Photo in the Carol M. Highsmith Archive, Library of Congress, Prints and Photographs Division.

research to life, populating it with personalities and ideas, highlighting tensions and complications.

To fulfill this golden rule, Ford practices a habit of mind characteristic of expert researchers: he takes whole texts into account rather than merely considering individual passages from those texts. Composition studies scholars Rebecca Moore Howard, Tricia Serviss, and Tanya K. Rodrigue describe this as a distinction between "writing from sources" and "writing from sentences." "Writing from sources" occurs when writers like Ford display an understanding of a whole source by offering summary and context (181–82). "Writing from sentences" occurs when the writer uses only individual sentences from the source without displaying their understanding of the whole source (181–82). Those who write only from sentences risk misrepresenting those passages by removing them from their context.

Writers Connect Ideas to Contexts, Authors, and Sources

As a thought experiment, imagine that a writer decided to use Jonathan Rauch's article in a study of gay marriage advocacy but had relied solely on quotation rather than incorporating other source use strategies. In

COMMON PITFALL

Sentence Mining

From 2008 through 2010, composition studies scholars Sandra Jamieson and Rebecca Moore Howard led the Citation Project, a study that mobilized researchers at sixteen American colleges and universities to investigate source use in first-year college students' writing (114–17). Their research found that while expert writers summarized whole sources frequently, first-year undergraduates tended not to summarize at all (114).

Jamieson's and Howard's study sheds light on why first-year undergraduates so seldom summarized: 69 percent of their citations referred to material that appeared on the first or second page of the source (124–25). Some writers may not have been reading sources beyond the first couple of pages, making accurate summary difficult. Certainly, Jamieson and Howard concede, many sources offer enough of their key ideas in the first few pages that a writer could credibly summarize from them. However, not all sources do. As proof, Jamieson and Howard point to the first few pages of their own book chapter and several others in the same collection that would have misdirected readers (129).

Takeaway: The Citation Project's findings suggest that writers should practice reading and writing strategies that address a whole source "rather than merely mine sentences from it" (130). Contextualizing and summarizing are the strategies writers can use to address whole sources.

other words, imagine if a writer were writing from sentences rather than writing from sources. They might have written a passage like this one. As you read it, see if you can determine what the writer wants you to take away from Rauch's article:

> Supporters of gay marriage exist across the political spectrum. "Marriage is the ultimate commitment for all: the destination to which loving relationships naturally aspire . . ." (Rauch 13). The "proliferation of alternatives (civil unions, domestic-partner benefits and socially approved cohabitation)" would cease if gay marriage becomes legal (Rauch 13).

RESEARCH ON WRITING

Ken Hyland on Source Integration Strategies in Different Fields

How do scholars decide which source integration strategies to employ? Linguist Ken Hyland argues that scholars favor strategies that align with how their fields of study view the role of research. Hyland examined 1,400 published texts from eight academic fields—sociology, marketing, physics, and so on (xi). He found a strong preference for summary and paraphrase over quotation in all fields (26). But key differences emerged as well: none of the science writing Hyland studied used quotation, but quotation made up a substantial percentage of source use in social science and humanities publications (26).

What's the logic behind the way that different fields use research? Hyland argues that different areas of study have unique understandings about how knowledge is constructed. Most science researcher want their studies to add to existing understanding (30–32). Thus, they prefer summary and paraphrase, which present previous studies as established knowledge to build upon (30–31). Humanities and social science researchers, alternately, assume that past studies invite reinterpretation (37–38). Therefore, they favor contextualization and quotation in order to open up a study's history and language to reconsideration (37).

Takeaway: To learn about the source integration strategies common in your field of study, we recommend reading examples of that writing and noting how they use sources.

Read the research: Hyland, Ken. *Disciplinary Discourses: Social Interactions in Academic Writing.* U of Michigan P, 2014.

This rewrite has the virtue of highlighting Rauch's voice. However, it's likely to disorient readers, who will wonder who said the words, for what purpose, and how they contribute to the writer's claim. Our rewritten passage contains an example of a "dropped quote": a quote that appears without introduction and neglects to help readers make sense of the quotation. Ford's passage, on the other hand, offers context, summary, and synthesis that tell readers how he wants us to make sense of Rauch's words.

Tools & Techniques: Incorporating Sources

When integrating others' ideas in their writing, scholars face a tension: on the one hand, they want to give others' voices their due; on the other hand, they don't want those voices to drown out their own. When making decisions about integrating sources, writers ask, "Am I representing others' ideas fully and fairly? Am I offering others' ideas in a way that readers can grasp? Am I staying in control of my own project?" The following chart describes why and when writers might favor various strategies for incorporating sources:

Contextualization describes a source's background.

Why?	*When?*
To situate ideas within intellectual or historical circumstances	Before delving into the source's ideas to introduce the reader to the source
To familiarize readers with new material	After presenting the source's ideas to
To justify the use of a source	show a tension between the source
To signal the function the source will perform	and its origins
To highlight a tension between a source and its historical or intellectual origins	

Summary distills the main takeaways of a source.

Why?	*When?*
To work with major ideas	Before moving toward a focused
To give an overview	analysis of a specific passage
To chart the intellectual terrain	When addressing the big picture of
To highlight a tension between a whole source and an individual passage within it	the source's scholarly contributions rather than specific details

Paraphrase rewords a passage from a source.

Why?	*When?*
To work with concepts but not the language they're conveyed in	After contextualizing and summarizing the source
To translate specialized language into words a non-specialist can understand	After quoting a source, as a way of explaining the quote
To maintain your writerly presence while representing another's ideas	

Quotation offers the exact language of a source.

Why?	*When?*
To set up an analysis of the source's language	Before analyzing the quote
To apply or redefine the source's key term or phrase	After contextualizing and summarizing the source
To present a source's distinct style and personality in order to convey something about the text	Not to end paragraphs, typically, because readers look for the writer to explain the quote
To emphasize the presence of the source's author	As an epigraph at the beginning of a text

Synthesis brings together ideas of multiple sources to convey something none of them could convey individually.

Why?	*When?*
To use a group of sources to note an intellectual trend or characterize a time period	Before situating a source within a larger conversation
To characterize the role a single source plays in a larger conversation in order to illustrate that the source is a precursor of a trend, an example of a larger set of ideas, or a break from the past	Early in your text to characterize the scholarly conversation you are entering
	After presenting more than one source in order to locate them within a scholarly conversation

Strategies to Contextualize Sources

In Chapter 6, we suggested that you can think of selecting sources as coming up with a guest list to a party that you're hosting. To extend this metaphor, let's think about how you might encourage lively conversation at the party. You will likely introduce guests to each other by saying their names and sharing something about them that will spark conversation. You might mention shared interests or something fascinating about a guest. On the page, this kind of introduction takes the form of contextualizing—giving readers enough background information to want to get to know the source better.

Here English studies scholar Michael Warner contextualizes a John Adams essay that plays a central role in his book *The Letters of the Republic: Publication and the Public Sphere in Eighteenth-Century America*. Before Warner summarizes Adams's text, what elements of contextualization does he offer?

year	In 1765, in the early stages of an imperial crisis and of his
historical context	career as a lawyer, John Adams wrote a brief retrospect
biographical context	of the political and legal history of the West. Appearing
publication context	unsigned and untitled in four installments in the *Boston Gazette*, the essay depicts the history of power as a history
summary	of knowledge. It tells modern history as a story of human self-determination rising through reflection. (1)

In the first sentence, Warner gives not only the year but also the relevant historical and biographical context. Then he cites the titles (or, in this case, the lack of titles) and the circumstances of Adams's publication. Finally, he tells us the source's genre (an essay in a newspaper), which leads into a brief summary. This careful contextualization followed by summary suggests that Adams will play a crucial role in Warner's text. Warner ensures that when readers encounter a quote by Adams, they will have the background knowledge they need to grasp the circumstances it rose out of.

Warner's passage signals several kinds of contextualization writers might use:

- *Historical context*: When did the source appear? Where? What was the social or political situation it emerged from and shaped?
- *Biographical context*: Who is the writer? At what point in their career did they create the source? What personal information might help readers understand the source?
- *Cultural context*: Is the source associated with an artistic or cultural group? Was it a response to an event or cultural circumstance?

- *Intellectual context*: How did the source respond to earlier thinkers? How did it influence later thinkers?

When making less substantial use of a source, scholars may use just a few words to quickly contextualize it. For instance, historian Drew Gilpin Faust uses just part of a sentence, which we've underlined, to contextualize a quote by renowned sociologist and civil rights crusader W. E. B. DuBois:

> <u>Writing the history of the black experience in war and Reconstruction in 1935, W. E. B. DuBois</u> found it "extraordinary . . . that in the minds of most people . . . only murder makes men. The slave . . . was humble; he protected the women of the South, and the world ignored him. The slave killed white men; and behold, he was a man!" (48)

Faust quickly contextualizes the quote with the author's name, the historical moment DuBois is responding to, and the year he published his writing. Faust calculates that her reader now understands enough to place DuBois's words within history and culture.

Strategies to Summarize Sources

To summarize a source is to tell readers the main takeaways of the whole source, but summarizing effectively means something more than describing how you experienced the source. Researcher Margaret Hill has observed that college students often begin composing summaries by simply recounting their experience of a source in sequence (first this happens, then this happens), which can fail to capture a text's main contributions and connect them to one's own project (538). What, then, are strategies for summarizing that can better capture a source? Let's examine three possible approaches to summarizing: 1) a topic-based approach, which highlights the subject matter; 2) a claim-based approach, which highlights the main argument; and 3) a project-based approach, which highlights the source's approach. To compare these approaches, we'll use each of them to summarize Richard Thompson Ford's *The Race Card*. Which summary gives you the best sense of what the book accomplishes?

- *Topic-based summary*: In *The Race Card*, Richard Ford examines racially charged events, including the reconstruction of New Orleans after Hurricane Katrina, businesses snubbing black celebrities, and Supreme Court cases about discrimination.

- *Claim-based summary*: In *The Race Card*, Richard Ford argues that the United States needs to better define "discrimination" in order to effectively deal with racism.
- *Project-based summary* (in Ford's own words from "A Scholar's Story"): "So I hoped to use legal analysis to clarify the debates around racism more generally. I also wanted to cut through the bad faith, denial, and political correctness around race— rhetorical strategies and displacement mechanisms designed to score points and win arguments at the expense of an honest account of the stakes of conflicts."

Each of these summaries is factually correct. But which offers the clearest explanation of what *The Race Card* does? The topic-based summary, while it explains the subject matter Ford discusses, tells us little about what Ford accomplishes by addressing those topics. The claim-based summary offers one of Ford's central arguments, but it doesn't tell us how he reaches this argument, and it potentially overlooks many other arguments in the book. The project-based summary—the approach we recommend—tells us what the book seeks to accomplish. Scholarly projects rarely have a single main claim, but they do have projects that we can describe. Project descriptions are impactful because they explain the text's aims and intellectual contributions.

As you set out to write a project-based summary of a source, consider the following questions (which we first introduced in Chapter 3) that will help you balance the source's project with your own:

- What is the source's purpose?
- What objects does the source analyze?
- What methods does the source employ?
- What is at stake in the source's study? For whom?
- What aspects of the source speak to my own project?

PRACTICE

Write a Summary that Advances Your Project

Writers summarize not only to distill someone else's ideas but also to advance their own projects. For example, here are two summaries of Martin Luther King, Jr.'s "Letter from Birmingham Jail." Each focuses on different aspects of King's work in order to speak to the writers' projects.

continued

Task 1: Read each and write down what you anticipate about the writer's project based on the way they summarize King's letter.

a. Legal scholar David Oppenheimer writes,

> The *Letter* is a powerful and important defense of civil disobedience. In it, King justifies violating unjust civil laws in order to obey moral law, an argument rejected by the Court in the *Walker* decision. (794)

b. Philosophers Larry May and Jill B. Delston write,

> King provides another extremely influential account of nonviolent civil disobedience. He defines a nonviolent campaign as one that has four stages: (a) a determination that injustice is occurring; (b) negotiation to try to end the injustice; (c) a cleansing process that steels one against hatred and revenge; (d) nonviolent direct action. He offers a defense of this strategy, as opposed to a strategy of violence, by reference to traditional Judeo-Christian moral principles. (233–34)

POSSIBLE ANSWERS: Both examples summarize King's project fairly, but each also stresses different aspects of King's work. a) Oppenheimer's summary suggests that he is interested in the legal aspects of King's work: he prepares readers to consider judicial responses to King's argument. b) May and Delston's summary suggests that they are interested in the ethical aspects of King's work: they focus on how King uses religious morals to justify his protest movement.

Task 2: Write a summary that advances your own project. Imagine that you are working on a project that examines how texts can carry different meanings when the authors write them while in jail or prison. Write a summary of Martin Luther King, Jr.'s "Letter from Birmingham Jail" that balances King's project with your own. You can find King's 1963 letter with a quick internet search.

POSSIBLE ANSWER: Martin Luther King, Jr. wrote "Letter from Birmingham Jail" to awaken communities to injustice, arguing that individuals should break unjust laws and accept the consequences—even if it means being imprisoned. He describes how he himself is writing from jail after being arrested for civil disobedience.

Strategies to Paraphrase Sources

When scholars paraphrase, they put a source's ideas into their own words. Literary studies scholar Philip Arrington points out that paraphrase, like summary, is a kind of "translation": "Because paraphrasing is 'another saying' or, more specifically, a rewriting of what someone else has written, it presupposes interpretation, revising another's vision, a creative *translation* of one text into another" (186). When scholars put someone else's language into their own words—when they translate—they emphasize aspects of the source that speak to their own projects. Doing this translation in a way that avoids plagiarism requires writers to transform both the source's language and its sentence structure (in other words, its syntax).

Paraphrase is one of the harder skills researchers perform. In fact, when psychologist Miguel Roig asked 104 professors from various fields to paraphrase a difficult technical passage from a psychology article, nearly a third produced paraphrases containing **patchwriting** and almost a quarter altered the meaning of the source ("Plagiarism and Paraphrasing Criteria" 310, 313–16).

COMMON PITFALL

Patchwriting

When writers work with jargon-laden sources in unfamiliar fields, they are especially susceptible to a potential form of unethical source use that Rebecca Moore Howard calls "patchwriting." Howard coined the term to describe "copying from a source text and then deleting some words, altering grammatical structures, or plugging in one-for-one synonym substitutes" (233). Patchwriting can also occur when a writer relies on a translation program to translate a passage from another language. The translation will retain the structure of the original language.

Howard argues that patchwriting indicates a developmental phase of writing: when writers are learning to engage with new ideas and new language, they may compose sentences that adhere too closely to the language and form of a source (240). Despite the fact that patchwriting is a transitional stage in learning to paraphrase, in many academic settings it constitutes plagiarism.

Let's consider an example of a passage that would be difficult to paraphrase because it contains advanced concepts and specialized language. We will take a passage from psychologist Gerd Gigerenzer's book chapter, "Moral Intuition = Fast and Frugal Heuristics?" In the chapter, Gigerenzer studies how to encourage people to make moral decisions. While most research approaches the topic by studying how individuals think and feel, Gigerenzer studies how larger social surroundings influence people's moral choices. How might you paraphrase these two sentences from Gigerenzer's chapter?

> Unlike theories that focus on traits, preferences, attitudes, and other internal constructs, the science of heuristics emphasizes the interaction between mind and social environment. Knowing the heuristics that guide people's moral actions can be of help in designing change that might otherwise be out of reach. (26)

If, upon first read, you're not quite sure what this passage means, that's understandable. We've picked sentences that convey complex ideas using specialized terminology precisely because these types of sentences are typically difficult to paraphrase. Indeed, writers are more likely to plagiarize when they encounter sentences like these where the meaning is difficult to ascertain (Roig, "College Students' Attempts at Paraphrasing" 978–79).

In paraphrasing Gigerenzer's passage, writers may encounter three pitfalls that raise ethical concerns: 1) retaining bits of the original language, called "patchwriting"; 2) retaining the original sentence structure; and 3) failing to cite the source. Consider these three examples of paraphrases of Gigerenzer's passage that raise ethical concerns, followed by an appropriate paraphrase.

Problematic Paraphrase #1: Patchwriting

> **To design social change that is otherwise out of reach**, Gigerenzer argues that we should look to **the science of heuristics** (26).

The bolded words in this paraphrase borrow Gigerenzer's words (or variations of them) without putting quotation marks around them. In order to avoid patchwriting, writers must use original language to convey the source's ideas. To generate this original language, the writer may have to do additional reading to help them fully grasp specialized concepts like "the science of heuristics."

Problematic Paraphrase #2: Retaining the Source's Sentence Structure

Gigerenzer argues that understanding the mechanisms that point individuals to ethical acts might be helpful in planning transformation that could in different circumstances be unattainable (26).

Even though this paraphrase of Gigerenzer's second sentence cites him and uses almost none of his language, it follows the sentence structure of the original. This paraphrase simply replaces Gigerenzer's words with synonyms. The result is a sentence that so closely conforms to the original's structure of thought that it would raise ethical concerns.

Problematic Paraphrase #3: Failing to Cite the Paraphrase

To tackle seemingly unsolvable social ills, do we have to intervene in each individual's decision-making? That would be a daunting undertaking. Instead we can create social systems that provide structures that encourage moral decision-making.

This paraphrase translates Gigerenzer's passage into original words and original syntax. However, it fails to cite Gigerenzer and thus constitutes plagiarism. The principle behind the logic of citation is that authors own not only their language and their structures of thought but also their ideas. To make this paraphrase ethical, the writer would need to cite Gigerenzer *in each sentence*; citations at the ends of whole passages obscure which sentences came from the source. To learn more about citation practices, see Chapter 13.

Ethical Paraphrase

In her book *The Self beyond Itself: An Alternative History of Ethics, the New Brain Sciences, and the Myth of Free Will*, religion scholar Heidi M. Ravven paraphrases Gigerenzer ethically. She writes,

Gigerenzer contends that it is the structure of the *context* that must be manipulated to produce morally desirable action from individuals, instead of relying on individual moral choice or moral training (26). (Ravven 264)

Ravven changes both the source's vocabulary and the sentence structure in her paraphrase. For instance, she replaces the difficult word "heuristics" with her own language of "structure." And Ravven credits Gigerenzer for his ideas, just as she also clarifies those ideas by putting them in her own terms.

Strategies to Quote Sources

Quotation appeals to writers because it is easy to do. It doesn't require translating others' ideas into your own language; you simply copy the source's exact language, place quotation marks around it, and cite the source. Quotation can be especially seductive when a source contains specialized language or difficult concepts. However, as we point out in the source integration chart at the beginning of the Tools & Techniques section, scholars use quotation not for their own ease, but to fulfill their readers' needs.

We had readers' needs in mind when we decided to paraphrase Miguel Roig's study in the preceding "Strategies to Paraphrase Sources" section. Although it would have been easier for *us* to use quotation instead of paraphrasing, we calculated that paraphrasing would be easier for *you* to understand. Read this quotation-heavy rewrite of the paragraph and compare your experience to that of reading the paraphrased version:

> Paraphrase is one of the harder skills researchers perform. In fact, when psychologist Miguel Roig asked 104 "professors from different disciplines" to paraphrase a "two-sentence paragraph taken from Zenhausern (1978)," he found that "thirty percent of the paraphrases (n=33) contained five-word strings from the original paragraph," and "a surprising 24% of the paraphrases evidenced some type of distortion" ("Plagiarism and Paraphrasing Criteria" 310, 314–15). To paraphrase ethically and accurately, we suggest these strategies . . .

How did your experiences of reading each passage differ? Certainly, the quotation-heavy version offers more details, but those details (the passage that professors paraphrased was two sentences long, Robert Zenhausern was its author, etc.) and Roig's specialized language (e.g., "five-word strings") may distract you from our purpose in citing Roig's study.

Ultimately, quotation comes with a cost: it shifts the readers' focus from your language and your project to someone else's. In order to sustain readers' attention, scholars strive to quote only when there's an advantage for readers. Here are four strategies for making quotation pay off for readers. They each integrate language from a source in a way that demonstrates how that language advances the writer's project.

Quotation Strategy #1: Focus on Language You Will Analyze

Writers frequently quote sources in order to emphasize and analyze the precise language of a source. For instance, in their article "Confronting the Challenges of Therapy Online: A Pilot Project," the scholars Dan Mitchell and Lawrence Murphy analyze the language of a woman interviewed about her experience with online counseling:

> At another point in the interview process, she wrote, "I felt that there was someone out there who cared about me and would help me." Her choice of words, "out there" is interesting. They suggest that the physical presence of the counsellor may not be necessary in order to communicate the warmth and caring that characterizes a healthy therapeutic relationship. (3)

Mitchell and Murphy make it clear why they are quoting (rather than summarizing or paraphrasing): they are interested in interpreting the precise language of the person they interviewed. Indeed, without quoting the phrase "out there," they would be unable to reach the conclusions they make about the effectiveness of therapists who are not physically present. Notice that the writers integrate the quotations into their own sentences using the phrases "she wrote" and "her choice of words." This brief contextualization helps readers understand the interviewee's larger idea and then focus on her language.

The most visible way of quoting a source is to use a block quote—a fully indented passage that is of significant length (at least four lines of prose in MLA style; at least forty words in APA style). Writers use block quotes to set off a long quotation that they will analyze substantially. In their book *SuperVision: An Introduction to the Surveillance Society*, political scientist John Gilliom and communications researcher Torin Monahan use a block quote of *Facebook's* privacy policy in order to set up their analysis:

> By 2009 the privacy policy read more like a lack-of-privacy policy:
>
> > Certain categories of information such as your name, profile photo, list of friends and pages you are a fan of, gender, geographic region, and networks you belong to are considered publicly available to everyone, including *Facebook*-enhanced applications, and therefore do not have privacy settings. You can, however, limit the ability of others to find this information through search using your search privacy settings.

> The deterioration of *Facebook's* privacy protections betrays that this medium isn't simply adapting to new conceptions of privacy as embodied by younger people—it is actively *shaping* those conceptions and slowly pushing users toward acceptance of further exposure and less control. (52)

We've included some of Gilliom's and Monahan's analysis beyond their block quote to demonstrate their interpretive work with this quote. They offer readers an intellectual pay-off for expending the extra energy it takes to read a block quote.

Quotation Strategy #2: Apply or Redefine a Key Term or Phrase

Writers quote key terms from sources in order to either apply the term to their own study or to redefine it. In her article "The Nanny Chain," sociologist Arlie Hothschild quotes a term coined by sociologist and gender studies scholar Rhacel Salazar Parreñas:

> In her forthcoming book *Servants of Globalization*, Parreñas, an affiliate of the Center for Working Families at the University of California, Berkeley, tells an important and disquieting story of what she calls the "globalization of mothering." The Beverly Hills family pays "Vicky" (which is the pseudonym Parreñas gave her) $400 a week, and Vicky, in turn, pays her own family's live-in domestic worker back in the Philippines $40 a week. (33)

By quoting "globalization of mothering," Hothschild credits Parreñas with a term in order to apply it. In this way, Hothschild retains her authorial presence, even as she makes use of Parreñas's concept.

Quotation Strategy #3: Highlight the Presence of a Source's Author

Writers use quotes to emphasize the presence of other researchers in the scholarly conversation. These quotes can foreground the roles of various participants in the conversation. In her book *The Deadly Life of Logistics: Mapping Violence in Global Trade*, geographer Deborah Cowen quotes scholar Michael Kempe, who studies piracy. How does Cowen frame Kempe's quote? What comes before and after?

> Michael Kempe emphasizes the non- or subhumanity of pirates . . . suggesting that "pirates were placed outside humanity, in a realm otherwise reserved for wild animals" (356). Piracy thus marked not simply an exceptional legal status; located outside the law, those labeled as such also lost their humanity. (137)

Cowen includes Kempe's own words to highlight his presence as a scholar and a key participant in the scholarly conversation. Notice that Cowen offers a brief summary of Kempe's work before she quotes him. After the quote, she offers a paraphrase and interpretation. By framing Kempe's quote with her own language, Cowen retains her authorial presence.

Quotation Strategy 4: Echo or Allude with Epigraphs

The only kind of quote for which readers do not expect analysis or explanation are epigraphs. Epigraphs are inscriptions that writers place at the beginning of a text to set a tone or to suggest commentary. Some epigraphs deal explicitly with the subject matter of the book. Other times, epigraphs suggest only an implicit connection and offer a more open-ended interpretation. For example, Annie Dillard's *Pilgrim at Tinker Creek*—a book that traces the writer's explorations of the natural world—uses an epigraph from the ancient Greek philosopher Heraclitus that suggests the mysterious workings of the cosmos:

> "It ever was, and is, and shall be, ever-living Fire, in measures being kindled and in measures going out" —Heraclitus (qtd. in Dillard).

Strategies to Synthesize Sources

When scholars synthesize, they bring together ideas from multiple texts to convey something that any one of the texts on its own could not convey. Synthesis requires imagining various networks that sources might form, asking, "What trends and patterns among texts emerge?" and "What moments of departure and innovation appear?" The following examples illustrate four common reasons why writers might synthesize texts:

1. *To make a claim about an intellectual trend.* In *God Is Not One*, religious studies scholar Stephen Prothero synthesizes a set of recent books that, he argues, take similar approaches to religion:

   The beginning of the twenty-first century saw dozens of bestselling books in both Europe and the United States by so-called New Atheists. Writers such as Richard Dawkins, Sam Harris, Daniel Dennett, Christopher Hitchens, and Michel Onfray preach their own version of Godthink, aping the perennial philosophers by loading all religions into one boat. This crew, however, sees only the shared sins of the great religions—the same idiocy, the same oppression. (9)

Scholars may use synthesis in this way in order to point out a limitation or gap in the existing conversation that calls for a response.

2. *To characterize the studies that you are building upon.* In "Simulating Coastal Migration in New-World Colonization," anthropologist Todd Surovell synthesizes scholarship that has established a methodology that he uses:

> This study follows in a long tradition of using computer simulation and mathematical modeling to investigate the plausibility of hypotheses concerning New World colonization (e.g., Alroy 2001; Anderson and Gillam 2000; Martin 1973; Mithen 1993; Mosimann and Martin 1975; Steele, Adams, and Sluckin 1998; Surovell 2000). (Surovell 580)

Scholars may use synthesis in this way to show how their research participates in a well-established conversation.

3. *To trace intellectual history.* In "Exploring Perceptions of Blame for Autism Spectrum Disorder," psychologists Linda McKenna Gulyn and Catherine Diaz-Asper trace the history of researchers' studies about the causes of autism symptoms. They write,

> The idea that the behaviors of parents themselves (particularly mothers) cause autistic symptoms has a long history. Beginning as early as the 1940s, Leo Kanner's (1943) diagnostic description of autism led psychoanalysts to attribute an infant's autism to mothers who are insensitive, emotionally cold, rejecting and distant (e.g., Bettelheim 1967). This psychological perspective persisted through the 1960s, until the emphasis shifted in the 1970s to the biological bases of autism (Chamak and Bonniau 2013; Baker 2013). (McKenna Gulyn and Diaz-Asper 588)

Scholars may use synthesis in this way to show how a conversation has evolved over time, often to point out that researchers today have different assumptions or interests than those of the past.

4. *To make a claim about a single author's body of work.* In *Unbearable Weight: Feminism, Multiculturalism, and the Body*, gender studies scholar Susan Bordo synthesizes the work of the anthropologist Mary Douglas:

The body—what we eat, how we dress, the daily rituals through which we attend to the body—is a medium of culture. The body, as anthropologist Mary Douglas has argued, is a powerful symbolic form, a surface on which the central rules, hierarchies, and even metaphysical commitments of a culture are inscribed and thus reinforced through the concrete language of the body. (165)

Bordo's footnote indicates that she is synthesizing two of Douglas's books: *Natural Symbols* and *Purity and Danger* (328). Scholars may use synthesis in this way to characterize the sustained thought of another scholar over the course of their career, lending more gravity to those ideas.

Now that we've explained some of the common ways that scholars integrate sources in their research, we recommend that you annotate the scholarship you read by noting strategies of contextualizing, summarizing, paraphrasing, quoting, and synthesizing that you can emulate. In the next chapter, we'll discuss analyzing sources, examining ways not only to integrate others' voices in your writing but to respond to them.

TURN TO YOUR RESEARCH
Strategies to Paraphrase and Synthesize

Paraphrase and synthesis are perhaps the most challenging ways to integrate sources in your writing. Here we offer strategies for doing each.

When a passage contains unfamiliar language or concepts, it can be challenging to paraphrase it in your own words. To paraphrase ethically and accurately, we suggest these strategies, which encourage you to get distance from the passage and then return to it:

- Read the passage multiple times.
- Read the sentences surrounding the passage to understand how the author arrives at the idea and how they apply it.
- Read other scholarly explanations of the source.
- Define key terms and jargon in your own words.
- Record yourself talking out your understanding of the passage.
- Step away from the source for long enough to forget its language.
- Draft a paraphrase by putting the source's ideas into your own words and citing the original text.

continued

- After you paraphrase, reread the source and compare it to your paraphrase, making sure that you are not inadvertently copying language or sentence structure.

Synthesis requires researchers to adopt habits of reading and writing across texts. To work with multiple sources at once, try using the following sentence templates as you take reading notes and draft:

- Taken together, these thinkers might lead us to characterize this [school of thought, this time period, this shift, this trend] as _____.
- Seen separately, it seems like _____, but taken together, we see that _____.
- This constellation of thinkers makes visible to us _____.
- Although they were working at different times and places, when we bring these writers together, we can see _____.

Though you may find that the exact language of these templates may not translate smoothly to your writing, they can push you to generate ways of synthesizing multiple sources.

Works Cited

Arrington, Phillip. "A Dramatistic Approach to Understanding and Teaching the Paraphrase." *College Composition and Communication*, vol. 39, no. 2, 1988, pp. 185–97. *JSTOR*, doi:10.2307/358027.

Bordo, Susan. *Unbearable Weight: Feminism, Western Culture, and the Body.* U of California P, 2003.

Cowen, Deborah. *The Deadly Life of Logistics: Mapping Violence in Global Trade.* U of Minnesota P, 2014.

Dillard, Annie. *Pilgrim at Tinker Creek.* Harper Perennial, 2007.

Faust, Drew Gilpin. *This Republic of Suffering: Death and the American Civil War.* Knopf, 2008.

Ford, Richard Thompson. *The Race Card: How Bluffing about Bias Makes Race Relations Worse.* Farrar, Straus and Giroux, 2008.

Gigerenzer, Gerd. "Moral Intuition = Fast and Frugal Heuristics?" In *Moral Psychology: The Cognitive Science of Morality: Intuition and Diversity*, edited by Walter Sinnott-Armstrong, MIT P, 2008, pp. 1–26.

Gilliom, John, and Torin Monahan. *SuperVision: An Introduction to the Surveillance Society*. U of Chicago P, 2013.

Highsmith, Carol M. *Scarecrow in Rural Farmland, Maryland*. circa 1980–2006, Carol M. Highsmith Archive, Library of Congress, Prints and Photographs Division, www.loc.gov/pictures/item/2011630204/.

Hill, Margaret. "Writing Summaries Promotes Thinking and Learning across the Curriculum: But Why Are They so Difficult to Write?" *Journal of Reading*, vol. 34, no. 7, 1991, pp. 536–39.

Hochschild, Arlie. "The Nanny Chain." *American Prospect*, vol. 11, no. 4, Jan. 2000, pp. 32–36.

Howard, Rebecca Moore. "A Plagiarism Pentimento." *Journal of Teaching Writing*, vol. 11, no. 2, Jan. 1992, pp. 233–46.

---. "Writing from Sources, Writing from Sentences." *Writing & Pedagogy*, vol. 2, no. 2, 2010, pp. 177–92.

Hyland, Ken. *Disciplinary Discourses: Social Interactions in Academic Writing*. U of Michigan P, 2014. *ProQuest Ebook Central*, ebookcentral.proquest.com/lib/columbia/detail.action?docID=3415133.

Jamieson, Sandra, and Rebecca Moore Howard. "Sentence-Mining: Uncovering the Amount of Reading and Reading Comprehension in College Writers' Researched Writing." In *The New Digital Scholar: Exploring and Enriching the Research and Writing Practices of NextGen Students*, edited by Randall McClure and James P. Purdy, *Information Today*, 2013, pp. 111–33.

May, Larry, and Jill Delston. *Applied Ethics: A Multicultural Approach*. Routledge, 2017.

McKenna Gulyn, Linda, and Catherine Diaz-Asper. "Exploring Perceptions of Blame for Autism Spectrum Disorder." *Journal of Developmental and Physical Disabilities*, vol. 30, no. 5, Oct. 2018, pp. 587–600. *Crossref*, doi:10.1007/s10882-018-9604-2.

Mitchell, Dan L., and L. M. Murphy. "Confronting the Challenges of Therapy Online: A Pilot Project." *Proceedings of the Seventh National and Fifth International Conference on Information Technology and Community Health*, 1998.

Oppenheimer, David Benjamin. "Martin Luther King, *Walker v. City of Birmingham*, and the *Letter from Birmingham Jail*." *University of California Davis Law Review*, vol. 26, no. 4, summer 1993, pp. 791–834.

Prothero, Stephen R. *God Is Not One: The Eight Rival Religions That Run the World—and Why Their Differences Matter*. HarperOne, 2010.

Rauch, Jonathan. "Power of Two." *New York Times Magazine*, Mar. 2004, p. 13.

Ravven, Heidi. *The Self Beyond Itself: An Alternative History of Ethics, the New Brain Sciences, and the Myth of Free Will*. New Press, 2013.

Roig, Miguel. "Plagiarism and Paraphrasing Criteria of College and University Professors." *Ethics & Behavior*, vol. 11, no. 3, July 2001, pp. 307–23.

---. "When College Students' Attempts at Paraphasing Become Instances of Potential Plagiarism." *Psychological Reports*, vol. 84, no. 3, June 1999, pp. 973–82. *Sage*, doi: 10.2466/pr0.1999.84.3.973.

Surovell, Todd A. "Simulating Coastal Migration in New World Colonization." *Current Anthropology*, vol. 44, no. 4, Aug. 2003, pp. 580–91. *Crossref*, doi:10.1086/377651.

Warner, Michael. *The Letters of the Republic: Publication and the Public Sphere in Eighteenth-Century America*. Harvard UP, 2009.

CHAPTER 12

Analyzing Sources

SCHOLAR'S STORY

Media Studies Researcher Kelly Kessler on Analyzing Hollywood Musicals

When I started working on my first book, my eye was focused on a study of shifting masculinity in the Hollywood musical. I started out my research process by watching every available Hollywood film (mid-1950s forward) in which people spontaneously burst into song. In a prestreaming and early DVD era, this was no easy task. I created a detailed database to track shooting styles, stars, types of songs and singers, styles of dance, numbers of songs/dances, and so on.

As I landed on the late 1960s, I noticed a pattern that I had not expected. Musicals like *Sweet Charity* clearly reflected the new and edgier form of the non-musical, visually stylized, anti-hero films of the New American Cinema like *Bonnie and Clyde* and *Easy Rider*. And instead of featuring classical Hollywood dancers like Gene Kelly and Fred Astaire, these new musicals starred men famous for their ruggedness or oddball comedy, celebrities like Burt Reynolds, Clint Eastwood, Steve Martin, and Robin Williams. They were non-musical superstars placed in unexpected genre pieces.

continued

As I tried to make sense of these shifting patterns of musical masculinity, I realized I needed to refocus my project. I began to examine systemic changes in the film industry—new shooting styles, the rise of the antihero and unresolved narratives, and the disappearance of studio system acting stables. I would then ask how these larger changes impacted masculinity within the musical genre. What started as a project focused almost solely on masculinity in the musicals themselves morphed into a project about larger transformations within Hollywood.

Read the research: Kelly Kessler is a professor of media and cinema studies at DePaul University. She is the author of *Destabilizing the Hollywood Musical: Music, Masculinity and Mayhem* and *Broadway in the Box: Television's Lasting Love Affair with the Musical*.

Mindset: Analysis Turns Observations into Evidence

Media studies scholar Kelly Kessler knew that writing a book about Hollywood musicals would, of course, require her to analyze films. In her research process, we can see her employ a method to lay the groundwork for this analysis, and it is a method that any researcher can emulate. Kessler started by observing details. She watched a lot of musicals and wrote down a lot of observations about them—so many observations that she needed a database to keep track of them all. As she gathered details, she examined them strategically by looking for gaps in understanding—things that didn't quite make sense or couldn't be explained easily. Kessler thus found "a pattern that [she] had not expected." She focused on one type of scholarly problem we describe in Chapter 2: a pattern appears that stands in tension with a break in that pattern. In particular, Kessler noticed that before the 1960s, the pattern for musicals was to feature male leads known for their graceful dancing (see Photo 12.1). But in the 1960s, that pattern broke when men known for their goofiness or macho personas took over the lead roles (see Photo 12.2).

Researchers Analyze to Address Gaps in Understanding

By compiling details and looking for gaps in understanding, Kelly Kessler formulated a scholarly project that led to an illuminating claim: depictions of masculinity shift in Hollywood musicals of the 1960s.

PHOTO **12.1**
Fred Astaire, here dancing with Adele Astaire in 1921, exemplifies the graceful, formal performance style that was popular in early musicals (Fred Astaire and Adele Astaire).

PHOTO **12.2**
Clint Eastwood, known for playing tough-guy roles like Dirty Harry, here plays the rugged but sensitive singing cowboy in the 1969 film *Paint Your Wagon* (Paramount Pictures).

The details she chose to study are specific to movie musicals: "shooting styles, stars, types of songs and singers, styles of dance, numbers of songs/dances, and so on." We can imagine that a literary studies researcher whose project involves studying print sources might instead focus on details like narrative style, language choices, or publication history. And an environmental biologist might have a project that focuses on water samples, population surveys, or climate data. Regardless of which details scholars pay attention to, in order to analyze, they look for a particular kind of scholarly problem: an *interpretive* problem. You'll remember from Chapter 2 that researchers generally seek out scholarly problems—difficulties that arise from gaps in understanding. By "*interpretive* problem," we mean a difficulty that can be addressed only by interpretation. Put another way, scholars use **analysis** in an effort to answer the question, "How should I interpret this?"

Details become evidence only after scholars analyze them—pointing out what is difficult to understand, offering an interpretation, and connecting that interpretation to their own project. In other words, through analysis, scholars turn observations into evidence.

When scholars analyze, they typically do three things seen in Figure 12.1:

1. *Focus* on particular details of a source that reveal an interpretive problem. See Chapters 2 and 7 for strategies that can help you find interpretive problems.
2. *Interpret* the details. Interpretation explains how a reader should understand the details in order to make sense of the writer's interpretive problem.

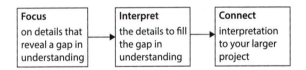

FIGURE **12.1**
Analysis typically consists of these three strategies. Although we've separated these tasks from one another in order to discuss them, you'll see that many scholars combine these tasks, put them in different orders, and so on.

KEY TERM

Analysis

Analysis (sometimes called "close reading" or "explication") refers to the process scholars use to examine and explain the meanings of sources. Scholars begin analysis with observations about a source, focusing on details that call for interpretation. By interpreting the details, scholars show how their observations support their larger project.

3. *Connect* the interpretation to their own project in order to advance that project. A project, as we explain in Chapter 3, is the approach the writer takes to making sense of the problem they've identified.

While we present analysis as three distinct steps that appear to proceed in order, it is helpful to remember that analysis, like writing, is recursive—that it involves returning repeatedly to the same details, rethinking your interpretations, and letting your project evolve as you come up with new ideas. It is likely, for instance, that your interpretation of some details will lead you to shift your focus to other details, that connecting the interpretation to your project will change your project's ambitions, and so on.

We can see Kelly Kessler employ these three aspects of analysis in her article "Broadway in the Box: Television's Infancy and the Cultural Cachet of the Great White Way." In the article, she seeks to understand how early American television gained viewership and cultural relevance by using music and staging from Broadway. Here, Kessler offers analysis of a television performance by two Broadway stars, Russell Nype and Elaine Stritch:

Focus on details that reveal an interpretive problem	Russell Nype . . . and Elaine Stritch's performance of Berlin's "You're Just in Love" from *Call Me Madam* uses costuming, staging, and camerawork to simultaneously evoke theatrical and concert performance. Nype and Stritch appear in costume on a partial set—with couch, chair, table, and telephone—and after a few lines of dialogue burst into
Interpretation of the details	song. Although they perform and dress in a manner the play would have dictated—wearing evening gown and tux, sitting and standing next to each other, making eye and physical contact—their repeated full-front positioning and formal dress, as well as choices made with regard to the camera's focal distance, project concurrent theatrical and concert settings. Medium long shots frame the duo's position among the set pieces, whereas a series of medium close-ups mirror a decontextualized style of performance . . . and the actors' gestures and bows project an out-of-character awareness of the
Connection to larger project	audience. They bring something for everyone: the ephemerality [brief existence] of the live theater and the familiarity of the pop charts. ("Broadway in the Box" 357–58)

1. *Focus on details that reveal an interpretive problem.* Noting that the details of a source or sources must be interpreted in order to be understood creates a need, or motive, for analysis. In essence, once the writer points out a place of potential confusion or misunderstanding, they raise a desire in readers to understand it through analysis.

   Kessler begins her analysis by focusing on details that reveal a gap in understanding: the performance "uses costuming, staging, and camerawork to simultaneously evoke theatrical and concert performance" ("Broadway in the Box" 357). Kessler points out the tension—the performance has characteristics of both a play and a concert—in order to raise a question in readers' minds: How can we make sense of these seemingly contradictory elements of the scene?

2. *Interpret the details to explain their meaning.* Writers address the gap in understanding by making sense of the details. Writers thus guide readers to new insights about how they can look at these details.

   Kessler's interpretation involves citing details and then explaining what they "project" and suggest: "Medium long shots frame the duo's position among the set pieces, whereas a series of medium close-ups mirror a decontextualized style of performance . . . and the actors' gestures and bows project an out-of-character awareness of the audience" ("Broadway in the Box" 358). Kessler explains how we can understand the varying camera perspectives: distant shots ("medium long") situate Nype and Stritch in a distinct setting apart from the audience, while the close-up shots position Nype and Stritch not in any specific setting ("decontextualized") but rather in the world of the audience.

3. *Connect interpretation to writer's own project.* Writers tell us why the new meaning raised by their interpretation is important. In other words, they explain how the interpretation advances their own project.

   Kessler uses her interpretation of camera perspectives to advance her larger project of understanding how American television used Broadway: "They bring something for everyone: the ephemerality of the live theater and the familiarity of the pop charts" ("Broadway in the Box" 358). Her initial observations revealed an interpretive problem—the theater aspects of the performance seem not to fit with the concert aspects of the performance. Her interpretation makes sense of that problem and advances her larger project: television purposefully used characteristics from both plays and concerts in order to appeal to a wide audience.

Sources Invite Multiple Interpretations

A team of writing studies researchers conducted a study examining how groups of college students approached the task of analyzing a poem. In their study, Nancy L. Chick, Holly Hassel, and Aeron Haynie found that their undergraduate subjects tended to read the poem in a way that limited how they were able to analyze it. In particular, many students gave what Chick, Hassel, and Haynie call "flattened-out responses" (409). By "flattened-out," they mean that the students looked for a single "true" meaning and rejected the validity of alternative interpretations, even when the text of the poem also supported those alternatives (400). Flattened responses limit writers' ability to present analysis that captures the kind of complexity that academic readers prize.

For scholars to resist analysis that narrows the interpretive possibilities of a source, they must embrace "negative capability": the ability to hold multiple and sometimes competing ideas in one's mind at the same time (a concept we explain in Chapter 1). What does this look like in scholars' writing? Film studies researcher Megan Woller demonstrates negative capability in her article about the 1967 film musical *Camelot*. The film's lead actor, Richard Harris, was a talented singer. Yet in *Camelot*, Harris, who plays King Arthur, adopted a talk-singing style often relied upon by bad singers. Woller offers analysis to make sense of Harris's singing style, but to do so, she first practices negative capability by acknowledging another possible analysis (Woller 7). She cites fellow media studies scholar Kelly Kessler's interpretation: that Harris's talk-singing invites viewers to question the normally cheerful optimism of musicals (Woller 7; Kessler, *Destabilizing the Hollywood Musical* 104). Woller then generates a second possible interpretation that serves her own project.

Woller focuses on two details in tension, revealing an interpretive problem	Although later a successful singer, [in *Camelot*] Harris has a slight voice and chose to talk-sing during portions of several songs. Kelly Kessler argues that this "restraint
She cites Kessler's interpretation	or ambivalent commitment to actual song forces him to remain connotatively distant from the accomplishments the Arcadian musical proves possible through song: love and social harmony" (104). Yet there is
She adds her new interpretation	another reading. While Julie Andrews out-sang Burton in the original stage production, Vanessa Redgrave's weaker voice more closely matches Harris in the film.... Redgrave sings in a pleasant though small voice with a breathiness that adds a layer of sex appeal to her character. Like Harris, she also talk-sings some of the more difficult passages.... Due to the similarities in vocal abilities, Arthur and Guenevere emerge as highly compatible aurally. (7)

Kessler and Woller start by focusing on the same interpretive problem: Harris was a skilled singer who, nevertheless, sings poorly in *Camelot*. But while Kessler responds to this problem by offering an interpretation of Arcadian musicals more broadly, Woller offers "another reading" of the relationship between *Camelot's* lead characters. Woller suggests that perhaps Harris sang below his ability in order to complement his costar's singing style and show their characters to be a good match.

Notice that Woller does not reject Kessler's analysis but instead adds a new possibility. This new possibility adds greater complexity to the conversation about the film. The fundamental assumption behind Woller's analysis is that texts are complex enough to offer multiple interpretations, each of which can further our understanding. In the next section, we'll detail some of the specific strategies that scholars use to generate analysis that advances scholarly conversations.

Sources Don't Speak for Themselves

When writers analyze, they typically begin by describing in great detail their observations about the source they are citing. Less-experienced writers sometimes stop there, assuming that their readers will interpret the source in the same way. Seasoned scholars, however, understand that a source doesn't speak for itself. Thus, they push beyond description into interpretation. Put another way, academic researchers do not merely call attention to details, they explain what those details mean and why they are important. Their interpretation turns observations into evidence that supports their projects.

The first step in pushing beyond description and into interpretation is learning how to distinguish between the two. Notice that description and interpretation each address different kinds of questions.

Description answers the following questions:

- What do you notice or observe with your own senses?
- What happened?

Interpretation answers a different set of questions:

- How should readers make sense of what you observed?
- Why are the conclusions you draw important?

PRACTICE
Distinguish between Description and Interpretation

One way to ensure that you are both describing and interpreting sources is to practice identifying description and interpretation in sources you encounter. You will then be primed to identify each in your own writing.

Task: The following two passages both describe and interpret. We've numbered the sentences. Using the questions in the bulleted lists from the previous section, identify which sentences offer description and which offer interpretation. Check your answers using the answer key that follows.

Passage #1 from Heather Chan's "From Costume to Fashion: Visions of Chinese Modernity in *Vogue* Magazine, 1892–1943":

(1) In the 1920s and 1930s, as *Vogue* increasingly represented Chinese women as lively and well dressed, the modern Chinese woman became a fashionable racial Other to Americans. (2) A 1936 article, "On the Face of the Globe," provides for its readers a contemporary depiction of Chinese beauty [see Box Figure 12.2]. (3) The article accompanied a collage of images of female beauty from commercial art around the world, gathered

continued

FIGURE **12.2**
Images from *Vogue Magazine's* 1936 article "On the Face of the Globe" (82).

so that readers could see that "every race holds up a different ideal . . . each one idealizing its own racial type." (4) The illustration representing China was front and center. (5) From what can be seen of her clothing, she appears less traditional than the Hungarian women in ethnic dress at the bottom, the seminude women in the illustration from India, and the Japanese women in kimonos. (6) "On the Face of the Globe" describes the ideal Chinese "racial type" as a "succulent Chinese girl with her long waiving [*sic*] hair, her Hollywood brows, her rouged cheeks— Chinese with a California patina." (7) This word choice suggests the influence of Western, specifically American, beauty ideals on the beauty standards of modern China. (Chan 222–23)

Passage #2 from Nicholas Carr's "Is Google Making Us Stupid?":

(1) The company [Google] has declared that its mission is "to organize the world's information and make it universally accessible and useful." (2) It seeks to develop "the perfect search engine," which it defines as something that "understands exactly what you mean and gives you back exactly what you want." (3) In Google's view, information is a kind of commodity, a utilitarian resource that can be mined and processed with industrial efficiency. (4) The more pieces of information we can "access" and the faster we can extract their gist, the more productive we become as thinkers. (Carr 62)

ANSWERS:

Passage #1. Chan alternates between interpretation and description. Sentences 1, 2, 5, and 7 interpret, while sentences 3, 4, and 6 describe.

Passage #2. Carr describes Google's mission in sentences 1 and 2. Then he interprets its mission in sentences 3 and 4. Carr carries out interpretation by going beyond what Google says and explaining how we should make sense of its mission statement.

Tools & Techniques: Generating Interesting Analysis

With any given source, scholars might make an endless number of observations. But which observations will lead to meaningful analysis?

Interpret Observations that Advance Your Project

Let's start with an object that many scholars have analyzed: photographer Gordon Parks's "American Gothic," a 1942 portrait of custodian Ella Watson (see Photo 12.3). How might you offer a fresh analysis of the image? Write down your initial observations. You might notice that Watson wears glasses, that the flag draped on the wall behind her has forty-eight stars, that a small dark triangle sits in the corner of the photograph, that the broom appears closer to us than the mop, and so on. How would a scholar decide which details to focus on? Here are two questions that scholars ask themselves when deciding which observations are useful:

1. Which observations are relevant to my project?

   If, for instance, you were working on a project that sought to understand how American fashion changed in the 1940s, you

PHOTO **12.3**
"American Gothic," Gordon Parks's portrait of Ella Watson (Gordon Parks Archive, Library of Congress Prints and Photographs Division).

might decide to focus on the pattern of Watson's dress, the number of buttons, the length of its sleeves, and other such details. If, however, you were working on a project that sought to understand how the photographer Gordon Parks represented his subjects, you might focus on the image's composition, its lighting, its perspective, and so on.

2. Which observations lead to interpretive problems?

Scholars focus on those observations that present a difficulty in understanding. By presenting to their readers something that is not easily understood, scholars motivate their readers to pay attention to a new interpretation. It would not be merely enough, then, to describe the pattern of the dress; a scholar would have to explain how the pattern calls for interpretation, perhaps because it does not adhere to expectations, for instance.

Let's look at an example of a scholar who analyzed Parks's photograph. In his 2016 essay "Harlem in Furs: Race and Fashion in the Photography of Gordon Parks," media studies scholar Jesús Constantino explores the tension between Parks's interest in fashion photography and his interest in politics. In this excerpt, he focuses on the dress Ella Watson is wearing. What details does Constantino point out?

Focuses on details that pertain to his project	Two buttonholes lay unused over her left breast; the two overlaying pieces of fabric have been sewn together instead. One of the unused buttons for an unseen third buttonhole has been folded inward at her neck to form a more comfortable v-line. At her waist, two buttons have been added to take in (albeit unevenly) what had once likely been a larger waistline. A single tear in the fabric just to the left of the lower of the two buttons testifies to
Interprets details that advance his project	the age and imperfection of the alteration. . . . [Parks] directly challenges the tactics of fashion photography itself. The image frustrates desire. The dress appears as though it could be used and reused forever through an endless series of minor alterations, standing defiantly outside the circulation of commodities. (794–95)

Because Constantino is interested in fashion, he dwells on precise observations about Ella Watson's dress—its style, fit, texture, and wear. These details help Constantino emphasize the tension between fashion and politics that he explores in his project. His interpretation—that the photograph challenges the consumerist culture of fashion by "standing defiantly outside the circulation of commodities"—comes only after he has guided the reader through a series of close observations.

When scholars interpret details—as when Constantino tells us how best to understand Watson's dress—they offer their own take on a source, explaining exactly what meaning they would like readers to take away. We find that interpretation is the most neglected part of analysis in the writing of less-experienced researchers. They can make the mistake of imagining that the reason for their focus on specific details is obvious to readers. Producing interesting analysis requires taking on the role of thoughtful guide for readers, using reasoning to show them how to interpret details.

It requires writers to ask the question, How must I interpret the details I've observed in order for them to act as evidence to support my project?

Let's look at an example of another scholar who examines the same photograph but focuses on different details in order to produce a new interpretation to serve his particular project. Here is an excerpt from American studies scholar Joseph Entin's 1999 article "Modernist Documentary: Aaron Siskind's 'Harlem Document.'" In his article, Entin seeks to understand how photographs carry both symbolic qualities and documentary qualities. What details does he observe that address his project? How do these details present a scholarly problem that calls for interpretation? Before you read Entin's excerpt, you may want to do an image search on the web for "American Gothic and Grant Wood." You'll find an image of the 1930 painting by Grant Wood that Gordon Parks's photograph takes its name from.

Focuses on details that pertain to the project	Entitled "American Gothic" because it recasts the famous Grant Wood painting of a farm couple, Parks's image depicts Watson, who worked as a night-time cleaner in the Federal building that housed the FSA [Farm Security Administration], where Parks was interning on a fellowship, standing in front of an American flag with a broom and a mop, the tools of her menial labor. . . . The tone of "American Gothic" is defined by Watson's
Interprets details that advance the project	conscious participation in the photographic act. She gazes straight into the camera, collaborating in the ironic subversion of the patriotism symbolized by the flag draped behind her. Her eyes pierce the photographic plane; her gaze is serious, steady, and straightforward, almost confrontational. The directness of her look and the solidity of her stance lend her an aura of strength and determination that belie her menial occupation. The frontality of Watson's pose and the eye-level position from which the photograph is taken establish equality between Watson and the viewer. (369)

This excerpt focuses on different details than the previous one. Entin emphasizes details that speak to his project about symbolism and realism: he focuses on the tension between the symbol-laden backdrop of the American flag and the everyday-ness of Watson's mop and broom. He calls readers' attention to Watson's "serious, steady, and straightforward" eyes, looking directly at the viewer and challenging them to grapple with the tension. These observations allow Entin to offer an interpretation of the photograph: the composition creates a sense of "equality between Watson and the viewer."

Entin's interpretation demonstrates how scholarly writers guide readers to the meaning of their observations. The more clearly writers lead readers from observation to interpretation—the more clearly they explain what their observations mean and why—the more likely readers will be convinced by the analysis. Writers do not simply reveal the meaning of their observations like a magic trick; they guide readers down a path, helping them reach the same conclusions.

PRACTICE

Observing and Interpreting Details that Advance Your Project

Imagine that you are working on a project that seeks to understand depictions of labor and nationalism in the United States. What details of Gordon Parks's photograph "American Gothic" might you want to focus on? And what interpretations might you begin to make?

Task #1: Observe details relevant to your project. List as many details as you can find.

Task #2: Focus on those details that, when grouped together, raise gaps in understanding, posing interpretive problems. To explain the gaps, try completing this sentence for each:

> In Gordon Parks's "American Gothic," we see [detail A]. And yet, we also see [detail B]. Taken together, these details may seem surprising because [explain the nature of the tension].

Task #3: Venture to offer interpretations that make sense of these interpretive problems.

Task #4: Connect your interpretations to your larger project.

ONE POTENTIAL ANSWER: In Gordon Parks's "American Gothic," we see a broom and mop in focus in the foreground. And yet we also see that the background is dominated by an out-of-focus American flag hanging from the wall. Taken together, these details may seem surprising because the broom and mop are everyday tools of domestic labor that we don't typically see set before a grand symbol of the nation. This surprising tension invites a new understanding of the photograph, namely, that the photograph elevates the humble labor of custodian Ella Watson above any grander notions of Americanness. Interpreted in this light, we can see that Parks's foregrounding and sharper focus on Watson's cleaning tools ask us to honor her contributions over a distant, hazy concept of nationhood.

Connect the Interpretation to Your Project

When writers connect an interpretation to their own project, they make the final, crucial step of analysis. If interpreting a source explains to readers what meaning they should take away, connecting that interpretation to a project tells them why that meaning is important. Writers tell readers what role the interpretation will play.

In the example that follows, linguist Paul Meara advances his study by connecting his interpretation to his project. The study, "The Importance of an Early Emphasis on L2 Vocabulary," asks what English language instructors should focus on when teaching their beginning-level students. Should they teach students just enough vocabulary (about 500 words) to read beginner-level texts or a lot of vocabulary words (about 2,000) from word lists? Meara examines the impact of increasing students' vocabularies on their ability to understand texts. He analyzes the data from a graph (see Figure 12.3) that compares the size of English language learners' vocabularies with the number of words they would recognize in common texts (9).

Focuses on details	The actual figures for English suggest that a basic vocabulary of about 2,000 words accounts for about 80% of what we see or hear. . . . What the graph does show is that a person with
Interprets details	a vocabulary of 2000 words is going to be able to recognise at least some of the words s/he hears. In contrast, the graph suggests that a person whose vocabulary is limited to only 500 words or so will meet a very large number of unfamiliar words in almost any common context. These unfamiliar words will be enough to prevent most learners at this level from understanding very much, except in very unusual circumstances. The obvious conclusion, from a linguistic point of view, is that a vocabulary of 500 words is pretty useless, while a vocabulary of 2,000 words goes a considerable way towards a realistic level of competence. The
Connects the interpretation to the study's project	linguistic evidence, then, suggests that it might be sensible to teach beginners a very large vocabulary very quickly and not restrict their lexical development to small vocabularies acquired over an extended period of time. (9)

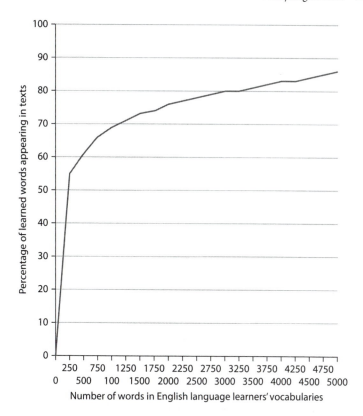

FIGURE 12.3
A graph in Paul Meara's study comparing the numbers of words in an English language learner's vocabulary (on the x-axis) to the percentage of words they would recognize in common texts (on the y-axis) (9).

When Meara analyzes this graph, he takes the same steps that scholars take if they were to analyze a poem, a photograph, or any source. In other words, even graphs and charts do not speak for themselves but require analysis. Notice that Meara's initial interpretation—that English language learners really need a vocabulary of about 2,000 words in order to grasp most of the common texts they encounter—relies upon observations and reasoning about the object he analyzes, a graph. But the connection he makes to his project goes beyond the graph: teachers should focus on building students' vocabularies very early in their English language learning. Connections like the one Meara offers create a sense of purpose that drives analysis, making clear to readers how a writer's interpretations advance a writer's project.

We want to close this chapter by noting that though we have presented analysis as a carefully defined three-step process, analysis is a notoriously slippery concept among scholars. While many argue that analysis is the fundamental practice of academic research, little consensus exists about how to define it or carry it out (Hayles 64; Smith 57–63). The definition and methods that we present here are therefore not universal. They rise out of our conversations with researchers like Kelly Kessler about what role analysis plays in their writing and what they actually *do* when they analyze. We suggest you have similar conversations with the researchers you encounter.

TURN TO YOUR RESEARCH

Analyze a Source

Once you identify which sources you want to analyze in your writing, complete the following prompts. They guide you through strategies for generating analysis that will advance your project.

1. *Focus* on details:
   a. I notice the following details that relate to my project:
   b. The details pose a gap in understanding that calls for interpretation because [name details that, when taken together, raise an interpretive problem].
2. *Interpret* the details:
   a. We can make sense of the details by understanding them as [fill the gap in understanding raised by the interpretive problem].
   b. We should interpret the details this way, because [offer reasons why your interpretation explains the gap in understanding].

3. *Connect* the interpretation to your project:
   a. This interpretation has implications for my larger project, namely . . .
   b. The project can now be understood as . . .

Works Cited

Carr, Nicholas. "Is *Google* Making Us Stupid?" *Atlantic Monthly,* vol. 302, no. 1, July 2008, p. 56.

Chan, Heather. "From Costume to Fashion: Visions of Chinese Modernity in *Vogue Magazine,* 1892–1943." *Ars Orientalis,* vol. 47, 2017.

Chick, Nancy L., et al. "'Pressing an Ear against the Hive': Reading Literature for Complexity." *Pedagogy: Critical Approaches to Teaching Literature, Language, Composition, and Culture,* vol. 9, no. 3, 2009, pp. 399–422. doi:10.1215/15314200-2009-003.

Costantino, Jesús. "Harlem in Furs: Race and Fashion in the Photography of Gordon Parks." *Modernism/Modernity,* vol. 23, no. 4, 2016, pp. 789–811. *Crossref,* doi:10.1353/mod.2016.0074.

Entin, Joseph. "Modernist Documentary: Aaron Siskind's 'Harlem Document.'" *Yale Journal of Criticism,* vol. 12, no. 2, Fall 1999, pp. 357–82.

Fred Astaire and Adele Astaire. 1921. *Wikimedia Commons,* commons. wikimedia.org/wiki/File:AdeleFred1921.jpg#filehistory.

Hayles, N. Katherine. "How We Read: Close, Hyper, Machine." *ADE Bulletin,* vol. 150, 2010, pp. 62–79.

Kessler, Kelly. "Broadway in the Box: Television's Infancy and the Cultural Cachet of the Great White Way." *Journal of Popular Music Studies,* vol. 25, no. 3, Sept. 2013, pp. 349–70. *EBSCOhost,* doi:10.1111/jpms.12036.

---. *Destabilizing the Hollywood Musical: Music, Masculinity, and Mayhem.* Palgrave Macmillan, 2010.

Meara, Paul. "The Importance of an Early Emphasis on L2 Vocabulary." *Language Teacher,* vol. 19, no. 2, Feb. 1995, pp. 8–11.

Paramount Pictures. *Paint Your Wagon.* 1969. *Unreality Magazine,* unrealitymag .com/evolution-of-clint-eastwood-in-movies/.

Parks, Gordon. *American Gothic.* 1942. *Gordon Parks Archive, Library of Congress Prints and Photographs Division,* www.loc.gov/pictures/ item/2016644280.

Smith, Barbara Herrnstein. "What Was 'Close Reading'?: A Century of Method in Literary Studies." *Minnesota Review: A Journal of Creative and Critical Writing*, vol. 2016, no. 87, 2016, pp. 57–75. *Google Scholar*, doi:10.1215/00265667-3630844.

Woller, Megan. "The Lusty Court of *Camelot* (1967): Exploring Sexuality in the Hollywood Adaptation." *Music and the Moving Image*, vol. 8, Apr. 2015, pp. 3–18.

Woolman Chase, Edna. "On the Face of the Globe." *Vogue*, vol. 88, no. 9, 1936, pp. 82–83.

....

CHAPTER 13

Citing Sources

Mindset: Scholars Rely on the Integrity of Their Peers

The anthropologist Evelyn A. Early spent years studying two communities of women in Cairo, Egypt: *afrangi* (modern) women and *baladi* (traditional) women (51). The communities lived in different urban landscapes, the *afrangi* women in a newer district laid out on a regular grid pattern and the *baladi* women in a district spiderwebbed by irregularly arranged streets (see Figures 13.1 and 13.2). Early found that each group navigated their neighborhoods differently but equally skillfully (38–39). *Afrangi* women relied on street names and numbered addresses that followed the logic of the grid. (Go five blocks north to such-and-such a street. Then turn left. The building is at 1505.) *Baladi* women navigated according to local landmarks, relying on their shared knowledge of the community's important sites. (Walk up the hill until you get to the market. Then follow the road toward the mosque.)

Early's research offers a metaphor for understanding citation styles—the guidelines that scholarly organizations issue to standardize text formatting and source citation in their fields. Like the navigation styles of the groups that Early studied, citation styles reflect different logics about how to best move through a space. Citation styles might strike writers who are unfamiliar with them as pointlessly arbitrary and fussy, sometimes interfering with a fluid writing process. However,

An *afrangi* (modern) neighborhood in Cairo, featuring streets arranged in grids. Map courtesy of the Bureau of Consular Affairs, U.S. State Department.

A *baladi* (traditional) neighborhood in Cairo, featuring streets arranged around local landmarks. Map courtesy of the Bureau of Consular Affairs, U.S. State Department.

to those who are familiar with them (presumably your readers), styles facilitate a fluid *reading* process, functioning like roadmaps to texts, placing key features exactly where readers in the scholarly community expect them to be.

What happens when experts encounter a text whose style doesn't conform to their field's guidelines? Early's research, again, is suggestive. She examined what happened when women accustomed to the logic of one district had to find their way in the other group's streets. When asked to navigate the irregularly laid-out *baladi* women's district, *afrangi* women found the streets "convoluted and confusing" (Early 38–39). And *baladi* women equally disliked navigating *afrangi* streets, which were laid out so regularly that they seemed indistinguishable (Early 39). Early's study suggests that no single ideal way exists to navigate neighborhoods and, to extend our metaphor, to navigate academic writing. Instead, the best navigation strategy conforms to the logic that readers expect in their field of study. When writers conform to a particular field's style, they present themselves as comfortable insiders in the scholarly community, researchers who know the territory and can guide readers through it.

Citation Styles Help Readers Navigate Texts

Citation styles offer guidelines about three aspects of research writing: page formatting, in-text citations, and bibliographies. Page formatting guidelines help writers make texts visually familiar to readers by dictating appropriate fonts, font sizes, page margins, line spacing, page numbering, title page formats, and so on. **In-text citation** and **bibliography** guidelines help readers navigate the text's use of sources and potentially locate the sources themselves.

You might expect a chapter titled "Citing Sources" to be filled with rules about how to cite various sources. You'll find many websites that spell out citation guidelines (we like the *Purdue OWL*), and you'll find citation generating programs (we used *Zotero* for this book). We recommend taking advantage of these free resources just the way that seasoned scholars do. Indeed, most scholars have not memorized the guidelines of source citation. There are just too many. Instead they focus on the principles behind those guidelines so that when they look them up, they can decide how to employ them in ways that satisfy readers. Thus our goal here isn't to spell out guidelines that are readily accessible

KEY TERM

In-Text Citation and Bibliography

In-text citations are brief notations included within the body of a text that indicate which sentences summarize, paraphrase, or quote from sources. Depending on the citation style, an in-text citation may appear in parentheses (called a "parenthetical citation") or as a superscript number that refers to a footnote or an endnote.

A *bibliography* appears on a separate page at the end of a research text. It contains detailed publication information about each source cited. Each citation style dictates specific formatting guidelines for various types of sources (books, journal articles, newspaper articles, films, and so on).

elsewhere but to show you how researchers use the available resources effectively.

The chart that follows introduces you to the four most common academic styles—APA, MLA, and two versions of Chicago Style. We use citations of Evelyn A. Early's book about *baladi* and *afrangi* women to illustrate differences among the styles.

Citation Styles Reflect Fields' Values

We began this chapter noting that two different Cairo communities—the *baladi* and the *afrangi*—navigate their neighborhoods quite differently. The ways these groups move through the world suggests something not only about how their streets are laid out but also about the values of each community. *Afrangi* (modern) navigation, following regular grids, suggests a community that values predictability and systematic logic. *Baladi* (traditional) navigation, following local landmarks in irregular patterns, suggests a community that values insider knowledge of the community's important sites. The way we navigate the world says what's important to us.

Just as we can discover a community's values by examining the way that community members navigate their world, we can get a sense of the values of specific scholarly fields by examining how members of that field use citation to navigate their scholarly conversations. Each citation style sets its guidelines to prioritize the information that those areas of study value most. They signal what they prioritize by 1) placing higher-value

Style	APA	Chicago, or CMS, author-date (A-D)	Chicago, or CMS, note-bibliography (N-B)	MLA
Established by . . .	American Psychological Association	University of Chicago Press	University of Chicago Press	Modern Language Association
*Published in . . .	*Publication Manual of the American Psychological Association*, 6th edition (2010)	*Chicago Manual of Style*, 17th edition (2017)	*Chicago Manual of Style*, 17th edition (2017)	*MLA Handbook*, 8th edition (2016)
Used in fields such as . . .	Social sciences and some sciences	Social sciences and natural and physical sciences	Humanities, particularly history	Humanities, particularly literature, cultural studies, foreign languages, philosophy, religion, and arts
In-text citations	When paraphrasing or summarizing, use parenthetical citations with author's last name and the year of publication, separated by a comma. (Early, 1993). When quoting, add "p." with the page number before the page number, separated by a comma. (Early, 1993, p. 51).	Use parenthetical citations with author's last name, the year of publication, a comma, and the page number of the material being cited. (Early 1993, 51).	Use footnotes or endnotes corresponding to superscript numbers in the text. Notes list full bibliographic information on the first citation and author and page number separated by a comma for subsequent citations. 1. Evelyn A. Early, *Baladi Women of Cairo: Playing with an Egg and a Stone* (Boulder, CO: Reinner, 1993), 51. 2. Early, 53.	Use parenthetical citations with author's last name and number of the page that the cited material appears on. (Early 51).
Bibliography title	References	Bibliography	Bibliography	Works Cited

*Listed here are the most recent editions available when this book was published. We recommend you check to see whether a more recent edition exists of the reference guide you are using; guidelines can change considerably from edition to edition.

information toward the beginnings of entries where readers see it first and 2) formatting higher-value information to make it stand out to readers (for example, with capitalization, italics, or parentheses).

Here are the first three elements in bibliography entries for Chanda Chisala and Dambisa Moyo's article "What's Ailing Africa?" in the major styles. Given what they prioritize, what hypotheses might you form to explain the values of the fields that use them?

APA   Chisala, C., & Moyo, D. (2009). What's ailing Africa?

CMS A-D   Chisala, Chanda and Dambisa Moyo. 2009. "What's Ailing Africa?"

CMS N-B   Chisala, Chanda and Dambisa Moyo. "What's Ailing Africa?" *Foreign Policy*

MLA   Chisala, Chanda, and Dambisa Moyo. "What's Ailing Africa?" *Foreign Policy*

Let's look at what conclusions we might draw about the order of each element.

First element of the bibliographic entries: One similarity jumps out: each style prioritizes authors first. This emphasis on authorship shows us that scholars experience research not as disembodied ideas but as a conversation voiced by real people who own their texts. No matter their area of study, scholars value authors' integrity and their ownership of ideas. Thus plagiarism, the act of separating an idea from its author, constitutes a serious violation of academic integrity.

Second element: After listing the author, the styles diverge. APA and CMS author-date styles list the year of publication second. By prioritizing the year, these styles speak to social science and science fields that value the timeliness of research; newer research is more relevant in these fields. In CMS note-bibliography and MLA styles, the article title appears second. These styles thus place greater emphasis on the subject of the research, helping readers in humanities fields answer the question, "Is the study's focus relevant?"

Third element: While APA and CMA author-date styles offer the article title third, CMS note-bibliography and MLA styles offer the title of the journal. Because the journal title is capitalized and italicized, readers can view all the journal titles in the bibliographies at a glance. In doing so, they gauge the prestige or credibility of the publication venue and therefore the importance of the conversation to others in the field.

PRACTICE

Find the Values That In-text Citations and Footnotes Reveal

We explained how bibliographic entries reveal the values of certain fields of study. In-text and footnote citation formats also reveal the values of the fields of study that use them.

Task: Determine the values that the following in-text and footnote citations suggest to you.

1. APA		For a summary or paraphrase: (Chisala and Moyo, 2009) For a quotation: (Chisala and Moyo, 2009, p. 14)
2. CMS A-D		(Chisala and Moyo 2009, 14)
3. CMS N-B		1. Chanda Chisala and Dambisa Moyo, "What's Ailing Africa?" *Foreign Policy* no. 173 (2009): 14, accessed March 5, 2018, http://www.jstor.org/stable/20684889.
4. MLA		(Chisala and Moyo 14)

ANSWERS: Like bibliographic entries, in-text and footnote citations from each style place the authors' names first, showing that all areas of study value most the reputation of the researcher(s) and their ownership of their work. Subsequent elements of the citations might suggest the following values:

1) and 2): The social science and science styles—APA and CMS author-date—emphasize the research's timeliness by listing the year of publication second.

3) The first citation of a text in CMS N-B style requires a full bibliographic entry whose format loosely echoes the other humanities-focused style, MLA. By footnoting that information, CMS N-B style values a fluid reading experience suited to historians' desire to create a compelling narrative about the past. Readers can glance at the bottom of the page to view a footnote rather than flipping to a separate bibliography page.

4) MLA style places the page number of the material being cited second. The fields that use MLA style—literary studies, philosophy, foreign languages, and so on—value careful textual analysis. Their readers may want to navigate directly to the passage being cited to examine the language and its context.

By analyzing citation styles, we see the field-specific logic underpinning each. We hope this perspective makes the styles' guidelines seem less like arbitrary rules and more like tools scholars wield to enact the values they share with other scholars in the field.

Citations Make Research Verifiable and Trustworthy

The grounding principle behind citing sources is that research is valid when it is verifiable. In other words, if readers examined the same sources or data that the researcher studied using the same methods to examine them, they could arrive at the same findings. Verifiability separates trustworthy scholarly knowledge from mere opinion or taste. It turns a scholar's research into a solid foundation that others can build on. To make research verifiable, readers need to know 1) which material in a text comes from sources and 2) how they can find that material in those sources themselves.

Research communities operate on the trust that writers have in each other's work. After all, for researchers to add to existing knowledge, they must first presume that they are building upon solid foundations. For this reason, plagiarism—the act of representing others' ideas, language, or data as one's own—undermines the value of scholarly writing. But instead of dwelling on the ill effects of plagiarism, we want to focus on the advantages of accurate source citations. When writers cite sources with integrity, they dramatize the mutual respect at the heart of even the most heated scholarly conversations.

Tools & Techniques: Citing Sources with Principle

Citation guides struggle to keep up with the times. Style guides regularly publish updated editions to include bibliographic formats for the newest forms of media. And citation generator programs like *EasyBib* and *Zotero* try to keep up with these updates. But media change too quickly. The most recent *MLA Handbook*, for example, explains how to cite Tweets but not *Instagram* posts. So writers who approach citation strictly as a task of memorizing rules can feel lost when they encounter cases that the rule books don't address. Here we want to offer principled strategies to help you cite any source with integrity, whether or not a citation guide addresses it explicitly.

When to Cite

Scholars cite every instance when they use any language, idea, or material drawn from another source (with the exception of common knowledge). Scholars cite not only print and digital texts but other media, like films and videos, paintings, performances, and so on. The format of the citation changes depending on the style you're using, but citation should always occur both 1) in an in-text citation at the moment when you use another's material—either as a parenthetical citation or a superscript number that corresponds to a footnote or endnote and 2) in a bibliographic entry at the end of the document on a bibliography page.

Scholars do not cite ideas that are considered "common knowledge." Common knowledge is a tricky term because it does not refer to the knowledge of the individual writer but instead to the knowledge of the scholarly community that the writer enters. Composition studies researcher Amy England says that we can only understand "common knowledge" within "the larger context of discourse community conventions and expectations" (112). If you're not sure what would be common knowledge to your reader, we recommend searching for the same idea in other scholarship in that field of study. Do other scholars cite it? If so, you should too. And as with all choices you make about whether to cite something, it's always best to err on the conservative side. If you're not sure whether to cite something, cite it.

How to Cite

What does it mean to know a citation style? Rather than memorizing a book full of formatting guidelines, "knowing" a style means understanding the values that inform it and being comfortable looking up the formatting guidelines that you need using a style guide's index or a trusted source like the *Purdue OWL's* "Research and Citation Resources."

Alas, style guides do not have all the answers. They will not, for instance, list guidelines for citing all possible types of sources. You can, however, use them to look up the guidelines for formatting *most* types of sources. Here are steps you can take when you're ready to cite a source:

1. In the most recent edition of the style's handbook or a trusted guide to the style, look up the guidelines for formatting the type of source you want to include in your bibliography. For instance, the 8th edition of the *MLA Handbook* gives the following example of how to format a book in the list of works cited (21):

    Jacobs, Alan. *The Pleasures of Reading in an Age of Distraction*. Oxford UP, 2011.

    And here is the *MLA Handbook's* example of a works cited entry for a tweet (24):

    @persiankiwi. "We have report of large street battles in east & west of Tehran now – #Iranelection." *Twitter*, 23 June 2009, 11:15 a.m., twitter.com/persiankiwi/status/2298106072.

2. *If the type of source you're citing isn't in a handbook, look it up on an authoritative website.* For instance, the 8th edition of the *MLA Handbook* has no information about how to cite a podcast. However, a quick search on the MLA website (style.mla.org/) yields the following example:

> Gladwell, Malcolm, narrator. "The Lady Vanishes." *Revisionist History*, season 1, episode 1, Slate Group, 2016, revisionisthistory.com/seasons?selected=season-1.

3. If you still can't find guidelines for your type of source, apply the style's larger principles of citation formatting to your source. For instance, neither the 8th edition of the *MLA Handbook* nor the MLA style website specifies the formatting rules for citing *Instagram* posts. However, we know that MLA formatting uses the following core elements in this order: 1) Author. 2) Title of Source. 3) Title of Container, 4) Other Contributors, 5) Version, 6) Number, 7) Publisher, 8) Publication Date, 9) Location (Modern Language Association of America 20). We can figure out, then, that an entry for an *Instagram* post would look like this:

> The Metropolitan Museum of Art. Photo of Joe Perry holding guitar. *Instagram*, photographed by Zach Whitford, 12 Apr. 2019, www.instagram.com/p/BwKW7qNF0Vo/.

For any citation, scholars adhere to the following principles: 1) readers should know who is responsible for producing the source, and 2) readers should be able to use the bibliographic entry to find the exact version of the source.

COMMON PITFALL

Trusting Citation Generators

Citation generating programs and apps like *Zotero*, *Google Scholar*, *NoodleBib*, and *Easy Bib* save researchers' time by gathering sources' publication information online at the click of a button and formatting that information into in-text citations and bibliographic entries. However, citation generators are seldom perfect. Compare, for instance, the following bibliographic entries. How many differences can you find between the two citation generated versions and the correct American Psychological Association-style, 6th edition, entry that follows them?

Entry generated by *Google Scholar*:

Chandrasekaran, P., Dallabetta, G., Loo, V., Rao, S., Gayle, H., & Alexander, A. (2006). Containing HIV/AIDS in India: the unfinished agenda. *The Lancet infectious diseases, 6*(8), 508–521.

Entry generated by *RefWorks*:

Chandrasekaran, P., Dallabetta, G., Loo, V., Rao, S., Gayle, H., & Alexander, A. (2006). Containing HIV/AIDS in india: The unfinished agenda. *The Lancet Infectious Diseases, 6*(8), 508–21. Retrieved from http://ezproxy.cul .columbia.edu/login?url=https://search.proquest.com/docview/2016128 41?accountid=10226

Correct entry:

Chandrasekaran, P., Dallabetta, G., Loo, V., Rao, S., Gayle, H., & Alexander, A. (2006). Containing HIV/AIDS in India: The unfinished agenda. *The Lancet Infectious Diseases, 6*, 508–21. doi:10.1016/s1473-3099(06)70551-5.

Given the mistakes that citation generators typically introduce, researchers proofread their bibliographic entries.

Forms of Plagiarism

Because all the major citation styles put authors' names first, we know that authors' reputation is one of the highest values of academic cultures. Knowing when and how to cite sources ensures that scholars maintain good reputations. However, we want to be clear that standards of academic integrity are not universal or unchanging. Intellectual property scholar Siva Vaidhyanathan finds that standards of integrity have changed over the course of American history (4). And scholars like English education researcher Joel Bloch demonstrate the complex ways that standards of integrity vary across cultures (3–10). How do scholars navigate differing standards? They follow the standards of their particular research community. These standards appear in the policies of their institutions and professional organizations. The standards we present in this chapter reflect the policies of American academic research communities.

For American researchers, plagiarism is an uncredited use of another's thoughts, words, or other material. Here are common varieties of plagiarism:

- *Passing off others' material as one's own.* This form of plagiarism might involve copying material or having someone else write the material.
- *Copying a passage from a source but omitting quotation marks.* When a writer omits quotation marks, even if they cite the source and list it in their bibliography, they falsely suggest to the reader that the language is their own.
- *Patchwriting.* Patchwriting occurs when writers attempt to paraphrase but echo too much of the original sentence structure or language without using quotation marks. For further explanation, see Chapter 11 on integrating sources.
- *Paraphrasing without citing.* This happens when writers put an author's ideas in their own words but fail to cite the author.
- *Collusion.* Collusion involves others dictating to a writer what language or ideas they should use. Collusion differs from collaboration, which entails getting help from others to draw out your own thinking. If your institution has a writing center, you can find writing collaborators there. Chapter 9 offers strategies for giving and receiving feedback that avoids collusion.
- *Self-plagiarism.* Self-plagiarism involves reusing one's own previously written work without permission. At a university, for instance, self-plagiarism might involve reusing a paper written for one class in another class without explicit permission from both instructors. In scholarly publishing, it may involve publishing the same material in two different journals.

Though some forms of plagiarism represent intentional cheating, unintentional plagiarism is still plagiarism. If you have questions about ethical source use, we recommend speaking with an instructor, an editor, or a research librarian.

Why Writers Plagiarize

Scholars such as Chris Park have articulated some of the reasons behind student plagiarism (Park 479). We've distilled reasons for plagiarism into five categories, all of which are fortunately avoidable:

- *Poor time management.* Writers may be tempted to plagiarize out of a sense of panic about a looming deadline (Park 479). A quick weighing of the pros and cons will likely convince writers that the consequences of a blown deadline will never be as severe as the penalty for plagiarism. Chapter 8 describes time management strategies.

- *Poor source management.* This unintentional form of plagiarism occurs when writers' research notes separate ideas from their sources, and those ideas end up uncited in the text. From the beginning of the research process, scholars' notes connect ideas and language to their sources. Chapter 5 details strategies to prevent this cause of plagiarism.
- *Lack of understanding.* Inexperienced writers sometimes plagiarize because they do not understand the rules of citation (Park 479). But ultimately the writer is responsible for understanding the rules. Thankfully, many resources—at educational institutions, libraries, and on the internet—exist to help writers learn proper citation techniques.
- *Desire to not cite every sentence.* Writers sometimes find that most sentences in a paragraph require citation. Out of a desire not to have their projects appear to be dominated by other voices, they may omit citations. In essence, they address an intellectual problem (the text is dominated by other voices) by creating a more serious ethical problem (the text does not credit the voices it uses). Instead, writers can ask themselves, "How can I contribute my own ideas to this scholarly conversation?"
- *Desire for recognition or better grades.* Some knowingly plagiarize to gain an unfair advantage (Park 479). Writers who find ways to make their research authentic and meaningful—rather than as merely a task to complete for others—remove the temptation to cheat.

Formatting

Besides offering the rules for citation, style guides also present formatting rules. When you format your text, paying attention to title page formatting, line spacing, margin size, font style, font size, indentation, heading styles, and page numbering will make a reader in your area of study feel like you have welcomed them into familiar territory.

TURN TO YOUR RESEARCH

Checking Your Formatting

We note earlier that citation generators can save time but can also introduce mistakes. Writers who rely on word processors' default settings for font, margins, and other features may similarly produce texts that don't conform to a style's formatting guidelines. As you polish your text and finalize your

continued

citations, this checklist will help you address commonly confused formatting features. For each, you might refer to the *Purdue OWL* website; it contains sample papers that demonstrate correct formatting for each major citation style.

Page formatting:

- ❑ *Title page format*: How should you present your name; the title of your project; the date; and, if applicable, your instructor's name and the course title?
- ❑ *Margin size*: How large should the margins surrounding your text be?
- ❑ *Line spacing*: Should paragraphs be single or double spaced? Should there be additional space between paragraphs? How should block quotes be spaced?
- ❑ *Font style and size*: Which fonts and type sizes are acceptable in your style?
- ❑ *Page numbering*: Where in the margins should the page number appear? Should your last name or a title header accompany the page number? Should numbering start with the first page or the second?

In-text citations:

- ❑ *Citation location*: Do you include citation information in each sentence containing source material that is not common knowledge rather than merely at the ends of whole paragraphs?
- ❑ *Citation information*: According to the citation style, what information should appear in the in-text citation?
- ❑ *Citation format*: Should you place in-text citations in parentheses at the ends of sentences or within sentences, in footnotes, or in endnotes?
- ❑ *Common knowledge*: If you present an idea that is not your own and is not cited, are you sure that it is common knowledge?
- ❑ *Paraphrases*: Have you cited not only quotations but also paraphrases of ideas or data pulled from sources?
- ❑ *Block quotes*: Some styles format the citations that accompany block quotes differently. Are you correctly placing and punctuating block quote citations?

Bibliography page:

- ❑ *Dedicated page*: Does the bibliography page start at the top of a new page that comes immediately after the last full page of text?

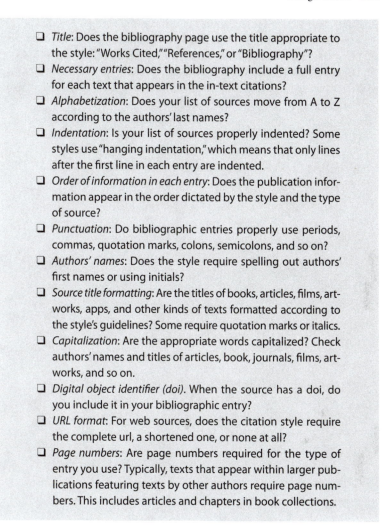

- ❏ *Title*: Does the bibliography page use the title appropriate to the style: "Works Cited," "References," or "Bibliography"?
- ❏ *Necessary entries*: Does the bibliography include a full entry for each text that appears in the in-text citations?
- ❏ *Alphabetization*: Does your list of sources move from A to Z according to the authors' last names?
- ❏ *Indentation*: Is your list of sources properly indented? Some styles use "hanging indentation," which means that only lines after the first line in each entry are indented.
- ❏ *Order of information in each entry*: Does the publication information appear in the order dictated by the style and the type of source?
- ❏ *Punctuation*: Do bibliographic entries properly use periods, commas, quotation marks, colons, semicolons, and so on?
- ❏ *Authors' names*: Does the style require spelling out authors' first names or using initials?
- ❏ *Source title formatting*: Are the titles of books, articles, films, artworks, apps, and other kinds of texts formatted according to the style's guidelines? Some require quotation marks or italics.
- ❏ *Capitalization*: Are the appropriate words capitalized? Check authors' names and titles of articles, book, journals, films, artworks, and so on.
- ❏ *Digital object identifier (doi)*. When the source has a doi, do you include it in your bibliographic entry?
- ❏ *URL format*: For web sources, does the citation style require the complete url, a shortened one, or none at all?
- ❏ *Page numbers*: Are page numbers required for the type of entry you use? Typically, texts that appear within larger publications featuring texts by other authors require page numbers. This includes articles and chapters in book collections.

Works Cited

Bloch, Joel. "Plagiarism Across Cultures: Is There a Difference?" *Indonesian Journal of English Language Teaching*, vol. 3, no 2, Oct. 2007, pp. 1–13. *Google Scholar*, doi:10.25170%2Fijelt.v3i2.133.

Bureau of Consular Affairs, U.S. Department of State. *Maps of Cairo, Egypt. Travel.State.Gov*, 8 Nov. 2019, travelmaps.state.gov/TSGMap/.

Early, Evelyn A. *Baladi Women of Cairo: Playing with an Egg and a Stone*. Lynne Reinner, 1993.

England, Amy. "The Dynamic Nature of Common Knowledge." *Originality, Imitation, and Plagiarism: Teaching Writing in the Digital Age*, edited by Caroline Eisner and Martha Vicinus, U of Michigan P, 2008, pp. 104–13. *Google Books*, 10.3998/dcbooks.5653382.0001.001.

Modern Language Association of America. *MLA Handbook*. 8th ed., Modern Language Association of America, 2016.

Park, Chris. "In Other (People's) Words: Plagiarism by University Students—Literature and Lessons." *Assessment & Evaluation in Higher Education*, vol. 28, no. 5, Oct. 2003, pp. 471–88.

Vaidhyanathan, Siva. *Copyrights and Copywrongs: The Rise of Intellectual Property and How It Threatens Creativity*. New York UP, 2003.

CHAPTER 14

Authority

SCHOLAR'S STORY

Theater Studies Scholar Elisabeth Heard Greer on Conveying Scholarly Authority

I remember stuttering my way through carefully crafted questions, barely listening to August Wilson's sage answers as he spoke on the other side of the phone. I had to put full trust in my recording device because my notes were incomprehensible. I was desperately trying to sound like a serious scholar, but the voice in my head was screaming, "You're just a graduate student, and you are interviewing the greatest living playwright of our generation!"

I tell this story every semester to my Composition II class. Composition II is the research writing class offered at Harold Washington College, a community college in Chicago where I've been teaching since 2008. The students often laugh at my hyperbolic retelling of the events—which end with me sweating and crying when I hang up the phone—but I use this example to illustrate the concept of *ethos*, and more importantly, to drive home the fact that they should never underestimate their own *ethos*.

I was in my mid-twenties when I interviewed Wilson. This bold idea was born of a conversation with my advisor when I mentioned that I loved Wilson's work. The set-up and follow through were surprisingly easy, and

continued

I tell my students that I was shocked that Wilson would give me—a lowly graduate student—a precious half hour of his day. My experience serves as an example that it does not matter how young you are, how inexperienced you are, or how insecure you might feel. If you conduct yourself like a professional, construct a rhetorically compelling argument, and write it well, people will take you seriously. Your *ethos* will be of a person who is confident, intelligent, and can be trusted. Even if, later on, you find yourself screaming, crying, and sweating.

Read the research: Elisabeth Heard Greer is an English professor at Harold Washington College. She is author of *Experimentation on the English Stage, 1695–1708: The Career of George Farquhar*. Her piece "August Wilson on Playwriting: An Interview" appears in the *African American Review*.

Mindset: Scholars Create Their Authority on the Page

When venturing on new projects, even experienced writers wonder to themselves: "Who am I to make a contribution to this scholarly conversation?" To discuss how writers gain authority, Elisabeth Heard Greer uses the word *ethos*, the Greek word for character. *Ethos* refers to the moral character or credibility of a writer or speaker. When readers consider a writer's *ethos*, they ask themselves, "Is this writer trustworthy?" Presumably, famed playwright August Wilson asked himself this question when then-graduate student Elisabeth Heard Greer requested an interview with him. Heard Greer was acutely aware that she hadn't yet developed a scholarly reputation that Wilson or her readers would recognize. However, she was able to focus on creating a trustworthy

RESEARCH ON WRITING

Aristotle on *Ethos*

In *On Rhetoric*, from the fourth century B.C.E., Greek philosopher Aristotle investigates the art of persuasion. Aristotle argues that people judge speech not only on its logic but also on their impressions of the speaker. Aristotle describes three qualities one must demonstrate to convey a compelling *ethos*, or character: "There are three reasons why speakers themselves are persuasive; for there are three things we trust other than logical demonstration. These are practical wisdom [*phronesis*] and virtue [*arête*] and goodwill [*eunoia*]" (112). In what follows, you'll see that our own chapter is inspired by Aristotle's categories, which we believe remain helpful for writers who want to show authority.

Takeaway: To craft persuasive texts, writers must attend not only to their reasoning but to the kind of character they convey on the page.

Read the research: Aristotle. *On Rhetoric: A Theory of Civic Discourse.* Oxford UP, 2007.

scholarly character by interviewing and writing in a way that projected the authority of a prepared professional.

How do less-seasoned writers craft an authoritative presence? When entering an unfamiliar scholarly conversation, it can be tempting, on the one hand, to mimic the persona of a senior scholar or, on the other hand, to try to erase one's presence from the text altogether. Both approaches can leave readers questioning the writer's authority. Those trying to sound like senior scholars often adopt inflated language or unfamiliar jargon that, according to writing studies scholar David Bartholomae, can sound to expert readers "more a matter of imitation or parody" than the voice of a seasoned scholar (11). The other extreme, making one's self invisible in a text by adopting a detached, clinical attitude, can fall equally flat: no writer is invisible. This writer becomes like the shy person at the party who stands quietly in the corner hoping nobody notices them.

Let's examine how Elisabeth Heard Greer tackled the challenge of presenting herself as an authority even when she was a less-seasoned scholar. In the introduction to her August Wilson interview, Heard Greer constructed a presence that conveys Aristotle's three qualities: wisdom, virtue, and good will. Yet she did so in a way that did not pretend that she carried authority she hadn't yet acquired. As you read the opening of Heard Greer's article, notice how she establishes authority by projecting character qualities that are trustworthy:

Opening with questions reveals **good will** toward her readers: she begins with humility and focuses on their mutual curiosity.	How does August Wilson view his plays and the process by which he creates them? Where does he start when writing a new play? Is August Wilson writing with a particular audience in mind? Joan Herrington, in *"I Ain't Sorry for Nothin 'I Done": August Wilson's Process of Playwriting,* attributes Wilson's success in playwriting to his influences, which he himself refers to as the "four 'B's'" (2)—the blues, the playwright Amiri Baraka, the painter Romare Bearden, and the short story writer Jorge Luis Borges. She also discusses what she calls Wilson's "new methodology of playwriting" (113), which entails revising the plays during the rehearsal process. Wilson first used this revision strategy with *The Piano Lesson* (1995) and decided to employ it again for the 1996 version of his play *Jitney,* originally written in 1979. . . . After seeing the Goodman Theatre's production of [Wilson's play] *Jitney,* which ran in the summer of 1999, I wanted to know more about Wilson's playwriting methods and how he came to revise a play that he originally wrote twenty years earlier. (93)
She demonstrates **virtue** with an accurate and generous characterization of a fellow scholar's argument.	
She demonstrates **wisdom** by offering context and evidence of her deep interest in Wilson's *Jitney* (see Photo 14.1).	

Elisabeth Heard Greer's example invites us to actively perform a writerly presence that conveys qualities of wisdom, virtue, and goodwill—even without yet having a lot of experience.

Writers Craft an Authority that Fits Their Projects

Aristotle's description of the "three things we trust" might seem to ask writers to convey a single, unchanging core self in every piece of writing. However, seasoned writers tend to consider their authority differently. They seek not to perform one unchanging persona in everything they write; instead, with each new writing task, they make choices about what kind of authority would suit that particular project.

To demonstrate the way that writers create different kinds of authority, let's look at two distinct pieces of writing. As you read the passages, ask yourself, "What does the writing tell us about the character of the writer?" As you read, underline the places in the text that you think indicate the writer's authority. Don't worry if you don't fully

PHOTO **14.1**
Actors Michole Briana White and Russell Hornsby performing August Wilson's *Jitney* at Chicago's Goodman Theatre in 1999 (photo courtesy of the Goodman Theatre).

understand the meanings of either text; the important thing is to consider what kind of authority the writing crafts.

Passage 1:
Black literature shares much with, far more than it differs from, the Western textual tradition, primarily as registered in English, Spanish, Portuguese, and French. But black formal repetition always repeats with a difference, a black difference that manifests itself in specific language use. And the repository that contains the language that is the source—and the reflection—of black difference is the black English vernacular tradition. (17)

Passage 2:
We always had a gas stove in the kitchen, in our house in Piedmont, West Virginia, where I grew up. Never electric, though using electric became fashionable in Piedmont in the sixties, like using Crest toothpaste rather than Colgate, or watching Huntley and Brinkley rather than Walter Cronkite. But not us: gas, Colgate, and good ole Walter Cronkite, come what may. (40)

What does each passage show about the writer's character? In the first passage, you probably noted that the writer is interested in intellectual, scholarly pursuits. You may have underlined the phrase "black English vernacular tradition" as an example of the writer's comfort with scholarly language. The writer carries the authority of an intellectual insider, a specialist.

In the second passage, the writer also shows a sense of insiderness, though a very different type of insider. In fact, the phrase "where I grew up" indicates a deep knowledge based on personal experience. We might describe the character of the second passage as informed, down-to-earth, and inviting. Notice that even though the passages convey very different character qualities, both feature a speaker who maintains authority; that authority arises from the way language conveys character.

So who wrote these passages? The first was penned by Henry Louis Gates, Jr., in his scholarly book *The Signifying Monkey: A Theory of African-American Literary Criticism*. The second passage was also written by Henry Louis Gates, Jr., from his book *Colored People: A Memoir*. The same person—a noted Harvard literary critic and historian—wrote both texts. So what should we make of the fact that the writer of the first passage seems different from the writer of the second passage? Does this mean that Gates is being inauthentic or fake in one of the passages? Of course not. In each, he demonstrates practical wisdom about his subject. Gates uses his writing to craft a character that speaks to the audience and purpose of each text. Put another way, he conveys an authority that fits his project.

These examples from Gates offer a powerful lesson in writing. Authority does not emerge from a single, rigid expression of your personality; rather, authority comes from the way writers shape and reshape their own character out of language. When scholars consider their authority, they don't ask "What kind of person am I?" Rather, they consider, "What kind of moral character do I want this piece of writing to show, given my project?" In turn, they consider how the authority that they craft positions their readers: "Am I asking them to be fellow scholars? Sympathetic listeners? Adversaries?"

Tools & Techniques: Conveying Authority

The examples from Elisabeth Heard Greer and Henry Louis Gates, Jr., demonstrate that professional researchers have multiple ways of crafting their authority, depending upon their projects and the public they'd like to address. Here we'll offer strategies for displaying a range of character qualities that signal your authority. But first, we'll turn to the three moral characteristics that, according to Aristotle, persuasive writing displays no matter what role the writer seeks to play: practical wisdom, virtue, and goodwill. We'll discuss these characteristics individually, but you'll see that wisdom, virtue, and goodwill can all overlap.

Practical Wisdom

How does a writer convey practical wisdom? A writer can demonstrate practical wisdom without being an expert in the field. The writer, though, will have to show that they have read attentively on their subject, that they have considered its full context, that they have considered multiple viewpoints, and that their approach is a thoughtful one.

One common way that writers establish their practical wisdom involves explaining their methods, demonstrating that they took a reasoned approach to arrive at their ideas. Here, for example, the historian Louis Marchand tells us about his method for examining advertising and consumer culture in the 1920s and 1930s in his book *Advertising the American Dream*:

> By examining the social backgrounds of those who shaped the advertisements and by listening to their shoptalk about themselves, their audiences, and their working conditions, I have tried to assess their biases and the accuracy of their perception of social realities. (xx)

Marchand describes his research methods not only so that we know what his study involves but also so that we trust that his study is a careful, deliberate one that accounts for "biases" and potential inaccuracies.

Scholars realize, of course, that it is not enough to display practical wisdom in their methods. Readers may think that the writer lacks wisdom if they encounter poorly formed sentences. Thus, in the later stages of a writing project, professional writers take pains to craft compelling, error-free sentences as further signs of their authority.

RESEARCH ON WRITING

Larry Beason's "*Ethos* and Errors: How Business People React to Errors"

Writing studies scholar Larry Beason conducted a small but evocative study of how errors in business writing influence perceptions of writers' authority in professional settings. Beason asked fourteen businesspeople to read five versions of the same document (36). Each version contained a single type of error—either misspellings, sentence fragments, run-on sentences, unnecessary quotation marks, or incorrect word endings—repeated in

continued

four different places (38). Participants then ranked how much each error bothered them and discussed their responses (38). Beason found that the readers' concerns about correctness extended beyond a desire to understand the document. Even when participants encountered errors that did not interfere with their understandings of the text, they made negative judgments about the writer's wisdom based on those errors (48).

Some businesspeople judged the writer to be hasty, careless, or professionally weak (Beason 49). Others labeled the writer a "faulty thinker" or one who fails to pay attention to details (49). Study participants also spoke passionately about the harm that an employee's errors could do to a company's image or in legal proceedings; even those who were not bothered by certain errors felt that business clients and courtroom juries would react negatively (56–59). Beason concludes that "the extent to which errors harm the writer's image is more serious and far-reaching than many students and teachers might realize" (48).

Takeaway: In professional settings, even errors that don't interfere with readers' understanding can harm a writer's ethos. To project practical wisdom, make time in the later stages of drafting to correct sentence-level errors.

Read the research: Larry Beason's *"Ethos* and Errors: How Business People React to Errors." *College Composition and Communications*, vol. 53, no. 1, 2001, pp. 33–64, *JSTOR*, doi:10.2307/359061.

Virtue

How does a writer convey virtue? Rhetoric scholars Edward P. J. Corbett and Robert J. Connors explain that writing that shows virtue must demonstrate its commitment to honesty by displaying the highest integrity and avoiding "unscrupulous tactics" (73). Here are some of the common ways that researchers seek to display virtue:

- *Acknowledging the limits of one's inquiry.* For instance, Ntsako Baloyi and Paula Kotzé write in their study of South African's attitudes toward digital privacy, "This study does not claim to be exhaustive of personal data protection related issues or to be a fully representative sample" (4). Writers acknowledge limits when they assess what kinds of claims their analysis can and cannot support.
- *Bringing forward evidence that might call into question one's claim.* Take this passage from psychologist Mick Cooper questioning whether his goal to get the clients he counsels to adopt a realistic picture of their situation is actually the most helpful approach:

[T]here is a growing body of evidence to suggest that most "well-adjusted" people tend to perceive their world with a certain degree of illusion, distortion, and self-deception (Baumeister, 1991), and that those who adopt an unrealistically optimistic outlook on life can often fare better than those who face up to the brute reality of their situation (Armor and Taylor, 1998) . . . As of yet, I am not convinced, but an engagement with the empirical research has stimulated me to question and reconsider my stance. (8)

Here Cooper shows that he's open to changing his mind based on new evidence; his scholarly virtue comes from his engagement with research rather than from unwavering convictions.

- *Representing others' ideas fully and generously.* Ian Bogost's review of Patrick Crogan's book about video games—*Gameplay Mode: War, Simulation, and Technoculture*—anticipates readers' objections to Crogan's argument and then offers an alternative interpretation that addresses those objections:

Some readers will rightly criticize the book for the relative absence of concrete examples and interpretations of specific games . . . But a more generous reading would allow Crogan a different goal: to characterize one of the modes of thought that underlies video games as a medium.

Bogost's expression of virtue follows a kind of scholarly golden rule: scholars strive to characterize others' writing as fairly as they would want their own characterized.

- *Accurate source citation.* As we explain in Chapter 13, scholars use citations not only to help readers find sources but also to demonstrate their own values: they respect others' ownership over their own ideas and honor their contributions to the scholarly conversation. In other words, accurate source citation is a way of expressing virtue.

COMMON PITFALL

Exaggeration

At some point, you may have been tempted to open your paper with the phrase, "Throughout history, humankind has always . . ." or "Since the dawn of time . . ." Or perhaps you've wanted to write, "This evidence proves

continued

beyond the shadow of a doubt that . . ." The desire to use such language often comes from well-intentioned thinking about authority. As composition studies scholars Zachary C. Beare and Marcus Meade suggest in their research on exaggeration in student writing, when student writers strive to "establish the importance" of their argument, they understand that their teachers value passion (81). Yet exaggerated statements can actually undercut one's authority, since they are usually imprecise, inaccurate, or difficult to prove. Indeed, exaggerated phrases can raise readers' skepticism at the very moment when the writer wants to demonstrate authority.

Goodwill

How, finally, does a writer convey goodwill? A writer must show that 1) they care about the welfare of their readers and 2) they share the reader's commitments, interests, or values.

For certain kinds of arguments, goodwill might come when writers express how their readers might benefit from their findings. Notice, for instance, how clearly medical researcher Siddhartha Mukherjee states the consequences of his argument that we should be more discerning when discussing possible cancer-causing agents. Mukherjee writes,

> If we lump everything into the category of "potentially carcinogenic," from toxic potatoes to McCarthy's grave, then our scientific language around cancer begins to degenerate. The effect is like crying "wolf" about cancer: the public progressively numbs itself to real environmental toxins and becomes disinvested in finding *bona fide* carcinogens. (MM35)

Mukherjee cares about the health of his readers. In fact, he names his concern: "the public." While he could easily grab attention by stoking fears about the pervasiveness of things that cause cancer, he instead suggests that readers should resist such fears. By clearly articulating the medical consequences of his research, Mukherjee conveys a desire not to score points with an audience but to foster their well-being.

Even in arguments that lack immediate practical benefits for readers, writers can express goodwill by showing that they share readers' values. In her book *Weapons of Math Destruction*, mathematician Cathy

O'Neil shows readers that she shares their values of fairness, even if those values make her rethink her long-held faith in her field. In recounting the role of mathematicians' algorithms in worsening the financial recession of the early 2000s, she writes,

> By 2009, it was clear that the lessons of the market collapse had brought no new direction to the world of finance and had instilled no new values. The lobbyists succeeded, for the most part, and the game remained the same: to rope in dumb money. . . . The drama pushed me quickly along in my journey of disillusionment. I was especially disappointed in the part that mathematics had played. I was forced to confront the ugly truth: people had deliberately wielded formulas to impress rather than clarify. (44)

When O'Neil describes her newfound realizations as pushing her along a "journey of disillusionment," we know that she once believed in the helpful power of big data before examining evidence that it in fact can be harmful. O'Neil shows a willingness to change her mind for the benefit of others. Thus she stresses that her research is guided by benevolence rather than self-aggrandizement.

MYTH VS. REALITY

Myth: Academics never use "I" in their writing.
Reality: Academics do use the first person pronoun.

People often characterize academic writing as impersonal and formal, and many newer writers are taught to avoid the word "I." However, scholars frequently use "I" or "we" in their writing to announce their presence. In a study of journal articles across a wide array of academic disciplines, researcher Ken Hyland found that every one of the 240 articles that he sampled included "at least one first person reference" (212).

Many disciplines value objectivity, but scholars do not automatically equate the use of "I" with a break from objectivity. Scholars use first person pronouns not to declare their personal beliefs but rather to articulate how they are contributing to the scholarly community in credible ways. Hyland's research finds that different disciplines have different conventions when it comes to the word "I." We encourage you to read research in your discipline with an eye toward how and why scholars use first person references.

Crafting a Persona that Fits Your Project

Rhetorician Wayne Booth writes that we cannot possibly expect speakers to sound the same way no matter their audience and their situation. He explains, "We depend, in all of our exchanges, on what might be called 'putting on masks': enacting, for *this* audience, a projected *ethos* that would never work on *that* audience. Every rhetor must choose from among the diverse 'personae' that might be projected" (51). Just as you likely play different roles when you speak to your friends, your parents, and strangers, writers play various roles depending on their project.

Remembering that "*ethos*" means character can help you keep in mind that, in many ways, writing is a performance in which you play various characters. It may seem that scholars seek to play, above all, a single role—that of expert. It is true that scholars can benefit from this role. For example, in "Cultural Constraints on Grammar and Cognition in Pirahã," an article that challenges mainstream thought on linguistics, the scholar Daniel L. Everett describes his authority to understand an obscure culture and language. He writes, "I have lived for over six years in Pirahã villages and have visited the people every year since 1977. I speak the language well and can say anything I need to say in it, subject to the kinds of limitations discussed in this paper" (621). Everett's article makes strong claims about the intricacies of language use among a small group of indigenous people in the Amazon rain forest, so he needs to establish his expertise. Writers typically craft an expert persona when they are writing about something that requires obscure or extremely specialized knowledge.

But we want to stress that "expert" is only one of many roles that professional writers play. Let's look at some other personae that scholars adopt to convey authority. The purpose of the four examples that follow is *not* to suggest that when you write you need to pick a single character and stick to it. Rather, we mean to open up a range of possibilities.

The experienced persona: a character who demonstrates that they are personally invested in the subject matter due to their background or experience. For example, in *Trans** (pronounced "trans asterisk"), a book that investigates how culture accounts for gender, Jack Halberstam writes,

> When I was a young . . . person . . . I was constantly taken for a boy, and my parents were frantic to intervene in the relentless gendering of me as male. I was forced to wear my hair long and dress in girlish clothing, and told to sit and stand in a certain way. . . . The presence of cross-gendered children and gender-ambiguous children within the family throws all kinds of assumptions about gender, childhood, and

embodiment into question and ultimately casts doubt on the validity of the family itself. (45–46)

Halberstam uses his own childhood experience to dramatize the effects of family life on conceptions of gender. He then goes on to make arguments that draw on evidence not from his own life but from dozens of scholarly sources. Writers adopt the experienced persona when they want to emphasize the personal stakes of their arguments and the ways that their lived experiences inform their analyses.

The learner persona: a character who emphasizes their own lack of knowledge in order to foster a sense of exploration and discovery. In *Being Mortal*, a book that urges hospitals and doctors to change the way they typically treat patients at the ends of their lives, medical researcher Atul Gawande writes,

> I learned about a lot of things in medical school, but mortality wasn't one of them. Although I was given a dry, leathery corpse to dissect in my first term, that was solely a way to learn about human anatomy. Our textbooks had almost nothing on aging or dying. How the process unfolds, how people experience the end of their lives, and how it affects those around them seemed beside the point. (1)

Gawande begins not with what he knows but with what he doesn't know, emphasizing the extent to which he had to position himself as a learner in order to gain new understanding. Writers display the learner persona to convey a sense of humility and to emphasize how their newfound knowledge is hard won.

The detective persona: a character who acts like a sleuth, searching for clues to solve a problem. In *Reading the Forested Landscape*, a book about the way that landscapes reveal human and natural history, ecologist Tom Wessels explains how he interprets visual clues to understand what happened in a forest:

> Further evidence allows us to eliminate some of these possibilities and provides us with clues to solve the mystery. For example, there is a downed tree in this forest. It could be the result of a *blowdown*—a wind event strong enough to uproot and topple live trees. Certain clues make this possibility questionable. If we look closer, the downed tree appears to be more likely the result of *deadfall*. (25)

Wessels uses many of the words we might find in a detective story—"evidence," "clues," "solve," "mystery"—giving readers a sense that he is an investigator equipped with a keen eye and powerful inductive reasoning.

Writers adopt the detective persona when they want readers to attend to the observations that lead to claims and when they want to cultivate in readers the same enjoyment the writer had in arriving at a fresh conclusion.

The experimenter persona: a character who forms a hypothesis and tests their ideas before they draw conclusions. In "Multiplex Genome Engineering Using CRISPR/Cas Systems," a team of scientists explains their testing of "genome-editing technologies":

> Next, we explored the generalizability of RNA-guided genome editing in eukaryotic cells by targeting additional protospacers within the EMX1 locus. (Cong et al. 820)

Even this straightforward explanation of a laboratory technique displays character traits. The word "explored" carries with it a sense of open-mindedness, suggesting that these scientists did not know exactly what the results of their experiment would be; we are thus more likely to trust their results. Writers adopt the experimenter persona when they want to emphasize the extent to which they have reached their findings only after having carefully assessed the data they gathered.

Notice two roles we have not mentioned in this list that you might have expected: the opponent or the judge. Certainly some scholars choose to adopt these roles. But these adversarial positions leave little room for ongoing scholarly conversations that invite next steps that other researchers might take. Indeed, an overly aggressive approach can diminish a writer's virtue, since readers might think the writer is more interested in winning an argument than in advancing understanding. Researchers usually perform roles that build up communities rather than shut down opponents.

We've listed only a small number of the possible personas that writers adopt as they establish authority. We encourage you to name other roles that you see scholars perform in their research. You will find that many writers perform multiple roles over the course of a single essay. We hope that the breadth of possibilities proves freeing as you establish your scholarly authority through wisdom, virtue, and goodwill.

TURN TO YOUR RESEARCH

Conveying Practical Wisdom, Virtue, and Goodwill

To check that you are conveying character attributes that will bolster your authority, turn to a draft of your paper and underline places that convey each trait.

Practical wisdom: Where are you showing that you . . .

- have thought deeply about the subject?
- consider multiple viewpoints?
- use reason to reach your conclusions?
- take into account the context of the subject?

Virtue: Where are you showing that you . . .

- rely on sound reasoning rather than trickery?
- acknowledge the limits of your research?
- bring forward and address evidence that calls your claim into question?
- represent others' ideas fully and generously?

Goodwill: Where are you showing that you . . .

- have sincere concern for the well-being of your readers?
- care how your readers will benefit from the new knowledge you're offering them?
- share the same interests, values, and commitments as your readers?

If you see significant sections of your paper that are not underlined, ask yourself how you might revise those sections so that your language bolsters your authority.

Works Cited

Aristotle. *On Rhetoric: A Theory of Civic Discourse.* Translated by George Kennedy, 22nd ed., Oxford UP, 2007.

Baloyi, Ntsako, and Paula Kotzé. "Do Users Know or Care About What Is Done with Their Personal Data? A South African Study." *IST-Africa 2017 Conference Proceedings*, edited by Paul Cunningham and Miriam Cunningham, IIMC International Information Management Corporation, 2017, pp. 1–11, researchspace.csir.co.za/dspace/bitstream/handle/10204/9677/Baloyi_2017.pdf?sequence=3.

Bartholomae, David. "Inventing the University." *Journal of Basic Writing*, vol. 5, no. 1, 1986, pp. 4–23.

Beare, Zachary C., and Marcus Meade. "The Most Important Project of Our Time! Hyperbole as a Discourse Feature of Student Writing." *College Composition and Communication*, vol. 67, no. 1, Sept. 2015, pp. 64–86.

Beason, Larry. "Ethos and Error: How Business People React to Errors." *College Composition and Communication*, vol. 53, no. 1, 2001, pp. 33–64. *JSTOR*, doi:10.2307/359061.

Booth, Wayne C. *The Rhetoric of Rhetoric: The Quest for Effective Communication*. Blackwell, 2004.

Cong, Le, F. Ann Ran, David Cox, Shuailiang Lin, and Robert Barretto. "Multiplex Genome Engineering Using CRISPR/Cas Systems." *Science*, vol. 339, no. 6121, Feb. 2013, pp. 819–23. *science.sciencemag.org*, doi:10.1126/science.1231143.

Cooper, Mick. "Viagra for the Brain: Psychotherapy Research and the Challenge to Existential Therapeutic Practice." *Existential Analysis: Journal of the Society for Existential Analysis*, vol. 15, no. 1, 2004, pp. 2–14. *Google Scholar*.

Corbett, Edward P. J., and Robert J. Connors. *Classical Rhetoric for the Modern Student*. Oxford UP, 1999.

Everett, Daniel L. "Cultural Constraints on Grammar and Cognition in Pirahã: Another Look at the Design Features of Human Language." *Current Anthropology*, vol. 46, no. 4, 2005, pp. 621–46. *JSTOR*, doi:10.1086/431525.

Gawande, Atul. *Being Mortal: Medicine and What Matters in the End*. Metropolitan Books, 2014.

Halberstam, Jack. *Trans*: A Quick and Quirky Account of Gender Variability*. U of California P, 2018.

Heard, Elisabeth J., and August Wilson. "August Wilson on Playwriting: An Interview." *African American Review*, vol. 35, no. 1, 2001, pp. 93–102. *JSTOR*, doi:10.2307/2903337.

Hyland, Ken. "Humble Servants of the Discipline? Self-Mention in Research Articles." *English for Specific Purposes*, vol. 20, no. 3, 2001, pp. 207–26. *ScienceDirect*, doi:10.1016/S0889-4906(00)00012-0.

Jitney. 1999. *Goodman Theatre*, www.goodmantheatre.org/90/index.php/august-wilson/.

Marchand, Roland. *Advertising the American Dream: Making Way for Modernity, 1920–1940*. U of California P, 1985.

Mukherjee, Siddhartha. "Do Cellphones Cause Brain Cancer?" *New York Times*, 13 Apr. 2011, pp. MM30–35.

O'Neil, Cathy. *Weapons of Math Destruction: How Big Data Increases Inequality and Threatens Democracy*. Crown, 2016.

Wessels, Tom. *Reading the Forested Landscape: A Natural History of New England*. Countryman Press, 1997.

CHAPTER 15

....

Style

Mindset: Scholars Make Stylistic Choices to Serve Readers

What counts as good academic writing style is up for debate. Most readers will likely have difficulty understanding the following sentence from gender studies scholar Judith Butler's *Gender Trouble*, a book that other scholars have cited over 60,000 times:

> The deconstruction of identity is not the deconstruction of politics; rather, it establishes as political the very terms through which identity is articulated. (203)

The sentence uses specialized terminology ("deconstruction" for instance) and doesn't contain any people doing actions (Who does the "deconstruction"?). The sentence is especially difficult taken out of context, but even in context, readers may need to work hard to understand what Butler means.

In an essay called "The Professor of Parody," philosopher Martha Nussbaum takes issue with Butler's writing style. She argues that Butler uses unnecessarily difficult language in order to make her ideas appear more impressive: "[O]bscurity creates an aura of importance. It also serves another related purpose. It bullies the reader into granting that, since one cannot figure out what is going on, there must be something significant going on, some complexity of thought, where in reality" there is not (39). Nussbaum experiences Butler's writing style as aggressive and empty.

Butler has responded to critics like Nussbaum by arguing that difficult language is necessary to take on the task of "challenging common sense" ("A 'Bad Writer' Bites Back" A27). Rather than presuming, as Nussbaum does, that the author's job is to offer clear statements that can be narrowly interpreted, Butler suggests that an intentionally challenging style asks readers to find meaning themselves and to reflect on the nature of meaning itself ("A 'Bad Writer' Bites Back" A27).

Typically, American academic writers do not intentionally use challenging language—though some who do, like Butler, are highly influential. Most scholars who write about **style** side with Nussbaum, valuing writing styles that readers find easy to interpret. In American academic writing, readers typically expect that they will not have to labor over sentences to grasp who is doing what action. And those readers typically expect writers to convey meaning clearly enough that a single interpretation emerges. But we open with the Butler-Nussbaum debate to acknowledge that no single ideal style of academic writing exists. Writers make stylistic choices based on what they want readers to experience.

Instead of dictating what style you should employ in your writing, this chapter describes the effects that various styles have on readers. Readers experience certain styles as challenging and others as easy; some styles invite only a single interpretation, and others invite many interpretations. Once you understand the effects of your stylistic choices, you can decide what you want your readers to experience.

Writers Use Different Styles at Different Moments in the Process

While scholars may start out with a firm idea about the style they want to craft in a project, they seldom attempt to produce that style in the

---

KEY TERM

Style

Style is the set of choices about language, sentence structure, and paragraph construction that writers make to affect the reader's experience.

MYTH VS. REALITY

Myth: Academic writing styles are not creative. They require writers to be formal and distant from their subjects in order to sound objective.

Reality: Scholars use many of the same stylistic techniques as creative writers.

Academic writers attempt to create compelling characters in tension-filled situations—even if those characters are cancer cells or mathematical formulas and even if those situations exist under a microscope or in a purely theoretical realm.

Some more adventurous styles even let readers *experience* the very ideas that the writing discusses. For one example, you might read "Save the Robots: Cyber Profiling and Your So-Called Life," a *Stanford Law Review* essay by Richard Thompson Ford, whom we featured in Chapter 11. Ford's essay questions whether people relying on algorithms to make decisions will give up their individual rights bit by bit (1583–84). Ford conveys his ideas not from a scholarly distance but through a narrator who talks himself into relying more and more on artificial intelligence to make decisions, even as those decisions require risking more and more freedoms, even democracy itself. By the end of the essay, the narrator asks, "In fact, why not dispense with cumbersome voting altogether?" (1579). Ford's narrator—and by extension Ford's reader—experiences the very problem his essay raises: they slide into technological dystopia as the result of a series of small, seemingly harmless decisions. Pieces like Ford's demonstrate how academic writing styles can be serious while still being creative.

early drafts. Composition researcher Linda Flower gives us a vocabulary to differentiate the kinds of styles that writers aim for at different moments of the writing process. She makes the distinction between "writer-based prose" and "reader-based prose" (19–20), terms we first explored in Chapter 10.

Writer-based prose is "written by a writer to himself and for himself. It is the record and the working of his own verbal thought" (19). Because it records the writer's initial thinking, writer-based prose captures the words that first occur to the writer. Common characteristics of this style include using pronouns like "it" or "this" without clarifying which noun they refer to, bulking up sentences with words that distracting repetition

When they want to think on the page, *writers write writer-based* prose
to record their words as *they* appear

"they" could refer to writers or words

FIGURE **15.1**
A sentence in writer-based prose helped us gather our ideas; we later revised it to clarify
those ideas for readers.

don't add to readers' understanding, repeating words often enough
to distract readers, and burying main ideas at the ends of sentences.
But rather than think of these stylistic choices as faulty, Flower argues
that they serve an important function: they help writers develop their
thinking. Figure 15.1 shows a sentence that did just that for us in an
early draft of this paragraph. How would you describe your experience
reading it?

Only after scholars have developed their thinking do they turn to
revising their style into what Linda Flower calls "reader-based prose."
Reader-based prose "is a deliberate attempt to communicate something
to a reader" (20). If writer-based prose answers the question, "What am
I thinking?," reader-based prose answers the question, "How do I want
my readers to experience my thought?" Reader-based prose considers
what language readers will find familiar and lively, what word order
readers will anticipate, and what sentence and paragraph lengths readers will find engaging. Writers' choices about these matters depend on
who their readers are and how they want those readers to encounter
their particular projects.

As an example of a shift from writer-based to reader-based
style, look at the way we revised the early draft of the sentence from
Figure 15.1. How does your experience of this reader-based style differ?

Because it records the writer's initial thinking, writer-based prose
captures the words that first occur to the writer.

Flower's study emphasizes the necessity of stylistic revision. The
lesson here is not that writer-based prose is bad. Rather, writer-based
prose is a necessary—but preliminary—step in the writing process.
Writers move from writing that will help them discover their ideas to
writing that will help them convey those ideas.

COMMON PITFALL

Polishing Sentences Too Early

Imagine that you are an architect who is designing a home for a family in Colorado. Which would be the most efficient process for producing a great home?

Option A: You imagine the ideal house in your mind, order the building materials you think you will need, and then go to the site and assemble the materials from the foundation up.

Option B: You approach the process like architect Scott Lindenau, who is responsible for the sketch and the home pictured here (see Figure 15.2 and Photo 15.3). You make many quick sketches. When you arrive at a

FIGURE 15.2
Architect Scott Lindenau's early sketch of Scholl House, a home he designed in Colorado.

PHOTO 15.3
The finished home designed by Lindenau.

continued

sketch you like, you refine it with computer-aided drawings. Once you and the client are happy with a formal drawing, construction can begin.

Though it has fewer steps, option A is extremely inefficient: as you build the home from the design in your memory, you will inevitably discover something you want to change—a window is badly placed or two walls don't meet correctly—and you'll have to disassemble and reassemble the building to make the changes.

Certainly option B is more efficient even though it produces a lot of sketches and drawings that you would no longer need once the home is built. It uses a lower-effort mode—sketching—in the earlier stages to allow ideas to develop; and it switches to a higher-effort mode—home construction—at the later stages to produce a finished building.

Writers, too, are more efficient if they use lower-effort, writer-based styles in the earlier, idea-generating stages of a project and higher-effort, reader-based styles in the later stages. Yet writing studies researchers find that less-experienced writers frequently use higher-effort, reader-based styles in the earliest stages of their writing: the equivalent of setting their initial idea in concrete rather than sketching it first (Faigley and Witte; Sommers). They tend to invest time and effort to find the perfect word, the cleverest phrase, and the most elegant sentence before fully developing their ideas. As a result, revising requires disassembling and reassembling sentences that required a lot of work. Less-experienced writers are thus more likely to resist substantial revising and stick with their initial thoughts.

Researchers find that experienced writers are more likely to employ lower-effort styles early on—sketching quick, unpolished sentences. They are thus more likely to revise and restructure their writing quite dramatically early in a project. Only after they have developed their best ideas do they turn to the hard work of polishing their style for readers.

Tools & Techniques: Reducing Ambiguity and Rewarding Attention

What follows are techniques that can help you move from "writer-based prose" to "reader-based prose." We've divided these techniques into two categories: 1) techniques that reduce possible misunderstandings of your work and 2) techniques that reward a reader's attention.

Techniques to Reduce Misunderstandings of Your Work

Poets, novelists, lyricists, and the like often use language that is richly ambiguous to invite readers to interpret their texts in multiple ways. Researchers, on the other hand, usually strive to have a single meaning emerge from their work. This single-minded purpose does not mean that researchers' styles need be dry and uninteresting, but it does mean that researchers typically seek styles that avoid unintended ambiguity. The following techniques will help you write in styles that reduce possible misunderstandings for readers.

Choose Words Strategically

Choosing words is the most frequent stylistic decision writers make. We sometimes see less-experienced writers select advanced-sounding words in order to project the persona of a brilliant thinker. Elaborate or specialized language comes with two risks, however: the writer may misuse less-familiar words, or the writer may alienate readers who don't share their expansive vocabularies. Experienced scholars also consider how their word choices shape their personae for readers, but they may have a broader conception of what sounds smart. Many view the ability to convey complex ideas in clear, accessible language as the highest display of scholarly skill. But what counts as accessible differs for different readers.

Experts make strategic decisions about when and how to use specialized language. Physicians might discuss an *acute myocardial infarction* with their colleagues but use the term *heart attack* with a patient. Baseball players might discuss a *breaking ball* or a *splitter* with a sports writer but simply talk about *pitches* with a young fan. With a specialized vocabulary, these insiders speak efficiently—conveying precise concepts in one or two words that might otherwise take much longer. With nonexperts, however, they choose words that laypeople would understand.

Writers make use of the specialized vocabulary of their disciplines, but they also keep in mind that specialized words often have contested meanings even among their fellow experts. Art historians debate what "modernism" means; musicologists debate what "minimalism" means; philosophers debate what "existentialism" means; and so on. Writers, thus, take time to define their specialized terminology. Notice, for instance, that many scholars use the following formulation when they use the specialized term "neoliberalism":

> The political scientist Cathy Cohen writes, "**By neoliberalism I mean** a commitment to increasing privatization of the public sphere." (26)

> The education scholar Heidi Pitzer writes, "**By neoliberalism, I mean** the set of ideas and policies that make the market paramount." (63)

> The legal scholar Malcolm Voyce writes, "**By neoliberalism I mean** policies of competition, deregulation and privatization." (2055)

Scholars define their terms not only to show their awareness of the debates within their disciplinary communities; they also define words in order to expand their scholarly communities. Writers define jargon in order to open up their ideas to more readers.

COMMON PITFALL

Trusting Spelling and Grammar Checkers

Error correction tools built into word processors and apps have drastically reduced certain kinds of common writing mistakes. However, they have also increased other kinds of mistakes. Writing studies researchers Andrea A. Lunsford and Karen J. Lunsford came to this conclusion by comparing two studies tracking errors in college students' writing: one done in 1986, before spell checkers and grammar checkers existed, and another in 2008.

The 1986 study by Andrea A. Lunsford and Robert J. Connors tracked errors in 3,000 handwritten first-year undergraduate papers. By far, the most common error they found then was spelling (Connors and Lunsford 400–01). Andrea A. Lunsford and Karen J. Lunsford repeated the study in 2008, this time with 877 word-processed papers. These papers, written with the benefit of spell checkers, reduced spelling errors: they moved from first to fifth on the list (Lunsford and Lunsford 782). "But," Lunsford and Lunsford lament, "every blessing brings its own curse"; spell checkers had caused increases in a different kind of error by 2008: using the wrong word (796). Wrong word errors typically occur when a spell checker flags a word it doesn't recognize and then suggests an inappropriate alternative. Even apps that claim to prevent more mistakes than word processors' tools tend to do poorly when researchers put them to the test (Dembsey 67).

Takeaway: Don't accept a spell-checker or grammar-checker's advice unless you understand it and agree with it.

Use Inclusive Language

You'll notice that throughout this book we use the plural pronoun "they" to refer to single people, such as "a writer" or "a researcher," whose gender is unknown. At one time, "he" was the preferred term to refer to an unspecified man or a woman (you likely noticed, for instance, that the sentence we quoted earlier from Linda Flower's 1979 study uses "himself" in this manner). Slowly, alternatives like "he/she," "s/he," and "one" became more popular because they more accurately represented more people. More recently, "they" is emerging as a preferred term, endorsed by organizations like the National Council of Teachers of English and the Associated Press, because it more accurately represents not only men and women but also nonbinary people.

Language evolves with culture. The following guidelines will help you select the most inclusive terms:

- *Call people what they prefer to be called.* For example, currently both "Black" and "African American" are used to refer to Americans who have African ancestry. However, to describe a member of the Congressional Black Caucus who has African ancestry, the preferred term would be "Black" because the organization chooses that term.
- *Favor more accurate terms over less accurate terms.* Instead of umbrella terms like "Latino," "Latina," or "Latinx," for instance, use "Puerto Rican," "Dominican," and so on whenever possible.
- *Foreground personhood before disability or illness.* Try "writers who are dyslexic" instead of "dyslexics."
- *Identify people in similar ways.* For instance, instead of "Edith Windsor and her wife," use "Edith Windsor and Thea Spyer, her wife" (using each person's name). This suggestion also extends to omitting differences when they are not relevant. For instance, when listing Los Angeles's Hall of Fame basketball players, instead of mentioning "Magic Johnson and his Muslim teammate Kareem Abdul-Jabbar," use "Magic Johnson and his teammate Kareem Abdul-Jabbar."
- *Stay up to date on preferred terms.* Professional organizations like the Modern Language Association, the American Psychological Association, and the National Council of Teachers of English issue recommendations on inclusive language.

Use Functional Signposts

Functional signposts are a form of metadiscourse, language that describes the purpose of a passage within a piece. Linguist Ken Hyland explains, "Metadiscourse reveals the writer's awareness of the reader and his or her need for elaboration, clarification, guidance and interaction" (20). Using functional signposts, writers can draw attention to their own stylistic choices, speak directly to the reader, and reflect upon their own language. (In Chapter 10, we show how functional signposts can guide readers through the structure of a piece.) Writers can thus clarify their own intentions and tell readers what to expect.

We offer here a list of situations when writers commonly use functional signposts (which we've bolded):

- *To articulate their project*: Military studies scholar Mitchell Zais writes, "[T]**his essay will argue** that there are at least two qualities which are essential for the most senior commanders" (59).
- *To focus attention*: Learning sciences researcher Miriam Gamoran Sherin writes, "**What I want to emphasize here is that,** through this process, I developed a professional vision of classroom events" (78).
- *To clarify meaning*: Psychologist Ed Diener writes, "**What I mean to say** is that each researcher needs to inform himself or herself about what causality means in the first place" (119).
- *To reiterate*: Social psychologist Paula Niedenthal writes, "**Put another way,** the grounding for knowledge . . . is the original neural state that occurred when the information was initially acquired" (1003).
- *To anticipate a misreading*: Education scholar Lester-Irabinna Rigney writes, "**I am not suggesting** in any way that critical research by non-Indigenous Australians should not continue . . . **I am saying** that Indigenist research by Indigenous Australians takes the research into the heart of the Indigenous struggle" (117).
- *To map structure*: Historian Craig Heron writes, "**This essay will move from** a description of the state of the two largest metalworking crafts . . . **to** a discussion of the efforts of employers to transform their factories" (9).
- *To anticipate objections*: Media production researcher Ruth Goldman writes, "**Although some might argue that** 'queer' could

include bisexual . . . **the fact that** Warner uses other essentializing categories . . . renders bisexuality noticeably absent" (176).

- *To offer a reading cue*: English studies scholar Elizabeth Tebeaux writes, "**In the following passage, notice that** every sentence uses active voice" (346).

Use the Passive Voice Judiciously

Readers anticipate that they will discover a lot about what a sentence conveys by tracking its main actor and main action. So readers' attention is high at the places in sentences where they expect those actors and actions to appear. When writers obscure the main actors, therefore, readers can miss crucial information. What is your experience of reading these two sentences, the first which puts the actor and action where readers expect it and the second which doesn't?

1) Maria kicks the ball.
2) The ball is kicked by Maria.

The first sentence is active, meaning that the subject ("Maria") performs the verb's action ("kicks"). The second sentence is passive, meaning that the subject ("ball") is acted upon by the verb ("is kicked"). Why do readers generally prefer the active construction? They expect it. The active construction tells us the main actor right away, while the passive construction makes us wait to find out the main actor. Indeed, some passive constructions may never even identify the main actor—for instance, if our sentence read simply "The ball is kicked."

The active voice follows this pattern: subject + verb (see Figure 15.4).

The passive voice follows this pattern: [no subject performing the action] "to be" verb + past participle (see Figure 15.5). "To be" verbs include "is," "are," "was," "were," "be," "being," and "been." And a past

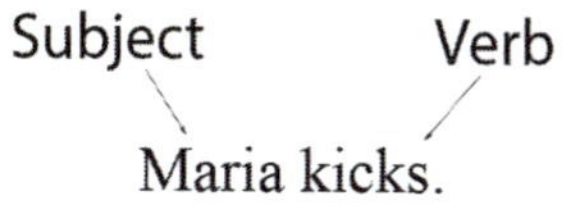

Subject   Verb

Maria kicks.

FIGURE **15.4**
A sentence written in the active voice.

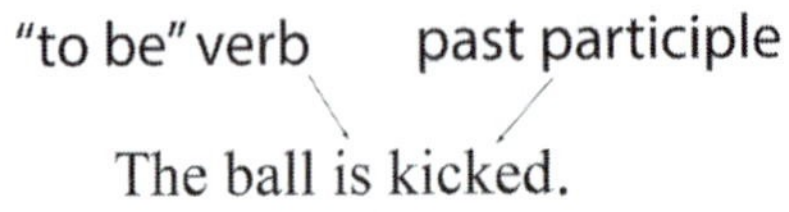

"to be" verb   past participle

The ball is kicked.

FIGURE **15.5**
A sentence written in the passive voice.

participle (like "kicked") is a past tense form of a verb that combines with the "to be" verb to form a verb phrase.

In some instances, readers find that hiding main actors by using the passive voice is not only unsatisfying but also unethical. Citizens often criticize politicians for making statements like the following (we've bolded the passive constructions):

> President Richard Nixon, in his 1974 resignation speech: "I regret deeply any injuries that **may have been done** in the course of events that led to this decision" (qtd. in Taft 1141).

> President Bill Clinton, in a 1997 news conference: "mistakes **were made**" (qtd. in Broder).

In each of these passive-voiced statements, readers are left to wonder the identity of the main actor. To assign responsibility, writers can place the actor before the verb. In Clinton's case, for example, "Mistakes were made" would become "I made mistakes."

We want to be clear that using the passive voice is not breaking a rule, but it is a stylistic choice that asks readers to expend energy to figure out the main actor. Therefore, we are not suggesting that writers always avoid the passive voice, only that they use it deliberately. Here are instances in which writers sometimes choose to use the passive voice:

- *When the actor is unknown or their identity doesn't matter.* In an article about Biblical translation, the New Testament scholar Bruce Metzger writes, "[W]ithin the first half of the twentieth century some part of the Bible **was published** in more than 500 languages" (36). Many different publishers performed the action, and listing their identities would get in the way of understanding Metzger's point.
- *To focus on the action rather than the performer.* In one study, bio-chemist George Ellman writes, "The hot solution **was filtered** and the black precipitate **was washed** with several hundred milliliters

of hot water" (71). Ellman wrote this widely cited article in 1959, and for many years it was common for scientific studies to favor the passive voice—directing attention away from the scientist and toward the experiment.

This usage is now changing in the sciences. Nature Publishing Group, a collection of some of the world's most often cited scientific journals, offers the following advice to writers who submit papers: "Nature journals prefer authors to write in the active voice ('we performed the experiment . . .')" (Nature). Indeed, many contemporary scientific articles favor the active voice. For example, in a recent paper on antipredatory responses in fish, a team of biologists writes, "**We then filtered** the solution through glass wool" (Ferrari et al. 516). We encourage writers to look at recent examples of writing in their field of study to discern when the passive voice is appropriate.

TIME SAVER

Learn Grammar by Using Your Own Writing

Although grammatical choices are a component of style, you'll notice that we don't offer exercises to improve your grammatical correctness. Does that mean that we believe grammatical correctness isn't important? Not at all. Writing studies researchers have found that grammatical errors can significantly damage writers' credibility (Beason; Hairston; Leonard and Gilsdorf). However, decades of research suggests that studying parts of speech or correcting sample sentences in isolation seldom improves a writer's grammar. (For a brief introduction to this research, see Amy Martinsen's "The Tower of Babel and the Teaching of Grammar.")

What is the most time-efficient way to improve your grammar? Writing studies scholar Constance Weaver argues that teaching grammar "in the context of writing is considerably more effective than teaching usage and mechanics in isolation" (180). Why? By using your own sentences as examples, you work within your own logic to understand your patterns of grammar usage. We recommend a two-step process to improving your grammar using your own drafts.

1. *Focus on high-impact grammar errors.* With the help of a seasoned writer (perhaps a writing center consultant, an instructor, or an editor), read your draft aloud to identify all

continued

the kinds of grammatical errors that appear. Then choose one or two higher-impact errors to focus on. After you have mastered those, go on to the next. Use these criteria to determine which grammar issues to prioritize:

a. Prioritize recurring errors rather than errors that may occur only once.

b. Prioritize errors that bother readers more. A small study by Larry Beason found that readers in professional settings were especially bothered by sentence fragments and fused sentences, even when those constructions didn't interfere with their comprehension (Beason 41, 48).

2. *Determine your stage of grammar learning.* Since detecting, diagnosing, and revising grammar errors are different skills (Hayes et al. 178), you need to identify your exact point of confusion and apply strategies to master that stage before moving to the next. Which of the following statements best describes your understanding?

a. *Detection*: When I read my sentences aloud, I don't notice that something is off.

Strategy: Strengthen your ear for writing by reading a lot, reading aloud, and reading along while listening to others read aloud. Admittedly, honing your ear is a slow process, so in the meantime, practice strategies that do not rely on your ear to hear errors. Use a grammar handbook or websites like the *Purdue OWL* to learn the features of the grammar issue in question that are easy to locate or track. Begin tracking those features in your reading and your own writing.

Example: If your recurring error is run-on sentences—two complete sentences that run together without appropriate punctuation—learn to draw slashes between each complete clause in your writing that has a main subject and verb. Noticing sentence boundaries is the first step in learning where sentences should begin and end.

b. *Diagnosis*: I notice that something is off, but I can't identify what.

Strategy: Recognize the way that you characteristically produce this error. Look for a pattern.

Example: Perhaps you create run-on sentences by throwing commas between what should be separate sentences. If that's the case, look for a comma in the sentence that seems off and check whether the clauses on either side of the comma could stand on their own as complete sentences.

c. *Revision*: I can identify what the error is, but I don't know how to fix it.

Strategy: Start by writing out your own logic for deciding what to do in this grammatical situation. Then consult a grammar website or a handbook to learn how others handle the grammatical issue. Compare the site's or handbook's logic to your own. Notice where your logic diverges and revise your description of your logic to incorporate the logic of the handbook. In other words, adjust your existing logic rather than trying to replace it with an entirely foreign logic.

Example: To revise your run-on sentences, you might describe your own logic for when to end a sentence like this: "By my logic, a sentence is a complete thought. To determine where to end sentences, I read my writing and listen for what sound like thoughts that could stand on their own. I place a period when I feel ready to go on to a new thought." Then you compare your logic with the *Purdue OWL* website's explanation: "An independent clause [the grammatical term for a complete sentence] is a group of words that contains a subject and verb and expresses a complete thought." Comparing your logic with the *Purdue OWL*'s, you can now say that your understanding of a complete sentence as a complete thought is accurate only when a subject and verb are also present. And you can adjust your revision strategy to place periods between multiple clauses that contain subjects and verbs.

Revise Nominalizations

Let's examine another potential writing pitfall that can obscure main actors and main actions. What makes the following sentence so difficult to understand?

> The argument of Kozinets in regard to the interest in consumer culture of scholars and marketing practitioners is that they must participate in the following of consumers online.

This sentence is bogged down by nominalizations—the noun forms of verbs and adjectives. "Argument," for instance, is the noun form of the verb "argues." "Following" is the noun form of the verb "follows." And "interest" is the noun form of the adjective "interested."

Readers expect the main actions in a sentence to be verbs; when the main actions come in the form of nouns, readers have trouble figuring out what is happening. As a simple revision technique, you can ask yourself two questions: 1) Who is the main actor in my sentence? 2) What is the main action that my actor is doing? Once you've answered these questions, you can revise your sentence so that the main actor is the subject and the main action is the verb.

Our sample sentence features a main actor doing an action—Robert V. Kozinets argues. After clarifying the main actor and main action, we can revise the other nominalizations ("following" to "follow," "interest" to "interested") to clarify the rest of the sentence. After these revisions, we are left with the following sentence, which comes from a book review by business researcher Stephanie O'Donohoe,

> Kozinets argues that scholars and marketing practitioners interested in consumer culture must follow consumers online. (328)

Compare this sentence to our sample sentence, and you'll be able to see how changing nominalizations to verbs and adjectives can help readers track what is happening in the sentence. O'Donohoe's sentence has clear actors that are responsible for actions.

Specify Pronoun Referents

Pronouns are words that refer to nouns. Writers typically use pronouns in order to avoid repeating the same nouns too often, which would bore readers. For instance, instead of writing, "Most **building owners** believe that they will never have a serious fire, so **building owners** are reluctant to engage in discussion with fire engineers during design of **building owners'** new buildings," fire engineer Andy Buchanan writes, "Most building owners believe that **they** will never have a serious fire, so **they** are reluctant to engage in discussion with fire engineers during design of **their** new buildings" (81). Buchanan replaces "building owners" with the pronoun "they" and the possessive pronoun "their" in order to keep his language fresh.

The English language has a number of flexible pronouns that can refer to nouns. For instance, the demonstrative pronouns "this," "that," "these," and "those" and the personal pronouns "it" and "they" take their meaning entirely from their referent (the noun they refer to). The inherent ambiguity of words like "this" and "it" make them flexible and useful, but their meaning can be unclear if writers do not specify their referents. Writers thus seek to clarify the meaning of pronouns by making sure that readers always know the precise referent.

As an example, can you identify the noun that the bolded pronoun refers to in the following sentence about a study examining cervical cancers during pregnancy?

> In our series of 2382 consecutive cervical cancers, only 2.1% of the cases were associated with pregnancy. Therefore, **this** can be analyzed best in a matched cohort study.

In this example, the word "this" could refer to multiple things: the series of cervical cancers, the percentage of cases, the association with pregnancy, the pregnancy itself, and so on. Writers often include a noun after the word "this" to get rid of any ambiguity. In fact, the actual study looking at cervical cancers during pregnancy specified the noun that the pronoun "this" referred to:

> In our series of 2382 consecutive cervical cancers, only 2.1% of the cases were associated with pregnancy. Therefore, **this rare combination** can be analyzed best in a matched cohort study. (Van Der Vange et al. 1024)

We've bolded the phrase "this rare combination" to emphasize how we know exactly what "this" refers to: the low occurrence of cervical cancers related to pregnancy.

Techniques that Reward Readers' Attention

Readers' attention is highest at the places where they expect to see the most information. Readers thus focus at the beginnings of sentences—where they expect to see an actor and an action—and at the ends of sentences, where they expect to see the main point. In their book *Style*, Professors of English Joseph Williams and Gregory Colomb write, "Just as you look at the first few words of your sentence for focus, you can look at the last few words for emphasis" (87). Writers want the beginning of a sentence to bring readers in and the end of a sentence to sustain them. In what follows, we'll offer some strategies that can help you craft prose that attracts and keeps your reader's attention.

Cohesion and Coherence

What does it mean for a piece of writing to flow? Most readers would likely say that writing flows when it moves smoothly from one sentence to the next and from one paragraph to the next. Linguists call this sense of connectedness "cohesion," and scholars have found that highly cohesive writing aids in reading comprehension (Irwin 331). Writing that is cohesive feels to readers like the smooth unfolding of connected ideas rather than a choppy series of disconnected thoughts.

What does cohesive writing look like? Let's look at an example that uses an identifiable technique. Here is a passage from neuroscientist Eric Kandel's *In Search of Memory*, a book that offers an intellectual history of the science of the mind. We've bolded the words at the beginning and ends of each sentence—the sites of cohesion:

> Plato, who rejected observations and experiments, believed that the only reason we can think about ourselves and our mortal body is that we have **a soul that is immaterial and immortal. The idea of an immortal soul** was subsequently incorporated into Christian thought and elaborated upon **by St. Thomas Aquinas in the thirteenth century. Aquinas** and later religious thinkers held that the soul—the generator of consciousness—is not only distinct from the body, it is also of divine origin. (378)

What is Kandel's strategy for writing cohesive sentences? He begins each sentence with the word or idea that ended the previous sentence. Readers thus revisit what they know (from the previous sentence) and feel primed for what they are about to find out.

Yet a fully cohesive set of sentences may still be nonsensical. Take, for instance, the following absurd example, in which we take a word from the end of a sentence and use it to begin the next sentence:

> Plato believed that we have **a soul that is immortal. Immortal beings** do not exist **on earth. The earth** revolves around **the sun. Sunny days** are perfect for going to the beach.

These sentences flow smoothly one to the next; they are cohesive. Yet they lack a sense of unified wholeness, or *coherence*. As linguist Andrew Kehler points out, we understand a text not simply by interpreting each part, but also by figuring out how all the parts relate to one another (2). Both cohesion and coherence are scalable notions, meaning that writers can think about the cohesion and coherence of small portions of text like sentences but also of larger chunks of text like paragraphs, chapters, and so on. When crafting reader-based prose, you can strive for cohesion and coherence by asking yourself two questions: 1) "Does each part of my text flow smoothly one to the next?" and 2) "Do the parts of my text, taken as a whole, offer a sense of unity?"

Concision

Wordy writing styles require readers to expend energy sorting through which phrases matter and which are fluff. As you revise your writer-based style to a reader-based style, you can practice certain strategies to reduce wordiness. To begin, how might you make the following sentence more concise?

> The fact is, it was in the year 1988 that the policy and set of rules regarding the control and regulation of illicit substances was actually considered again by the main legislative body of the United States.

Eliminate fillers. Get rid of empty words and phrases that carry no information. In the sample sentence, we can delete "the fact is" and "actually" without any substantial loss of meaning.

Avoid wordy sentence constructions. Writers can revise expletive constructions (vague subject-verb phrases such as "it is," "there are," and so on) and passive constructions (like "the ball was kicked by Maria" instead of "Maria kicked the ball") to get to their point more quickly. In the sample sentence, we can get rid of the expletive "it was," and we can revise the passive construction "was considered again."

Replace wordy expressions. Writers can often replace unnecessarily long phrases with single words. The phrase "At this moment in time," for instance, can become "now." Negative constructions can often be replaced by single words: "not true" is "false," "not paid attention to" is "ignored," "not mean" is "kind." In the sample sentence, we can replace "considered again" with the single word "revisited," "illicit substances" with "drugs," and "the main legislative body of the United States" with "Congress."

Get rid of redundancies. Writers can eliminate unnecessary repetition often simply by deleting one of the redundancies. For example, "cheerful and upbeat" can become "cheerful" without any loss of meaning. In the sample sentence, we can replace "the year 1988" with "1988," and we can replace "policy and set of rules" with "policy."

Consolidate long phrases. Writers can sometimes replace lengthy phrases with shorter, punchier ones. In the sample sentence, we can replace "the policy and set of rules regarding the control and regulation of illicit substances" with "drug policy."

After applying these techniques to our sample sentence, we are left with the following sentence, which comes from legal scholar Michelle Alexander's book *The New Jim Crow*: "Congress revisited drug policy in 1988" (53). Alexander's sentence is not only shorter, but it is much clearer than our sample sentence. She respects her reader's time and sustains their attention.

Avoid Expletive Constructions

Expletive constructions are phrases that take the form of "it is," "there is," "there are," and so on. Expletive constructions give no information about what the sentence is about; "it" or "there" could refer to almost anything, and "to be" verbs convey very little about what is happening. These constructions can waste a reader's valuable attention. Notice, for instance, what happens if we replace a famous piece of writing with expletive constructions. Here is an expletive-laced version of Abraham Lincoln's "The Gettysburg Address," followed by the actual version. We've bolded the prominent nouns and verbs that readers will first encounter in each sentence:

> **It was** fourscore and seven years ago our fathers brought forth on this continent a new nation, conceived in liberty and dedicated to the proposition that all men are created equal. **There is** now engagement in a great civil war, testing whether that nation or any nation so

conceived and so dedicated can long endure. **It is** that we are met on a great battlefield of that war.

Fourscore and seven years ago **our fathers brought forth** on this continent a new nation, conceived in liberty and dedicated to the proposition that all men are created equal. Now **we are engaged** in a great civil war, testing whether that nation or any nation so conceived and so dedicated can long endure. **We are met** on a great battlefield of that war. (Lincoln)

If we are to look at the beginnings of sentences to find actors and actions, the "Gettysburg Address" gives us crucial information: "our fathers brought forth," "we are engaged," "we are met." Our rewrite using expletive constructions gives us virtually no information: "It was," "There is," "It is." Not only is the original paragraph more concise and direct, it places crucial information in places where readers' attention is highest.

Avoid Clichés

What is a cliché? Originally, a cliché referred to a plate used over and over again in the mechanical printing process. Now, clichés refer to phrases so overused that they have lost their power. "Time-honored traditions," "fatal flaws," "thinking outside the box," "just desserts," and "sighs of relief" are all clichés. Individuals who use clichés are using prefabricated language and, even worse, prefabricated thought. The famous writer George Orwell warned of the dangers of clichés in his 1946 essay "Politics and the English Language": "By using stale metaphors, similes, and idioms, you save much mental effort, at the cost of leaving your meaning vague, not only for your reader but for yourself" (361). If you write with clichés, you are not only using language without thinking, you are also asking readers not to think. For Orwell, a world of clichés can have dangerous political consequences, for stale language fosters a citizenry not used to making mental effort.

TURN TO YOUR RESEARCH

Gaining Critical Distance

Why is moving from writer-based style to reader-based style so challenging? As philosopher Rebecca Newberger Goldstein writes, "It's hard, once you've understood something, to remember what it's like not to understand it." Moving to reader-based prose demands that writers see their writing not through their own eyes but through the eyes of their readers. Crafting reader-based prose is especially difficult when writers have been sitting for a long time with their own thoughts and writing. Writers, then, will strive to gain critical distance from their own writing, trying to see it with fresh eyes. Here we offer a few strategies to help you assess your own writing.

Read aloud or listen to someone else read aloud. Hearing your words can give you a distance from them that helps you imagine how a reader will experience your work.

Ask for feedback. We've already suggested ways to elicit productive feedback from readers (see Chapter 9).

Read backward. It can be easy to miss errors because you read what you expect is on the page rather than what is actually there. Try instead reading from the last sentence of the text and moving up. That way, you won't have contextual clues that might lead you to make false assumptions about what's actually in your sentences.

Use the "find" tool. Rather than scanning the whole draft for a problematic word or punctuation mark, use the "find" command in your word processor to locate every instance.

Read for one issue at a time. To avoid splitting your attention, try rereading your almost-final drafts several times, attending to just one or two issues per reading.

Works Cited

Alexander, Michelle. *The New Jim Crow: Mass Incarceration in the Age of Colorblindness.* Perseus, 2010.

Beason, Larry. "Ethos and Error: How Business People React to Errors." *College Composition and Communication*, vol. 53, no. 1, 2001, pp. 33–64. *JSTOR*, doi:10.2307/359061.

Broder, John M. "Familiar Fallback for Officials: 'Mistakes Were Made.'" *New York Times*, 14 Mar. 2007, www.nytimes.com/2007/03/14/washington/14mistakes.html.

Buchanan, Andy. "The Challenges of Predicting Structural Performance in Fires." *Fire Safety Science*, vol. 9, 2008, pp. 79–90. *Google Scholar*, doi:10.3801/IAFSS.FSS.9-79.

Butler, Judith. "A 'Bad Writer' Bites Back." *New York Times,* 20 Mar. 1999, archive.nytimes.com/query.nytimes.com/gst/fullpage-950CE5D61531F933 A15750C0A96F958260.html.

---. *Gender Trouble: Feminism and the Subversion of Identity.* Routledge, 2011.

Cohen, Cathy J. "Obama, Neoliberalism, and the 2012 Election: Why We Want More than Same-Sex Marriage." *Souls,* vol. 14, no. 1–2, Jan. 2012, pp. 19–27. *Crossref,* doi:10.1080/10999949.2012.721707.

Connors, Robert J., and Andrea A. Lunsford. "Frequency of Formal Errors in Current College Writing, or Ma and Pa Kettle Do Research." *College Composition and Communication,* vol. 39, no. 4, 1988, pp. 395–409. *JSTOR,* doi:10.2307/357695.

Dembsey, J. M. "Closing the *Grammarly* Gaps: A Study of Claims and Feedback from an Online Grammar Program." *Writing Center Journal,* vol. 36, no. 1, 2017, pp. 63–100.

Diener, Ed. "What Is Positive about Positive Psychology: The Curmudgeon and Pollyanna." *Psychological Inquiry,* vol. 14, no. 2, 2003, pp. 115–20.

Ellman, George L. "Tissue Sulfhydryl Groups." *Archives of Biochemistry and Biophysics,* vol. 82, no. 1, 1959, pp. 70–77. *ScienceDirect,* doi:10.1016/0003-9861(59)90090-6.

Faigley, Lester, and Stephen Witte. "Analyzing Revision." *College Composition and Communication,* vol. 32, no. 4, 1981, pp. 400–14. *Google Scholar,* doi:10.2307/356602.

Ferrari, Maud C. O., et al. "Turbidity as an Ecological Constraint on Learned Predator Recognition and Generalization in a Prey Fish." *Animal Behaviour,* vol. 79, no. 2, Feb. 2010, pp. 515–19. *ScienceDirect,* doi:10.1016/j.anbehav.2009.12.006.

Flower, Linda. "Writer-Based Prose: A Cognitive Basis for Problems in Writing." *College English,* vol. 41, no. 1, 1979, pp. 19–37. *JSTOR,* doi:10.2307/376357.

Ford, Richard T. "Save the Robots: Cyber Profiling and Your So-Called Life." *Stanford Law Review,* vol. 52, May 2000, pp. 1573–84.

Goldman, Ruth. "Who Is That 'Queer' Queer? Exploring Norms around Sexuality, Race, and Class in Queer Theory." In *Queer Studies: A Lesbian, Gay, Bisexual, and Transgender Anthology,* edited by Brett Beemyn and Mickey Eliason, New York UP, 1996, pp. 169–82.

Goldstein, Rebecca Newberger. "Scholars Talk Writing: Rebecca Newberger Goldstein." Interview by Rachel Toor. *Chronicle of Higher Education,* 6 Oct. 2015, www.chronicle.com/article/Scholars-Talk-Writing-Rebecca/233639.

Hairston, Maxine. "Not All Errors Are Created Equal: Nonacademic Readers in the Professions Respond to Lapses in Usage." *College English*, vol. 43, no. 8, 1981, pp. 794–806, doi:10.2307/376679.

Hayes, John R., et al. "Cognitive Processes in Revision." *Advances in Applied Psycholinguistics*, edited by Sheldon Rosenberg, Cambridge UP, 1987, pp. 176–240.

Heron, Craig. "The Crisis of the Craftsman: Hamilton's Metal Workers in the Early Twentieth Century." *Labour/Le Travail*, vol. 6, autumn 1980, pp. 7–48.

Hyland, Ken. *Metadiscourse: Exploring Interaction in Writing.* Continuum, 2005.

Irwin, Judith Westpbal. "The Effect of Linguistic Cohesion on Prose Comprehension." *Journal of Reading Behavior*, vol. 12, no. 4, Dec. 1980, pp. 325–32. *SAGE Journals*, doi:10.1080/10862968009547385.

Kandel, Eric R. *In Search of Memory: The Emergence of a New Science of Mind.* Norton, 2006.

Kehler, Andrew. *Coherence, Reference, and the Theory of Grammar.* Center for the Study of Language and Information Publications, 2002.

Leonard, Donald J., and Jeanette W. Gilsdorf. "Language in Change: Academics' and Executives' Perceptions of Usage Errors." *Journal of Business Communication*, vol. 27, no. 2, 1990, pp. 137–58. *Google Scholar*, doi:10.1177/002194369002700202.

Lincoln, Abraham. *Gettysburg Address.* 1863. *Project Gutenberg*, www.gutenberg .org/0/4/4-h/4-h.htm.

Lindenau, Scott. *Scholl House, Drawing.* "Architects That Can Draw! Scott Lindenau, FAIA." *Jim Leggitt/Drawing Shortcuts.* jimleggitt.typepad.com/ jim-leggitt-drawing-shortcuts/2011/07/architects-that-can-draw-scott-lindenau-faia.html.

---. *Scholl House, Photograph.* "Architects That Can Draw! Scott Lindenau, FAIA." *Jim Leggitt/Drawing Shortcuts.* jimleggitt.typepad.com/jim-leggitt-drawing-shortcuts/2011/07/architects-that-can-draw-scott-lindenau-faia.html.

Lunsford, Andrea A., and Karen J. Lunsford. "'Mistakes Are a Fact of Life': A National Comparative Study." *College Composition and Communication*, vol. 59, no. 4, 2008, pp. 781–806.

Martinsen, Amy. "The Tower of Babel and the Teaching of Grammar: Writing Instruction for a New Century." *English Journal*, vol. 90, no. 1, 2000, pp. 122–26. *JSTOR*, doi:10.2307/821742.

Metzger, Bruce M. "Important Early Translations of the Bible." *Bibliotheca Sacra*, vol. 150, no. 597, 1993, pp. 35–49.

Nature. "How to Write a Paper." *Nature.com*, www.nature.com/authors/author_resources/how_write.html.

Niedenthal, Paula M. "Embodying Emotion." *Science*, vol. 316, no. 5827, 2007, pp. 1002–05. *Google Scholar*, doi:10.1126/science.1136930.

Nussbaum, Martha C. "The Professor of Parody: The Hip Defeatism of Judith Butler." *New Republic*, vol. 220, no. 8, Feb. 1999, pp. 37–45.

O'Donohoe, Stephanie. "Netnography: Doing Ethnographic Research Online." *International Journal of Advertising*, vol. 29, no. 2, 2010. *Business Source Complete*, doi:10.2501/S026504871020118X.

Orwell, George. "Politics and the English Language." In *The Orwell Reader: Fiction, Essays, and Reportage*, Houghton Mifflin Harcourt, 1956, pp. 355–66.

Pitzer, Heidi Katherine. "'What's Best for Kids' vs. Teacher Unions: How Teach for America Blames Teacher Unions for the Problems of Urban Schools." *Workplace: A Journal for Academic Labor*, vol. 17, 2010, pp. 61–74.

Purdue Writing Lab. "Independent and Dependent Clauses." *Purdue OWL*, owl.purdue.edu/owl/general_writing/punctuation/independent_and_dependent_clauses/index.html.

Rigney, Lester-Irabinna. "Internationalization of an Indigenous Anticolonial Cultural Critique of Research Methodologies: A Guide to Indigenist Research Methodology and Its Principles." *Wíčazo Ša Review*, vol. 14, no. 2, 1999, pp. 109–21. *JSTOR*, doi:10.2307/1409555.

Sherin, Miriam Gamoran. "Developing a Professional Vision of Classroom Events." In *Beyond Classical Pedagogy: Teaching Elementary School Mathematics*, edited by Terry Wood, et al. 2014, pp. 75–94.

Sommers, Nancy. "Revision Strategies of Student Writers and Experienced Adult Writers." *College Composition and Communication*, vol. 31, no. 4, Dec. 1980, pp. 378–88. *JSTOR*, doi:10.2307/356588.

Taft, Lee. "Apology Subverted: The Commodification of Apology." *Yale Law Journal*, vol. 109, no. 5, 2000, pp. 1135–60. *JSTOR*, doi:10.2307/797485.

Tebeaux, Elizabeth. "Franklin's Autobiography—Important Lessons in Tone, Syntax, and Persona." *Journal of Technical Writing and Communication*, vol. 11, no. 4, 1981, pp. 341–49. *SAGE Journals*, doi:10.2190/F2GW-HDJY-LYFB-L3PE.

Van Der Vange, N., et al. "The Prognosis of Cervical Cancer Associated with Pregnancy: A Matched Cohort Study." *Obstetrics & Gynecology*, vol. 85, no. 6, June 1995, pp. 1022–26. *ScienceDirect*, doi:10.1016/0029-7844(95)00059-Z.

Voyce, Malcolm. "Shopping Malls in India: New Social 'Dividing Practices.'" *Economic and Political Weekly*, vol. 42, no. 22, 2007, pp. 2055–62.

Weaver, Constance. *Teaching Grammar in Context.* Boynton Cook, 1996.

Williams, Joseph M., and Gregory G. Colomb. *Style: Lessons in Clarity and Grace.* 10th ed., Longman, 2010.

Zais, Mitchell M. *Strategic Vision and Strength of Will: Imperatives for Theater Command.* Army War College, 1985.

CHAPTER 16

Going Public

Mindset: Published Writing Shapes the Public Sphere

Santiago Tobar Potes was a first-year college student in a precarious position when he decided to publish a piece of his writing. Tobar Potes was a "dreamer"—someone who came to the United States as a child without official authorization and who was protected from deportation under the Deferred Action for Childhood Arrivals (DACA) immigration program. The DACA program was under threat in 2017, so the stakes were high for him when he published an article for the *Fox News* website titled "DACA Student: Deporting Me and 800,000 Dreamers Is a Man-Made Disaster That Will Be Terrible for U.S." In his piece, Tobar Potes argues that the American president should continue the DACA program, ensuring that dreamers could remain in the United States:

> [T]hose of us protected by DACA have no idea if we will be able to stay here or if we will be deported to countries where we have few if any memories.
>
> This is torture for all 800,000 of us—a giant question mark hanging over our heads.
>
> Almost all of us have jobs or are in school. We have friends, relatives, partners and many ties to our communities. And we love America. We desperately want to stay.
>
> But it's not just we Dreamers who would be hurt by the end of DACA. America would suffer.

The Center for American Progress estimates that ending DACA would remove about 685,000 workers from the U.S. economy over the next 10 years—creating hardships for employers who would have to replace them.

And the center estimates ending DACA would reduce the U.S. gross domestic product—the total value of all goods produced and services provided—by about $460 billion over a decade. . . .

I ask everyone born in the U.S. to look at us as you looked at your parents, grandparents or earlier ancestors who came to this land of immigrants, making your lives possible. Do you think the Native Americans, who were here first, should have deported members of your families?

Tobar Potes uses many of the strategies that we've discussed throughout this book: he presents a clear problem, uses evidence to support a claim, and establishes his own authority. But beyond these moves, Tobar Potes did something brave: not only did he place his work in a public forum, he submitted his piece to a news site where many readers would disagree with him. Most of the readers on the politically conservative site *Fox News* would likely have a stance on DACA that opposed his own. His task then was to invite readers to consider an alternative perspective.

How does Tobar Potes reach potentially opposed readers? When he asks "everyone born in the U.S. to look at us as you looked at your parents, grandparents or earlier ancestors who came to this land of immigrants," he urges *Fox News* readers to relate their experience to his. Further, he cites research showing that ending DACA would have negative economic consequences for all *Fox News* readers. Tobar Potes respectfully assumes that his readers can change their minds in the face of compelling evidence. He believes that readers do not exist in a static community but rather in one that can respond and change. He calls into being a collection of people who recognize a shared interest and can act on that interest. With his words, Tobar Potes forms what scholars call a **public**.

As the philosopher J. L. Austin says in his influential book *How to Do Things with Words*, we can use words not only to describe the world or state facts, but we can also use them to "do things"—words themselves perform actions like marrying, naming, betting, and promising (7–9). Austin suggests that we should ask ourselves not only what our

> **KEY TERM**
>
> **Public**
>
> A public is a community that writers bring into being through their writing (Eberly 165–66). Readers become a public when they identify a shared interest and recognize that their pursuit of that interest affects other members of that public (Dewey 51–54). Whereas terms like "audience" or "readers" presume pre-existing demographics of people who will consume a text, the notion of a public offers a way to understand the power of writing to spur people to enact social change.

words are saying, but what they are accomplishing. What work does writing do? Writing does not just put forth a story or an argument; it also changes how we conceive of our relationship to the writer and to other people. This is the work Tobar Potes does with his *Fox News* piece. With his words, Tobar Potes signals how readers might identify themselves as a part of a public. Writers who form publics with their words take on the role of active citizens. When they seek to publish their work, they ask themselves, "How will people think, feel, and act in reaction to my words? Will these responses shape publics in ways that I value?"

The Public Sphere Is Missing Crucial Voices

Santiago Tobar Potes chose to publish in a venue where his argument and his voice were uncommon. He likely thought to himself that in order to have the largest influence, he needed to contribute to a community where his thoughts might inspire rethinking. Indeed, many thinkers have noted that citizens in a democracy make better decisions when they encounter as many diverse ideas as possible. The influential sociologist W. E. B. DuBois argued that democracy "cripples itself" when it excludes voices (144).

Alas, a small subset of the American public has a disproportionately loud voice. In higher education, for instance, faculty of color are underrepresented (Turner and González 1). And women are underrepresented in academic publications and are cited less frequently than their male counterparts (Samuels and Teele 2). Popular publications like newspapers and magazines suffer from similar imbalances.

In 2019, the Women's Media Center reported that men authored 69 percent of the news articles issued by the Associated Press and Reuters News Service. And the *New York Times* acknowledged in 2019 that "women have long been underrepresented on the letters page" (Feyer and Mermelstein). Such underrepresentation can create blindnesses to others' ideas and experiences; *New York Times* public editor Liz Spayd argues that "a gender, or racial, imbalance changes what's considered news." For example, men were the subjects of three-quarters of the newspaper's obituaries in 2016 (Spayd). In the academic world, health researcher Frances K. Del Boca argues that sex and gender imbalances in scientific research and publishing have detrimental, even dangerous, consequences (1323).

Yet blaming publications for not including a wider range of voices is overly simplistic. Writers themselves share responsibility. The OpEd Project, a nonprofit that strives to promote diversity among editorial authors, notes that most newspapers report that between 80 and 90 percent of their submissions come from men (OpEd Project). Rob Spillman, editor of the literary magazine *Tin House*, explains that the overrepresentation of male authors in his publication is partly due to the authors themselves: "males submit 100% of the time after being solicited, versus 50% of females, [and] men are four times more likely to resubmit after an encouraging rejection" (qtd. in Diamond). Further, fewer women apply for certain writing jobs. *New York Times* sports editor Jason Stallman notes that fewer than one percent of applicants for jobs in his section are women (Spayd).

In response to such statistics, a number of scholars and organizations like the OpEd Project and the feminist literary arts organization VIDA have devoted themselves to ushering more diverse voices into the public sphere. These organizations encourage everyone to submit their writing more frequently and to resubmit revisions when editors invite them to.

Tools & Techniques: Making Ideas Public

Submitting a piece of writing to a publication takes courage for any writer. Here we share the perspectives of editors and published authors aimed at making the process less mysterious and more accessible. Their advice will help you make strategic decisions about writing for publication in order to shape publics that you care about.

Selecting a Publication

Authors balance two factors when choosing a publication to submit their writing to: 1) the piece's fit for the publication and 2) the impact it could have. However, authors assess each factor in ways that might not be intuitive. For instance, we might assume that the best fit is the publication that regularly features pieces that echo the writer's ideas. Yet Santiago Tobar Potes chose to submit his editorial to a publication whose editors have long opposed his stance, and they found his piece to be a good fit.

Further, we might imagine that the publication with the biggest audience will always have the biggest impact. Yet when Jeffrey Sachs and Pia Malaney were choosing a publication to submit their study on malaria—an article we described at the beginning of Chapter 3—they didn't choose a newspaper or magazine with vast readerships. Instead they chose *Nature*, a respected academic journal with a smaller readership of science and technology specialists. Measuring impact involves more considerations than simply the number of readers reached.

Find a Good Fit

Why was Santiago Tobar Potes's editorial a good fit for *Fox News* even though the piece offered a different perspective from the site's typical coverage? Editors of popular and academic publications alike think articles fit not when they echo what's already been said in the publication but when they *respond to* what's been said and then add something new and significant. Newness and significance aren't universal standards but rather are judged within the particular publication. Tobar Potes responded to issues that had already been raised in *Fox News*—the publication regularly covers immigration issues—but he also added something new: a different perspective on those issues.

How do writers figure out whether a publication is a good fit for their writing? "The answer is really quite simple," advise Michael Levy and Dhruv Grewal, long-time editors of the *Journal of Retailing*: "read the articles it publishes" (247). Sociologists John P. Bartkowski, Carma S. Deem, and Christopher G. Ellison echo Levy and Grewal's advice and offer a more specific strategy: "Consider the quality of the match between your paper and a specific journal's identity by reviewing what has been published in that journal for the past five to seven years. A very good match is typically found in a manuscript that meaningfully extends a line of research for which a journal is known" (109). Their advice applies to popular publications like newspapers and magazines too, though because they publish issues more frequently, you may want to track just the last few months of the publication's coverage about your subject. As you review the coverage, ask yourself, "Does the publication address the issue I've written about?" "Does my writing advance the conversation there?"

Make an Impact

Sustainable development scholar Jeffrey Sachs publishes his writing in a wide variety of venues: everything from hyper-specialized academic journals to widely read newspapers and best-selling popular books. We have noted that Sachs chose to publish his malaria study with coauthor Pia Malaney in a specialized academic journal. However, Sachs has written other articles about malaria for popular audiences. Along with Guido Schmidt-Traub and Vanessa Fajans-Turner, Sachs published an article about the subject in a United Arab Emirates newspaper called *Khaleej Times*. Why this publication? This time, Sachs and his collaborators wanted to have a different kind of impact: they wanted to press wealthy countries to fund United Nations efforts to eradicate malaria. Thus, they chose a publication that would reach policymakers in one of the richest countries in the world: the public that could make the kind of changes the researchers want to see.

How do writers decide where they will have the most significant impact? Here are some questions that writers ask themselves when looking for a venue to publish their work:

- *Where will I reach readers who can act on my ideas?* Writers seek venues that will reach the most influential potential publics. When scholars seek to shape future research about an issue, they publish in specialized academic journals. When they want to reach a general readership located in a specific geographical area, they'll seek to publish in local newspapers. Likewise, when they want to reach a geographically diverse set of readers, they'll look for publishing venues with a national or international reach.
- *What is the publication's mission?* Some publications advocate for a specific mission or political stance. *National Review*, for instance, describes itself as a "magazine of conservative opinion," while *The Christian Century* calls itself "a progressive, ecumenical magazine."

Most journals have a section or link called "About" that describes the publication's mission. Writers can then check to see if their writing will reach the readers they want to engage.

- *How influential is the publication?* Many writers want to publish in the most influential venue they can. To measure the impact of journals, scholars turn to the metrics featured in databases like the *Eigenfactor* database, *Google Scholar Metrics, Scopus,* and the *Web of Science Journal Citation Reports* (see Figure 16.1). A research librarian can show you how to access these databases.
- *How quickly will the piece come out?* Scholarly book and article publishing can take many months because the texts undergo intensive peer review and editing. As a result, they are more likely to be respected as serious scholarly work. On the other end of the spectrum, blogs, newspapers, and magazines that are not peer reviewed will publish pieces more quickly. Writers who want to share their ideas immediately—especially if they deal with current events—may choose to publish in these venues even though they may not carry the same scholarly weight.
- *Who writes for the publication?* By looking at bylines at the top of the articles and biographies at the bottom, writers can learn who writes for the venue. Perhaps the writers all have professional degrees, perhaps they are all on the publication's staff, or perhaps they come from a range of backgrounds and experiences. Writers typically choose publications where their profiles would be valued.
- *How accessible will the publication be to readers?* Some publications exist only online, while others exist only in print. Writers consider how easy their articles will be to search for and how long they will remain available.

$$\begin{array}{l}\text{2017}\\\text{Journal}\\\text{Impact}\\\text{Factor}\end{array} = \dfrac{74{,}090}{1{,}782} = 41.577$$

FIGURE **16.1**
This graphic from *Web of Science Journal Citation Reports* calculates the "impact factor" of the science journal *Nature*, where Jeffrey Sachs and Pia Malaney published their article about malaria. *Web of Science* uses data from the previous two years, dividing the number of times other scholars cited *Nature* articles (74,090) by the number of articles the journal published (1,782). *Nature* articles from 2015 and 2016 were cited an average of 41.6 times by 2017. This makes *Nature* the most influential science journal during that time period.

Writers also consider a second kind of impact when they choose a publication to submit their work to: the impact on their public profiles (see Figure 16.2). Whether they choose academic publications, newspapers, magazines, or social media, writers look for venues that have good reputations. After all, these publications will pop up any time someone searches their names online.

Writers who have yet to be published might consider writing in unvetted venues like a personal blog (or even *Twitter* or *Instagram*), but they can have a bigger impact if they tap into already existing readerships of edited venues like news publications, professionally edited blogs, and so on. We encourage first-time authors to try a variety of venues to share your ideas: undergraduate academic journals, newspaper op-ed sections, academic conferences, college newspapers, letters to the editor, even the comment sections of online publications.

Write for Your Chosen Publication

Once writers choose a publication, they take pains to write their piece in such a way that the editors of the publication can envision it there. To understand what signals whether a submission belongs, we can turn to the voices of editors. Many publications, both academic and popular media, post submission guidelines—often under headings like "Advice for Authors" or "Submissions"—that spell out what the editors look for. Duane Roen, a long-time academic journal editor, encourages writers to "Follow the journal's guidelines religiously" (239).

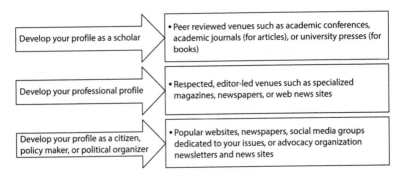

FIGURE **16.2**
Various publication venues raise writers' profiles in different ways.

COMMON PITFALL

Self-Publishing without Attracting Readers

Free website, blog, social media, and video platforms make publishing your work easy. But those free venues are often flooded with voices, and yours may be drowned out. However, certain strategies can increase your chances of finding readers. Your first step is to decide whether self-publishing will have the impact you want. Established publications, whether on the web or in print, come with established readerships. Further, publications that are vetted by editors and peer reviewers typically carry more credibility for readers.

If you decide that self-publishing is the best way to go, consider these strategies for getting readers to your site:

- Use meta tags. Meta tags are words that describe a webpage's content but don't appear on the page itself, only in its code. These descriptors tell internet search engines what your page is about. Use those same words periodically in your posting. Search engines promote pages whose postings echo its meta tags.
- Announce your newest content on social media.
- Include social media share buttons to your posts so that readers may share them with their networks.
- On each new post, link to related past posts.
- Make your website accessible for users with sensory and mobility impairments. Online tools like the World Wide Web Consortium's *Web Accessibility Initiative* analyze a site's accessibility and offer advice for web design that works for all users.

Search engines continually update the algorithms that control which results appear near the top. To learn the latest strategies for moving your site up in the results, search the web using the term "search engine optimization."

Submission guidelines, however, don't tell the whole story about what will appeal to editors. Ultimately, a submission needs to appear both familiar and new to editors: familiar enough that readers would recognize it as belonging in the publication and new enough that it adds something fresh to the conversation there.

Be Familiar

Although Santiago Tobar Potes offers an opinion that runs counter to typical coverage in *Fox News*, his article demonstrates respect for his politically conservative readers. He addresses the economic downsides of deporting undocumented immigrants brought to the United States as children, and he mentions that he interned for a conservative senator. Further, Tobar Potes's article shares characteristics that would be familiar to *Fox News* readers: it cites current events covered on the site, uses nonspecialized language appropriate for a general readership, and features short sentences and paragraphs typical of news articles.

Be New

Once Tobar Potes meets his readers on common ground in his DACA article, he can then add his fresh perspective to the conversation. Editors want to see this new perspective spelled out clearly in any submission. Business journal editors Michael Levy and Dhruv Grewal explain that the absence of a clearly spelled-out new contribution to a conversation is "[t]he number one reason cited by reviewers for their rejection of an article" (249). Magazine and newspaper editors likewise look for new, significant ideas. *Smithsonian Magazine* Senior Editor Jennie Rothenberg Gritz says, "There has to be something surprising and narratively interesting there." Writers can ask themselves, "What will feel fresh to readers of this publication?"

TURN TO YOUR RESEARCH

Targeting a Particular Publication

First Media Editor-in-Chief Gina Vaynshteyn underscores the importance of reading the publication that you plan to submit your writing to: "Pitching me something that doesn't make any sense for the publication, subject-wise or tonally, shows me you haven't read through the site. If you haven't done your homework, I wonder how diligent you'll be about your story" (qtd. in Herrera). What kind of "homework" do writers do to craft an article for a particular publication? After you select a publication, read articles in it to identify the following:

- *Form*: What do the articles look like? How long are they? Do they contain headings? How much space do writers devote to introductions, methods, conclusions, and so on? How long are individual paragraphs? Is there a common structure?

- *Scholarly problem*: What kinds of problems do the articles tackle? Are they problems of interpretation (common in humanities research)? Problems of definition (common, for instance, in legal scholarship)? Problems of missing facts or data (common in scientific and social scientific research)? Practical problems (common in engineering and business research)? Policy or proposal problems (common in political science or public policy research)?

- *Project*: What approaches do the articles take to address the problems they raise? Are their approaches theoretical, based on data gathering, premised on textual analysis, or reliant on some other method? How much material do they typically analyze?

- *Evidence*: What counts as evidence for this publication? Are the articles driven by statistical analysis, by textual analysis, case studies, or other kinds of evidence? Do they contain anecdotes? Are there charts and graphs? How many sources do articles cite?

- *Claim*: Do the claims ask us to reinterpret material, redefine a concept, rethink the causes or effects of a problem, consider a new proposal, or some other common stance?

- *Authorial presence*: Is the writer a major character within the articles? When and how frequently does the writer use first-person pronouns?

- *Citation style*: How do the articles credit others' ideas?

- *Presumed background of readership*: How much knowledge do articles assume that readers possess? How much do articles summarize sources? How much specialized terminology do they use? How often do they define those specialized terms? Do articles explain fundamental principles or background information?

Navigating Digital Spaces

Scholars have frequently pointed out that digital spaces offer tremendous opportunity for putting ideas into the public sphere but may also carry risks to an author's reputation, privacy, and sometimes safety

(Palfrey et al. 2). Writers are increasingly careful about controlling their digital footprint—the information trail they leave on the internet.

The internet has a "perfect memory," argues digital media scholar Viktor Mayer-Schönberger. Images or writing that you post in a weak moment will forever pop up when someone searches your name on the web. In his book *Deleted: The Virtue of Forgetting in the Digital Age*, Mayer-Schönberger tells the story of Andrew Feldmar, a Canadian psychotherapist who was barred from entering into the United States because a border guard's web search turned up an academic article in which Feldmar wrote that he took illegal drugs in the 1960s (Mayer-Schönberger 11). Feldmar cautions others not to put themselves in similar situations: "I should warn people that the electronic footprint you leave on the Net will be used against you. It cannot be erased" (qtd. in Mayer-Schönberger 12). Feldmar's advice is a reminder to post only the material on the web that you wouldn't mind being seen by employers, coworkers, admissions committees, your loved ones, and others.

Andrew Feldmar's advice also extends to where you choose to publish online. In Chapter 14 we considered factors that readers take into account when they judge an author's credibility. One factor was the reputation of the venue a writer publishes in. Even if your writing demonstrates a commitment to accurate research, publishing it on a site that trades in conspiracy theories or false reporting damages your reputation by association. Why is this so? The company we keep is a reflection of our characters. Authors who choose online venues with track records of publishing well-researched, accurate pieces show themselves to be worthy of readers' confidence.

But no matter how careful you are about what you publish online and where you publish it, you can't control how others will respond. Some publications offer opportunities for readers to respond to articles in a comments section. At their best, comments can open up conversations among many users and encourage active citizenship. Unfortunately, many comment sections are not moderated. As a result, researchers have found that a significant number of online comments are irrational and/or hostile (Ksiazek et al.). In 2016, news website *Vice.com* decided to eliminate reader comments on its articles. Editor-in-Chief Jonathan Smith explained that "too often" comments "devolve into racist, misogynistic maelstroms where the loudest, most offensive, and stupidest opinions get pushed to the top and the more reasoned responses drowned out in the noise."

Certain writers are more at risk of receiving comments from trolls, whose sole aim is to provoke outrage. Political scientist Christina M. Greer, a black female professor who publishes articles for both scholars and the general public, explains that she does not reply to comments posted to her online editorials because "It is best to preserve your energy for the long fight; choose your battles wisely. . . . Internet 'trolls' and online harassment are very real and can unfortunately spiral into dangerous territory and safety concerns, especially for faculty in marginalized and underrepresented groups" (152). We urge writers to participate in online commenting in ways that move conversations forward but also heed Greer's advice to ignore the trolls.

Putting Your Words in the World

We began this book with a Scholar's Story about the opening stages of research, and we emphasized the way that scholars seek out shared ignorance to motivate meaningful conversation. We close with a Scholar's Story about the final stage of research, publication, to emphasize that the push toward meaningful conversation remains at the heart of academic writing. Here, creative nonfiction writer Briallen Hopper reflects on a piece called "On Spinsters," which she published in the *Los Angeles Review of Books*. As you read Hopper's story, notice that her article came into being through the conversations she sought out with friends, her editor, and other authors' texts. But publication wasn't the end of conversation. Once her piece was published, it invoked a public that carried the conversation forward, a hallmark of successful writing.

We've chosen to end this book not with advice about turning in assignments for a grade but rather with considerations about how you might contribute to the public sphere. Our loftiest goal is to inspire you to use your writing to contribute to the conversations around you. The philosopher John Dewey declared, "Communication can alone create a great community" (118). We agree that society is better off when its citizens hear a diverse range of ideas and contribute their own thoughts in response.

In her story, Briallen Hopper reminds us that scholarly practice does not mean placing a lone voice in the world but rather involves deeply social activities of listening and responding. Hopper's story suggests the many ways that writing shapes and invigorates communities.

SCHOLAR'S STORY

Briallen Hopper on Writing Communities

People often say that writing is a solitary affair, but for me, writing is social. I rely on others for advice and encouragement. And I'm not alone: take a look at a book's acknowledgments section, and you'll see shout-outs to colleagues, librarians, editors, friends, family, and anonymous readers.

When I look at my essay "On Spinsters," I can see traces of my writing community everywhere. Before I even started writing, conversations helped me figure out what I wanted to say. I talked with my friend Dixa about single women and race, and I talked with my friend Merve about spinsters in the movies. When I was finally ready to write, I called up my friend Cathy to set up some writing dates.

My friend Mary is responsible for the liveliness of the lede: she told me to move a paragraph from the middle up to the beginning, and it got things off to a quicker start. My editor Sarah helped me trim down references to book reviews in the introduction to keep the focus on my own argument.

My friend Lindsay said that instead of paraphrasing Henry James, I should quote him, and she was right. I could never write "She was a spinster as Shelley was a lyric poet, or as the month of August is sultry," and thanks to Lindsay and Henry James I didn't have to. I could just steal it (with proper citation, naturally).

Publishing the essay marked the end of a certain phase of social life for "On Spinsters" and the beginning of a new one. Now that it's out in the world, readers email me about it, teachers teach it, and editors get in touch and ask me to write follow-up pieces. The conversation continues, and my writing community expands.

Read the research: Briallen Hopper is assistant professor of creative nonfiction at Queens College, CUNY and the author of *Hard to Love* (Bloomsbury, 2019). You can read her essay "On Spinsters" in the July 12, 2015 issue of the *Los Angeles Review of Books*.

As Hopper describes, conversations went into the creation of her piece, and conversations emerged from her piece. Scholars rely on evolving communities of thinkers to shape their writing. It is our job as students, teachers, readers, and writers to acknowledge this community, enter it ourselves, and help shape it in ways that matter.

Works Cited

Austin, J. L. [John Langshaw]. *How to Do Things with Words*. Harvard UP, 1975.

Bartkowski, John P., et al. "Publishing in Academic Journals: Strategic Advice for Doctoral Students and Academic Mentors." *American Sociologist*, vol. 46, no. 1, Mar. 2015, pp. 99–115.

Del Boca, Frances K. "Addressing Sex and Gender Inequities in Scientific Research and Publishing: Editorial." *Addiction*, vol. 111, no. 8, Aug. 2016, pp. 1323–25. *Crossref*, doi:10.1111/add.13269.

Dewey, John. *The Public and Its Problems: An Essay in Political Inquiry*, edited by Melvin L. Rogers, Pennsylvania State UP, 2012.

Diamond, Jason. "A Tale of Two Literary Magazines: *The Believer* and *Tin House* Respond to the VIDA Count." *Flavorwire*, 26 Feb. 2014, flavorwire. com/442334/a-tale-of-two-literary-magazines-the-believer-and-tin-house-respond-to-the-vida-count.

DuBois, William Edward Burghardt. *Darkwater: Voices from Within the Veil*. Harcourt, Brace and Howe, 1920.

Eberly, Rosa A. "From Writers, Audiences, and Communities to Publics: Writing Classrooms as Protopublic Spaces." *Rhetoric Review*, vol. 18, no. 1, autumn 1999, pp. 165–78. *JSTOR*, doi:10.1080/07350199909359262.

Feyer, Thomas, and Susan Mermelstein. "The Editors Respond: We Hear You." *New York Times*, 2 Feb. 2019. *NYTimes.com*, www.nytimes .com/2019/01/31/opinion/letters/letters-to-editor-new-york-times-women. html.

Greer, Christina M. "Scholarly Engagement With the Public: The Risks and Benefits of Engaging Outside of the Classroom." *Political Communication*, vol. 35, no. 1, Jan. 2018, pp. 150–53. *Taylor and Francis+NEJM*, doi:10.1080 /10584609.2017.1406589.

Gritz, Jennie Rothenberg. "The Pitch: How to Get the Attention of a Senior Editor at Smithsonian Magazine." Interview by Katia Savchuk. *NiemanStoryboard*, 14 Nov. 2017, https://niemanstoryboard.org/stories/ the-pitch-how-to-get-the-attention-of-a-senior-editor-at-smithsonian-magazine/.

Herrera, Tim. "How to Successfully Pitch *The New York Times* (or, Well, Anyone Else)." *Nieman Lab*, 22 Oct. 2018, www.niemanlab.org/2018/10/how-to-successfully-pitch-the-new-york-times-or-well-anyone-else/.

Ksiazek, Thomas B., et al. "Discussing the News." *Digital Journalism*, vol. 3, no. 6, Nov. 2015, pp. 850–70. *Taylor and Francis+NEJM*, doi:10.1080/21670811.2 014.972079.

Levy, Michael, and Dhruv Grewal. "Publishing Perspectives from the Editors." *Journal of Retailing*, vol. 83, no. 3, 2007, pp. 247–52. *ScienceDirect*, doi:10.1016/j.jretai.2007.06.001.

Mayer-Schönberger, Viktor. *Delete: The Virtue of Forgetting in the Digital Age.* Princeton UP, 2009. *ProQuest Ebook Central,* ebookcentral.proquest.com/ lib/columbia/detail.action?docID=534065.

OpEd Project. "Op-Ed Writing: Tips and Tricks." *OpEd Project,* www .theopedproject.org/oped-basics/.

Palfrey, John G., et al. "Response to FCC Notice of Inquiry 09-94: Empowering Parents and Protecting Children in an Evolving Media Landscape." *Berkman Center Research Publication No. 2010-02; Harvard Public Law Working Paper No. 10-19,* 2010. *Google Scholar,* papers.ssrn.com/sol3/ papers.cfm?abstract_id=1559208.

Roen, Duane H. "Revising for Publication: Advice to Graduate Students and Other Junior Scholars." *Rhetoric Society Quarterly,* vol. 25, no. 1, 1995, p. 237–426. *JSTOR,* doi:10.1080/02773949509391047.

Samuels, David J., and Dawn Teele. "New Medium, Same Story: Gender Gaps in Book Publishing." *SSRN Scholarly Paper, ID 3283107, Social Science Research Network,* 12 Nov. 2018. *SSRN,* papers.ssrn.com/abstract=3283107.

Spayd, Liz. "The Declining Fortunes of Women at The Times." *New York Times,* 22 Dec. 2017. *NYTimes.com,* www.nytimes.com/2017/03/04/public-editor/ the-declining-fortunes-of-women-at-the-times.html.

Tobar Potes, Santiago. "DACA Student: Deporting Me and 800000 Dreamers Is a Man-Made Disaster That Will Be Terrible for US." *Fox News,* 5 Sept. 2017, www.foxnews.com/opinion/2017/09/05/daca-student-deporting-me-and-800,000-dreamers-is-man-made-disaster-that-will-be-terrible-for-us.html.

Turner, Caroline Sotello Viernes, and Juan Carlos González. "What Does the Literature Tell Us About Mentoring Across Race/Ethnicity and Gender?" *Modeling Mentoring Across Race/Ethnicity and Gender: Practices to Cultivate the Next Generation of Diverse Faculty,* edited by Caroline Sotello Viernes Turner and Juan Carlos González, Stylus Publishing, LLC, 2015, pp. 1–42.

Web of Science. *Journal Profile: Nature.* InCites Journal Citation Reports, Clarivate Analytics, 2019, apps-clarivate-com.

INDEX

....

Note: Figures and tables are indicated by "f" and "t" following page numbers. Photographs are indicated by page numbers in italics.